ROBERT SAXTON: *CARITAS*

For Kathy –

Fervens illa mea
ignis est, sed suavitas
et bonitas
renitent ex ea.

[She is my blazing fire, but sweetness and goodness radiate from her.]
(twelfth-century)

Robert Saxton: *Caritas*

WYNDHAM THOMAS
University of Bristol, UK

ASHGATE

Published by
Ashgate Publishing Limited
Wey Court East
Union Road
Farnham
Surrey, GU9 7PT
England

Ashgate Publishing Company
Suite 420
101 Cherry Street
Burlington
VT 05401-4405
USA

www.ashgate.com

British Library Cataloguing in Publication Data
Thomas, Wyndham.
  Robert Saxton: *Caritas*. – (Landmarks in music since 1950)
  1. Saxton, Robert, 1953– *Caritas*.
  I. Title II. Series
  782.1-dc23

Library of Congress Cataloging-in-Publication Data
Thomas, Wyndham.
  Robert Saxton : *Caritas* / Wyndham Thomas.
    p. cm. – (Landmarks in music since 1950)
  Includes bibliographical references and index.
  ISBN 978-0-7546-6601-1 (hardcover : alk. paper) 1. Saxton, Robert, 1953–
Caritas. I. Title.
  ML410.S2134T46 2012
  782.1–dc23

2012002950

ISBN 9780754666011 (hbk)

Bach musicological font developed by © Yo Tomita

Printed and bound in Great Britain by
MPG Books Group, UK

Contents

List of Figures and Tables

Figures

Tables

List of Music Examples

General Editor's Preface

In commending this book on Robert Saxton, I am conscious of some slight embarrassment in that I write as both series editor and author. However, above all else, it is the composer and the chosen work that are being recommended, for *Caritas* is a remarkable opera – the more so for being based on a play by one of the world's greatest contemporary dramatists. Sir Arnold Wesker (who celebrates his eightieth anniversary in 2012) also adapted his original stage-play as the libretto, and must be credited with creating a splendidly researched narrative that explores medieval (but timeless) issues of faith, disillusionment, power, vocation and social structure. When Saxton was commissioned to compose an opera for the 1991 Huddersfield Festival of Contemporary Music, he was immediately attracted by the challenge of cooperating with such a distinguished playwright. The resulting music-drama demonstrates his profound insight into the psychological fabric of the plot and its leading characters, while the score displays a masterly synthesis of traditional and modern musical techniques.

Ever since the inception of the series of Landmarks in Music Since 1950, I have wanted to contribute a volume myself, should a suitable opportunity arise. It is my good fortune that this study of *Caritas* has brought together my scholarly interests in medieval music, liturgical drama and the analysis of twentieth-century music. This is the first monograph on the music of Robert Saxton and it will be published in good time to celebrate his sixtieth birthday in 2013. It is also the third volume in the Landmarks series to be devoted to a single opera or musical theatre piece. I sincerely hope that my book will inspire readers to explore Saxton's fascinating output more fully, and that the group of opera studies will stimulate more performances of the works concerned.

Wyndham Thomas
Corsham

Preface

Opera as a genre receives a very mixed press.[1] On the one hand it is considered to be the acme of musical and dramatic perfection – the ultimate artistic experience. On the other hand, it has been dismissed as a vastly over-rated indulgence of the rich and privileged – caricatured with pot-bellied heroes and received anecdotes of audience diversions. I shall neither attempt to balance these extremes, one against the other, nor to adjudicate between them, since opera at its best *can* be wonderfully stimulating and overwhelmingly moving – although so expensive to mount professionally that ticket prices are frequently beyond the means of those who wish to attend. There is a division of opinion, too, between commentators (and producers) who argue in favour of employing singers who are accomplished actors, as opposed to casting more established operatic stars whose greater experience and vocal stamina might, or might not, compensate for less credible acting – especially in youthful (or consumptive) roles. If one adds the observation that, with a few notable exceptions, opera company repertoires are heavily weighted in favour of works composed before the twentieth century, it is hardly surprising that there appears to be so much variation in the reception of new productions, together with generally conservative or guarded reviews of new operas.

However, one of the benefits of our contemporary society is that we now possess the technological means to (repeatedly) experience opera on film, recordings and television at substantially lower costs than for live performances. This has obvious advantages for study and is a convenient method of acquiring an overview of a large and complex repertoire. But an important – one might say essential – feature of operatic experience is that it is (or can be) enhanced by its social context. Certainly, the lively tradition of spontaneous applause (or other less generous critical response) is indicative of the passion (and politics) of audience involvement, while the annual pilgrimages to festivals as contrasted as Bayreuth and Glyndebourne are evidence of the value that is placed on historic (and/or fashionable) locations and an appropriate atmosphere. The survival of so many European opera houses also suggests that they can still attract funding and viable audiences, albeit often with a repertoire that gives only token recognition to present-day (or recent) composers. Even when new operas *are* commissioned (and the policies of companies such as Opera North are demonstrably enlightened in this respect), new works seldom run for more than a dozen performances before being replaced by yet another *Figaro* or *Bartered Bride*.

---

[1]   For the purpose of this generalised paragraph, the author does not enter into the Wagnerian debate about opera and music drama.

So, the question must be asked – why write a book about a modern opera? The answer is simple – because, with the help of the enclosed CD, it provides an opportunity for readers to reconsider their first impressions or else to be introduced to the work(s) in an informed and coherent way, with the overall aim of building a new and potentially very large audience. Presumably, these are also the reasons why opera companies invest in education programmes. A second question then presents itself, related to the selection of the work to be studied. Again, the reasoning is disarmingly straightforward – the choice is likely to be based on the conviction that a work is 'special' in a number of varied ways – whether because of the originality of its plot or its unusual reworking of a well-known legend; because of the originality of its musical language or the quality of its melodies; perhaps on account of the novelty of its staging, the prominence (or otherwise) of the chorus, or its relationship with other operas by the same or different composers; or, possibly, because of an historical coincidence that links performances with some aspect of current/world affairs.

The following chapters will address such issues – and others, related to the singling out of Robert Saxton's opera for detailed study. They will propose that *Caritas* is central to the composer's output to date; that it is a work of exceptional skill and quality; that it has integrity as a work of art; that it poses important questions about human ambition and motivation; that it both challenges traditions and, in some ways, extends them; that it does not provide glib answers to questions asked of the human condition or of religion itself. In deciding to base the work on a recorded historical figure and an ancient Christian vocation in which the anchoress lives apart from society (yet is still within it), Wesker has chosen to relate his subject to broader contemporary issues of idealism and dogma and to isolate practice from period. For his part, Saxton (while remaining faithful to his librettist's narrative) has distilled a musical language that has enabled him to blend medieval themes and locations with universal concerns of love, faith, disillusionment and redemption. In the broadest of terms, both Wesker and Saxton have searched for the true meaning of *caritas*.

The opera is without doubt a landmark in Saxton's *oeuvre* and a key work in the development of its genre. This book aims to provide insights into its 'special' qualities – its nature and status – through a blend of detailed analysis and contextual study. It is not an isolated work. It evolved out of more than a decade of major orchestral and vocal works by Saxton and is central to a significant development in the composer's style, leading to his second opera (*The Wandering Jew*), which was completed and first performed just as this volume, itself, was nearing completion.

Acknowledgements and Permissions

Acknowledgements

I am deeply indebted to all who have assisted in the preparation of this book. My thanks go especially to Heidi Bishop and Laura Macy and their editorial colleagues at Ashgate Publishing; to Martyn Imrie who has set the music examples; to Liz Webb (Robert Saxton's agent); to Joe Vaněk for his permission to reproduce photographs of the model of his original set design and for providing captions, together with a brief reminiscence of the production; to Alastair Muir for allowing Ashgate to use his photograph of the production of *Caritas* in the cover design; to the Rector and Wardens of St James' Church, Shere, for permission to quote from their pamphlet on Christine Carpenter; to Professor Paul Moorcraft for checking an early draft of Chapter 2; and to Professor Raymond Warren for providing ongoing criticism of the first three chapters. Needless to say, any shortcomings in the final text are solely my own responsibility.

Above all, I wish to thank Robert Saxton's publishers – Chester/Novello; York University Press and Ricordi – for donating scores of his published works to assist with my research. Music Sales Ltd has also given permission for me to quote from the works detailed in the 'List of Music Examples'. Sir Arnold Wesker has replied to my queries with tact and patience and I would like to thank him, in admiration, for allowing me to quote from the libretto of *Caritas* and the two versions of his play. Robert Saxton has been an invaluable (and utterly impartial) respondent to my frequent enquiries about his life, compositions and writings. He has generously loaned pre-compositional notes and sketches of *Caritas* and has given permission for some of these to be published as illustrations.

Finally I would like to express my loving thanks to my family for tolerating my various musical and historical obsessions. Their understanding and support have been invaluable.

Permissions

I am grateful for permission to reproduce the following copyrighted material:

CARITAS
Music by Robert Saxton
Libretto based on the play 'Caritas' by Arnold Wesker
Music © 1991 Chester Music Limited
Libretto © Copyright 1981 by Arnold Wesker reproduced by permission of Jonathan Cape, an imprint of the Random House Group Limited
All Rights Reserved. International Copyright Secured.
Reprinted by Permission.

Robert Saxton has generously loaned pre-compositional notes and sketches of *Caritas* and given permission for some of them to be published as illustrations.

Photographs of Set Design reproduced by kind permission of Joe Vaněk.

Extracts from *Caritas* (play and libretto) reproduced by kind permission of Sir Arnold Wesker.

Grateful thanks to the Rector and Churchwardens of St James's Church, Shere, for permission to quote from the pamphlet 'Christine Carpenter, Anchoress of Shere'.

Note on References

References to the Full and Vocal Scores of *Caritas* have been included in order to facilitate further, more detailed, study of the work. Unfortunately, there is some inconsistency of bar numbering between the two scores – the likelihood being that the bar numbers in the Full Score are correct in Act 1, and those in the Vocal Score correct in Act 2.

In order to avoid ambiguity (especially when comparing sections in the two sources), the following formulae need to be applied to bar numberings.

Act 1 (Vocal Score Only)

Bars 1–837:	as printed
Bar 841 (i) at top of p.88 =	bar 838, then consecutively to
Bar 841 (ii) in second system of p.88 =	bar 842, then consecutively to
Bar 843 (p.89/scene 10) =	bar 845, then consecutively to
Bars 847–1,150 =	as printed

Bar references within the critical text (Chapter 4, especially) use the modified numberings as above. The other (very rare) misprints are noted within the commentary.

Additionally, there is a discrepancy between the two opera scores in the locating of the start of Christine's Lullaby in Act 2. The Vocal Score places this title at bar 221 whereas the Full Score locates the title above bar 232 (bar 229 adjusted). The Full Score is assumed to be the correct version in this case.

Act 2 (Full Score Only)

The bar numbers in the Full Score are correct up to bar 190, which is printed three bars late. Therefore, all bar numbers from, and including, bar 190 need to be adjusted by the addition of three (three bars) to correspond with the Vocal Score. Bar 190 becomes 193; bar 200 becomes 203, and so on. The final bar is number 373 (*not* 370 as printed). The numbering throughout this volume has been adjusted where necessary to ensure conformity between the two scores.

Chapter 1

Introduction: Operatic Context

In a *Musical Times* article of 1986,[1] Paul Griffiths bewailed the fact that there were, as yet, no commercial recordings of Robert Saxton's compositions. As the author rather cryptically proclaimed, 'One ought to be able to refer readers to recordings so that words and sounds could be two channels of communication, completing a circle of light, perhaps.' The composer himself was then in his thirty-third year[2] and, to quote Griffiths again, 'had been producing music of a widely remarked fascination and substance for more than a decade'. From his first published composition, *Ritornelli and Intermezzi*[3] up to *The Circles of Light*[4] (the most recent of the works discussed in Griffiths' article), Saxton had, indeed, established an enviable reputation for both the originality and fecundity of his output. He had been awarded first prize at the prestigious International Gaudeamus Festival in Holland[5] and subsequently received numerous commissions including that from the BBC for his Concerto for Orchestra.[6] The commissioning of Saxton's chamber opera, *Caritas*,[7] just a year or so after the publication of the *Musical Times* essay, was no doubt based largely on the consistently high quality of this corpus of accomplished and evocative scores.

Whether prompted by Griffiths' advocacy or as a result of public and critical acclaim, a CD containing a selection of Saxton's works (composed between 1982 and 1985) soon followed.[8] Taken as a whole, the four featured pieces[9] reveal many of Saxton's recurring extra-musical obsessions and some of his characteristic compositional methods. For example, one might cite the concept of journeying

---

[1]   Paul Griffiths (1986) 'A Little Light on Robert Saxton', *Musical Times* 127(1717), pp. 145–7.

[2]   Born 8 October 1953.

[3]   *Ritornelli and Intermezzi* for piano (1972).

[4]   Chamber Symphony, *The Circles of Light* (1985).

[5]   In 1975 for his *What Does the Song Hope For.*

[6]   Composed 1983–84; first performed on 13 August 1984, at the Royal Albert Hall Promenade Concerts.

[7]   *Caritas* was commissioned by Opera North and the Huddersfield Contemporary Music Festival in 1987 and first performed at Wakefield Opera House on 21 November 1991.

[8]   EMI: CDC 7 49915 2 (1990). For details see the 'Recordings' section of the 'Bibliography' and below (n. 9).

[9]   *The Ring of Eternity* (1982/rev.1983), Concerto for Orchestra (1983–84), *The Sentinel of the Rainbow* (1983–84), and *The Circles of Light* (1985).

towards Light and the Divine Presence,[10] or the fascination with hexachords and tritones and the prominent use of sustained pitches to mark structural landmarks. For Saxton, whose Jewish ancestry coexists productively with his traditionally English schooling and Oxbridge education, there is no paradox or conflict between the varied sources that constitute his rich cultural identity. As more than one commentator has observed, he is as likely to draw on the New Testament as the Old; to make use of medieval Roman chant as Hasidic dance stimuli; to be influenced by the motets of Byrd and Tallis as by Schoenberg and Berg; or to accept a commission to write for the Anglican liturgy as to base an opera (*The Wandering Jew*) on a book by the German-Jewish writer, Stefan Heym.[11]

In a very real sense, the nature and dating of Saxton's two operas provide us with clear, albeit contrasting, landmarks in the composer's own artistic journey as he nears the end of his sixth decade. On the one hand, *Caritas* (1990–91), based on Arnold Wesker's eponymous stage-play,[12] is set over a comparatively short period of four years[13] within a relatively restricted Christian context – although one that abounds in violent profane elements and challenging politico-religious questions; on the other, *The Wandering Jew* (2010), described by Saxton as 'a dramatic radio operatic fantasy', is a time-travelling 'take' on the mythical legend of the Jewish cobbler who was condemned to a nomadic eternity after refusing Christ shelter on the way to his crucifixion. Although very different as dramatic exercises and separated by twenty years or so,[14] the two works nonetheless share several common themes (such as the use of historical or mythical events as reference points in a temporal framework) with the concluding reconciliation in the second opera being a gratifying complement to the despairing loss of faith at the end of *Caritas*. Whereas one might justifiably observe that Saxton's characteristic journey from darkness into light is reversed in *Caritas*, it is equally obvious that the *Sukkot*-inspired[15] last scene of *The Wandering Jew* represents the kind of spiritual transcendence found

---

[10]   Henry Vaughan's *The Ring of Eternity*, the Jewish *Kabbala* [Concerto for Orchestra], the Rainbow Bridge to Valhalla [*The Sentinel of the Rainbow*], and Dante's vision of God seen through Beatrice's eyes in *The Divine Comedy* [*The Circles of Light*].

[11]   Pseudonym of Helmut Flieg (1913–2001) whose novel *Ahasver* (1981) was translated into English as *The Wandering Jew* (1984).

[12]   First performed at the Cottesloe Theatre, London, 7 October 1981.

[13]   The play and opera both carry the start-date of July,1377, and the last date (of the Travelling Priest's sermon) of 17 June 1381 (four years later). The documents relating to the 'real' Christine Carpenter, however, extend over a three year period (July 1329–6 August 1332) – see Chapter 2, below.

[14]   Although their premieres date from 1991 and 2010, respectively, the idea for *The Wandering Jew* dates from 1984, if not earlier (see Chapter 6). Eventually, it was commissioned to celebrate the millennium.

[15]   *Sukkot*: the third seasonal festival in the Jewish celebration of Exodus – a reminder of the wanderings in the wilderness on the way to the promised land.

in *Verklärte Nacht*, and sought, perhaps, by Christine Carpenter in her frustrated anticipation of a 'showing'[16] – a vision of unity with God.

That *Caritas* is also a landmark in twentieth-century British opera requires rather more specialized, not to say sophisticated, argument. The following sections of this introductory chapter set out to place the work in its historical and generic contexts and to assess the unique contribution that it makes to the repertoire of chamber opera and to opera composed within the tradition of religious and liturgical drama (which has its origins in medieval Christian worship). Comparison with other similar or related contemporary works is inevitable but, in general, will be initiated only to explore common or differing elements rather than to imply direct influence (in either direction). However it would be unlikely if Saxton, who was advised in his early compositional efforts by Benjamin Britten,[17] had not picked up some professional 'tricks of the trade' from such a consummate master of operatic techniques – particularly at a time when Britten was producing *Curlew River* (1964) and the other parables for church performance.[18] We know little about Saxton's first excursion into opera (*Cinderella*), composed when he was twelve, but, whatever its merits, it should have provided him with invaluable experience in word setting and large-scale structural planning – and, no doubt, brought home to him the inherent difficulties of writing for the stage since, of all the media available to a composer today, opera is probably the one that makes the most exacting demands in terms of sheer technical expertise and the ability to work in partnership with other creative artists.

From the outset, Saxton was fortunate in that Arnold Wesker agreed to revise his original text as a libretto for the new opera. The play relates the true (but scantily documented) story of a fourteenth-century anchoress[19] who moves towards insanity as her desire for a divine revelation continues to be unfulfilled after a four-year period of seclusion. Although physically isolated, she is aware of the worldly life and love that she has abandoned. The very essence of the drama is the dogmatic refusal of her bishop to release her from her vows. Set against the backcloth of the Peasants'

---

[16]   The term used by the fourteenth-century recluse, Julian of Norwich, for her revelations. See: Julian of Norwich (1986) *A Revelation of Love*, ed. Marion Glasscoe (Exeter: University of Exeter), and Elizabeth Spearing (2002) *Medieval Writings on Female Spirituality* (London: Penguin Classics) for useful extracts from the Short Text, referred to in Chapter 4 of this volume.

[17]   From c.1963. Saxton has revealed further information about Britten's mentoring in the interview included later in this volume (Chapter 7).

[18]   The others were composed in 1966 (*The Burning Fiery Furnace*) and 1968 (*The Prodigal Son*).

[19]   Female anchorite, or recluse, who is voluntarily locked into a small cell attached to a church. Apart from basic provisions and the services of a priest, she normally has no direct contact with the outside world for the rest of her life, although sources suggest that such women were frequently approached for advice and religious mentoring.

Uprising (1381),[20] the play and libretto juxtapose sacred and secular worlds, the relative power and servitude of rulers and serfs, and the terrifying ordeal of Christine Carpenter (the youthful anchoress) who is caught between the inflexibility of the established church and her personal religious expectations. Such a narrative was to offer rich opportunities for musical characterization and evocation of the historical context of the action, as well as substantial challenges in pacing and integrating the sequence of dramatic 'snap-shots' that culminate in a scene of total despair.

Saxton's approach to these challenges and the significance of *Caritas* in his overall output will be subjected to more detailed examination in later chapters, but it is worth exploring now some of the operatic precedents that would have been absorbed by the developing composer. The oft-repeated aphorism – that twentieth-century opera was founded upon the legacy of the two towering figures of Wagner and Verdi – is difficult to fault. However, much was to change between the early works of Richard Strauss and Puccini (the main inheritors of these traditions) and the neoclassical experiments of Stravinsky and Hindemith; between the 'psychological' music dramas of Berg and Britten and the more exotic sound worlds of Maxwell Davies and Birtwistle. While individual operas (such as *Pelléas et Mélisande, Salome,* and *Wozzeck,*) have been accorded iconic status and continued to exert profound influence during the second half of the century, revivals of early works (by Monteverdi and Handel, especially) provoked a reaction to the sensuous textures of 'grand opera' and (informed by the varied traditions of baroque opera, medieval drama, dance and pantomime) led to the creation of new genres such as music-theatre and chamber opera – the latter most clearly defined in the works composed by Benjamin Britten for his English Opera Group. In Saxton's case, it seems that it was the assimilation of a number of varied operatic conventions rather than the legacy of a single composer or 'school' that provided the basis for the structure and choice of musical techniques in this, his first 'major' theatre work. *Caritas* juxtaposes religious ritual with scenes of violent punishment and madness. Although there are traces of the traditional elements of aria and ensemble, there are very few 'set-numbers' as such or choruses – apart from the chanting of plainsong (by members of the cast) and the external group of children whose insistent questioning of Christine punctuates many of the short scenes that make up Act 1 of both play and libretto, and are subsequently distorted in Act 2 of the opera. For the most part, Saxton's setting of Wesker's libretto is through-composed with few phrases repeated for emphasis. Not until the orchestral interlude and Ricercar that separate the two acts does the audience have time to contemplate the dire dilemma of the (anti-)heroine and prepare for the accelerated crisis that closes the work.

---

[20]   Wesker sets his drama about 50 years later than the documented life of Christine of Shere (and in Norfolk rather than Surrey) to achieve this historical juxtaposition.

Opera in England after World War II

The production of *Peter Grimes* at Sadler's Wells in 1945 – and its overwhelming critical acclaim[21] – is now seen as a defining moment in the (re)birth of opera in a country that had for too long been dominated by a Central European repertoire and continental imports. Paradoxically, *Grimes* is constructed on the model of a three-act 'grand opera', albeit dealing with a theme (social isolation) more akin to Berg's *Wozzeck* than to the amorous intrigues of Puccini's *Tosca*, or the ill-starred lovers of *La Bohème* and Verdi's *La Traviata* – although the role of anti-hero does find a precedent in Verdi's *Rigoletto*. Britten would certainly have known all of these operas and we know that he admired Berg and would have tried to study with him had circumstances (and advice) been favourable. It is also more than possible that, while in America,[22] he had discovered Gershwin's theatrical masterpiece, *Porgy and Bess* – a work with which *Peter Grimes* shares several significant features.[23]

Despite the theatrical prominence given to such well-used conventions as thrilling choruses, naturalistic orchestral interludes, and dramatic character confrontations, perhaps it was the essential intimacy of *Peter Grimes* – the exploration of the interior world of a social misfit – that persuaded Britten that his immediate future was to lie in a form of opera that eschewed large orchestral forces and choruses (other than the 'classical' chorus/commentator in *The Rape of Lucretia*). Crucially, he introduced the piano to accompany recitative in the manner of a baroque continuo and presented his narrative through the interaction of individuals rather than by creating a series of large-scale pseudo-pageants. Of course, a key factor in this decision was the composer's desire to increase his control over the finished production – to eliminate the potential hazards and uncertainties associated with established opera companies; to create a form of opera that could be easily transported to new venues and that reduced problems of staging and production. Britten would also have been aware of Holst's *Sāvitri*[24] (which uses only three singers and a dozen instrumentalists) and the success of comparable ventures by Stravinsky during the economic restrictions of the first World War,[25] although works such as *L'Histoire du Soldat*, together with Schoenberg's *Pierrot lunaire*, had a more potent influence subsequently on Maxwell Davies and his music-theatre compositions written for the *Fires of London*.[26] In Britten's hands, chamber opera emerged as a most effective alternative to its

---

[21]   The rather carping criticisms by 'senior' composers are not typical of the work's reception.

[22]   1939–42.

[23]   The setting in a fishing community; a cathartic storm scene; and a 'flawed' (crippled) main character (anti-hero).

[24]   Composed 1908; first staged 1916.

[25]   *Renard* (1915–16), *L'Histoire du Soldat* (1918) and *Pulcinella* (1919–20), especially.

[26]   Notably, *Revelation and Fall* (1968) and *Eight Songs for a Mad King* (1969).

grander brother without sacrificing anything of its dramatic intensity or depth of characterization. In the composer's own words:

> I am keen to develop a new art-form (the chamber opera, or what you will) which will stand beside the grand opera as the quartet stands beside the orchestra.[27]

Implicit in this 'manifesto' is the fact that chamber opera was not limited by a particular size of performing space, just as a string quartet could be played effectively in both small and large halls. The important factors were the nature of the sonority, the clarity of its textures, the intimacy and (in many cases) the pace of its action. It is significant, but should come as no surprise, that Britten (with Imogen Holst) made a performing edition of Purcell's *Dido and Aeneas* to include in the English Opera Group's repertoire along with *Albert Herring* and *The Turn of the Screw* (whose systematic structural use of tonal centres resonates in Act 1 of *Caritas*, especially).

Undoubtedly, Saxton was aware of these developments and (as has been mentioned earlier) was familiar with Britten's operatic output, including the later Church Parables, which represented yet another departure in music drama, and one whose biblical[28] and *Noh* sources created links with medieval Liturgical Drama as well as with a more recent tradition of operas based on religious subjects. *Caritas* itself tells a story set in a Norfolk church during the late Middle Ages and, like *The Burning Fiery Furnace*, for example, it makes reference to a plainsong antiphon as a means of establishing period and location. It is easy to find such parallels between Saxton and Britten, not least in the fact that the action of both *Curlew River* and *Caritas* was relocated to East Anglia (a region beloved of both Britten and Wesker)[29] and in the transformation of the chosen plainsong sources (the Compline hymn *Te lucis ante terminum* and *Alleluia. Te martyrum candidatus*, respectively) to provide much of the melodic material of each work. There is another significant point of comparison, of course, in the treatment of madness in both works – although the differences are profound. Unlike Christine's disillusioned descent into catatonic insanity in *Caritas*, Britten's Madwoman is a lost soul searching for her son within a ritualistic narrative presented in a pseudo-monastic setting that eschews naturalistic representation. Together with the other protagonists, the Ferryman and Traveller, she[30] wears a mask (a convention of *Noh* theatre) further to distance her depiction from reality; her unstable character is reflected in a musical line that is more angular than the plainsong-derived norm, while still refraining from the overt expressionism of a European *angst*-laden psychotic. The emphasis is on stylized restraint, consistent

---

[27]   Letter to Ralph Hawkes, 30 June 1946, cited and quoted in Mervyn Cooke (ed.) *The Cambridge Companion to Benjamin Britten* (Cambridge: Cambridge University Press), p. 95.

[28]   This applies only to *The Burning Fiery Furnace* and *The Prodigal Son*. See n. 29.

[29]   *Curlew River* is based on the Japanese Noh play *Sumidagawa*. The 'original' Christine Carpenter lived in Shere in Surrey during the mid-fourteenth century.

[30]   The role of the Madwoman (like all in the Noh tradition) is taken by a man.

with the essential characteristics of its Japanese model – but what has changed is the conclusion of the play where William Plomer (the librettist) replaces the bleak conclusion of *Sumidagawa* with a cathartic resolution (that owes more than a little to Chaucer's *Prioress's Tale*)[31] in which the Madwoman witnesses a vision of her dead son who promises that they will be reunited in heaven. After *her* vision, madness leaves her.

The underlying sense of restraint in Britten's Church Parables is a world away from the more public emotionalism of *Caritas*; whereas Britten achieves an atmosphere of relative timelessness – not to say overall tranquillity – *Caritas* is populated by eminently human and credible characters. There is a sense in which we are content to believe in the Abbot, the Ferryman, the Madwoman (and even the appearance of the spirit of her son) because of the artifice of the drama and its final resolution, whereas the tragedy of *Caritas* is vividly realistic and is not limited to the anchoress herself. Everyone, to some extent, is a victim: Mathew (the rector), Christine's parents, Robert Lonle (her former lover), even Bishop Henry who is as much imprisoned by his own preconceptions of his status as is Christine by the confines of her narrow cell.

Religious Opera

Without delving back too far into detailed operatic history, it is clear that librettos have covered a wide spectrum of themes and aspects of European culture. Classical myths (*Orfeo* and *Dafne*), lives of saints (*Sant'Alessio* and *The Martyrdom of Saint Magnus*), fairytales and legends (*The Flying Dutchman* and *Faust*), ancient history (*The Coronation of Poppea* and *Julius Caesar*), social/political satire (*The Marriage of Figaro* and *The Beggar's Opera*), stories from Shakespeare and Romantic literature (*Othello* and *Lucia di Lammermoor*), allegory and fantasy (*The Magic Flute* and *The Golden Cockerel*), the celebration of great events (*Gloriana* and *Aida*) – even the exoticism of the East (*Madama Butterfly* and *The Mikado*) – are amongst the recurring subjects deemed fit for musical setting and public entertainment. It is hardly surprising, therefore, that great adventure stories from the Bible such as Moses or Salome should have attracted composers from Rossini to Richard Strauss and Schoenberg. The list would be even longer if Handel's oratorios ('veiled operas') on the stories of Belshazar, Esther, Joshua, Judas Macabeus and Saul were included, and there is no doubt that the traditional division between church-based and theatre-based performance has prevailed against a more general acceptance of biblical themes, especially in early opera. However, this is not to say that the Church itself (or its music or monastic establishments) has been excluded from the corpus

---

[31]   In the *Canterbury Tales*, the Prioress narrates the story of a missing novice/singing boy who joins in *Alma redemptoris mater* from his grave. It is thought that the legend dates from the twelfth century.

of opera – whether it be to provide central themes (as in Pfitzner's *Palestrina*, which focuses on the impact of the Council of Trent on liturgical music) or local colour (as in the 'Nuns' Chorus' from Mascagni's *Cavalieri rusticana*). 'The Good Friday Music' from *Parsifal* is, probably, one of the best-known examples of a sacred occasion being depicted within an otherwise mythical context, and Puccini's *Suor Angelica* of a monastic setting enclosing a very human tragedy. This latter one-act opera (included in Puccini's *Il trittico*) treads a delicate line between poignant drama and overt sentimentality as (in a vision) the Virgin Mary leads the nun's (dead) son towards his dying mother (Angelica) to the accompaniment of 'The Royal March of the Madonna'. Angelica's aria, 'Senza mamma, bambino tu es morto', is similarly more a romantic threnody than a monastic prayer.

Perhaps the most successful antecedent of *Caritas* within this hybrid genre of secular history and monastic ceremony is Poulenc's *Dialogue des Carmélites*, set in the French Revolution and the subsequent Terrors. Composed in 1957, after its composer's return to Catholicism,[32] the opera relates the story of the Carmelite Nuns of Compiègne who were expelled from their convent and ultimately guillotined as martyrs in Paris. As in *Suor Angelica* (and to a lesser extent in *Caritas*), aristocratic characters (Blanche de la Force) and low-born (Sister Constance) are juxtaposed within the Church as well as without, albeit with the two being joined in death. Poulenc, perhaps anecdotally, is said to have claimed that his nuns only sang tonal music, and this work certainly uses a more conventional idiom (in both senses) than do his contemporary instrumental works.[33] In particular, the composer introduces plainsong in Act 1 to establish a monastic context, and the culminating points of each of the three acts are signalled with moving settings of the *Ave Maria*, *Ave Verum Corpus* and *Salve Regina*, respectively.

Whereas *Dialogue des Carmélites* is characterized by the overall dignity and restraint of its musical language, the same could hardly be claimed for Maxwell Davies's remarkable opera based on his interpretation of the life of the sixteenth-century composer John Taverner.[34] Its inclusion within this brief survey of the religious in opera is justified by a number of factors – the use of a church musician as hero/anti-hero and the selection of ecclesiastical and secular characters as archetypes (The White Abbot and King). The duality of its themes (Catholicism and Protestantism; faith and heresy; trial and punishment) and the duality of its musical language (tonal and atonal; authentic and parody) are also significant precursors of similar features in *Caritas*, although *Taverner* is more obviously satirical – more fantastical – than the tightly organized discipline of Saxton's work, which is essentially a cumulative drama in two connected acts rather than a reflective symmetry of opposites. What the two operas share most is the uncompromising expressivity (not to say expressionism) of their musical language and word setting

---

[32]   In 1936.
[33]   The Sonatas for Flute, Oboe and Clarinet, for example.
[34]   *Taverner* (1962–68), rev.1970, first performed 1972.

– and it is the second of these two features that will be explored in more detail in Chapter 4 as well as being touched on at the end of *this* chapter.

Finally in this section, mention should be made of two works composed on either side of *Caritas*. Both Jonathan Harvey's *Passion and Resurrection* (1981) and James MacMillan's *Visitatio Sepulchri* (1993), illustrate the post-1950 fascination with medieval drama, much of which survives in musically notated sources. Although current thinking would be opposed to including such sung plays in the operatic canon,[35] many medieval liturgical dramas do, however, contain comparable features of recitative, extended aria-like melismatic solos, ensembles, and choruses (derived from plainsong or strophic hymns). The profound influence of this genre on Britten's Church Parables has already been mentioned and it is worth adding that Britten was familiar with Karl Young's monumental volumes that made available the literary texts of this repertoire in a single collection for the first time.[36] Harvey and MacMillan both make use of a seminal medieval text (the dialogue-trope *Quem queritis in sepulcro*)[37] that is traditionally associated with the Introit of the Mass for Easter Morning.[38] Neither composer appears to draw on the received music of *Quem queritis*[39] but Harvey, certainly, acknowledges Young (1933) as his literary source. As his title suggests, Harvey also sets the events leading up to (and including) the Crucifixion,[40] with the 'Resurrection Garden Scene' (*Visitatio Sepulchri* itself) forming the (shorter) second section of the work. The entire ritual (sung in English throughout) is framed by words from the Book of Common Prayer (Holy Communion) and (at the end) versicles and responses from the Russian Orthodox order for Easter Sunday Matins. By comparison, MacMillan sets only the simple dialogue between the Angel(s) and the Three Marys (*Quem queritis …*) rather

---

[35]   Britten's children's 'pageant' *Noye's Fludde*, for example, is modelled on the fifteenth-century Chester Miracle Play (which does not contain music).

[36]   Britten owned an annotated copy of Karl Young (1933), *The Drama of the Medieval Church* (2 vols, Oxford: Oxford University Press), cited in M. Cooke (1998) *Britten and the Far East* (Woodbridge: Boydell & Brewer), pp. 162–64.

[37]   Q: 'Whom do you seek in the sepulchre [O Christians]?' [A: 'The crucified Jesus of Nazareth, O heavenly one.']

[38]   See Karl Young, *The Drama of the Medieval Church* (Vol.1, pp. 393-97) for the twelfth-century *Fleury Playbook* (Latin) version used by Harvey in English translation. Young's publication does *not* include music. MacMillan cites a thirteenth-century Latin Easter play from Notre Dame in Paris – but not the MS details. For other information and theories about the origin of the trope, see John Stevens (1986) *Words and Music in the Middle Ages* (Cambridge: Cambridge University Press), p. 330, n. 53 for a neat summary of the main arguments.

[39]   Found, for example, in Orléans ms 201. A modern edition is included in W. Thomas, transcr./ed. (2001) *Plays for Christmas and Easter* in *The Fleury Playbook*, Vol. 2 (Newton Abbot: Antico Edition).

[40]   Setting text from a twelfth-century Latin Passion Play from Montecassino in translation. See Sandro Sticca (1969) *Origins and development of the Latin Passion Play* (Albany, NY: State University of New York Press, 1969), pp. 66–77.

than the substantially extended drama from St Benoît-de-Fleury, used by Harvey. Significantly, he labels his work 'a sacred opera' designed for the stage, whereas *Passion and Resurrection* is conceived as a biblical *historia* to be performed in a church or cathedral within a liturgical context in which the audience/congregation participates in the singing of the two great hymns, *Pange Lingua* and *Vexilla Regis,* and the concluding Alleluias that punctuate the work. MacMillan also augments his basic Latin sentences by including the Easter sequence, *Victimae paschali laudes* (whose text provides a gloss on the Easter story), and the hymn *Te Deum,* which concludes many medieval liturgical-dramas – but these are sung onstage by the half-dozen or so performers, thus emphasizing the impression of an observed rather than involved ceremony. Indeed, with its obsessive *ostinati* and fanfares, its rapid 'Stravinskian' declamation and animated orchestration, *Visitatio Sepulchri* occupies a position closer to staged oratorio than either opera or liturgical drama, whereas Harvey's *Passion and Resurrection*, although cast as a sustained religious narrative, at times approaches operatic dimensions in its instrumental '*entracts*' as Christ is brought to Calvary and during his death and deposition. The hybrid nature of these two works is yet another aspect of the ways in which mutation of genres has contributed to the development of opera in the second half of the twentieth century.

Although, at first sight, *Caritas* shares little of the sustained Christian devotion of *Passion and Resurrection* or the intense paschal focus of *Visitatio Sepulchri,* it contains numerous references to hymns, prayers and sermons – not to mention heresies. Most of the action takes place in or close to the church and it opens with a liturgically authentic Office for the Enclosing of Anchorites. Of course, much of this detail is the work of Wesker[41] (who even specifies the use of the plainsong *Alleluia. Te martyrum* and the Pentecost hymn *Veni, Creator Spiritus*) but it is Saxton who weaves these references into a cohesive and convincing score that is further enhanced by additional liturgical quotations, such as the instrumental *Kyrie eleison* introduced in the transition between the two acts (and identified at the start of the Act 2 Passacaglia). In the course of this volume, *Caritas* will be examined as an opera with strong religious, political, social and historic elements. Its devotional and psychological aspects will be explored and its musical techniques will be analysed. Saxton's skill in orchestration and word-setting will be highlighted, as will his transformation of the conventions of staged-drama into opera where narrative and action can be sustained in the orchestra as well as through the spoken or sung word and gesture.

---

[41]   A full discussion of Wesker's research and literary genius in constructing his play and libretto follows in Chapter 2.

Saxton and Musical Narrative

One might well ask how Saxton made the transition from the relatively inexperienced composer of his early opera *Cinderella* to the accomplished professional who produced *Caritas*. Where did he develop the necessary skills to set a narrative of such interleaved detail and to create such a terrifying finale of darkest hopelessness? Some of the answers may be found, perhaps, in the above surveys and/or within the educational experiences of opera going, of student life, and of expert tuition by composers of the stature of Elisabeth Lutyens, Robin Holloway and Luciano Berio. Certainly, he would have been aware of other 'mad scenes' – in *Lucia di Lammermoor* and, possibly, Purcell's *Bess of Bedlam*[42] – and would have analysed their disjunct lines and frequently changing metres. Alan Bush's opera *Wat Tyler*[43] also deals with the peasants' rebellion against State authority, but Saxton would have learned little from its sweeping dramatic arch or its rather simplistic depiction of 'primitive' England through the use of parallel fourths and a predominantly diatonic language. Although this historic uprising provides a significant parallel with the story of Christine Carpenter in *Caritas,* its function overall is contextual rather than central, as in the plot of Bush's splendid masterpiece – a symptom of tragedy, perhaps, rather than its focal point.

Saxton, like any composer, would have been informed (and enriched musically) by the experience of such precedents, but it is his innate ability to tell stories through music that emerges in so many of his vocal and instrumental compositions leading up to *Caritas* and demonstrates his readiness for operatic challenges. His mastery of musical narrativity is refined through the experience of composing texted works – his three cantatas,[44] choruses such as *Child of Light* and *I Will Awaken the Dawn*, and works for vocal soloists and ensemble such as *Brise Marine*, *Eloge* and *La Promenade d'Automne*. It also lies behind the 'programmes' of instrumental works, a couple of which are given titles (*Carmen Natale* and *Choruses to Apollo*) that imply a song-like identity and an unsung text. A number of the orchestral pieces from this period, if not actual rehearsals for *Caritas,* certainly demonstrate the composer's ability to evoke striking sonorities and, more especially, to convey a sense of momentum – of musical travel – that takes us on journeys inspired by concepts of creation, birth and rebirth (*In the Beginning*, 1987) and the Resurrection itself (*Music to Celebrate the*

---

[42]   Purcell's song (printed in Playford, *Choice Ayres and Songs*, 1683) is just one example of the popular genre of 'Mad Songs', composed by Henry and Daniel Purcell, John Eccles, John Blow and others in the Restoration Period. Further examples include anonymous settings of 'Tom of Bedlam' (1673), 'Mad Maudlin' (1713), and H. Purcell's 'From Rosy Bow'res' (1695). See T. Roberts, ed. (1999) *Thirteen Songs of Passion and Madness* (2vols, London: Voicebox).

[43]   Published 1959.

[44]   1979, 1980 and 1981.

Resurrection, 1988–89).[45] The parallel with Christine's journey of self-discovery and disillusionment in *Caritas* needs no further emphasis, although, as has already been mentioned, the opera depicts the passage from the light of her dedication to a life of prayerful solitude towards a metaphorical crucifixion as her faith is shattered, rather than the progression from darkness to light, so prominent a feature of the two above-cited orchestral works. In a sense, this reversal of Saxton's favoured emotional path poses far greater challenges – in the place of great affirmative unisons and joyous orchestral dancing, we witness a cruel parody of normality as the musical material from Act 1 (including the plainsong) progressively disintegrates in the final scene until all disappears into a chanted monotone: 'This is a wall ... and this is a wall .. and this is a wall ...'.

Robert Saxton's own voyage of discovery from his artistic nativity up to *Caritas* has only been touched on here but there is no question but that this opera marks the culmination of the first major period of his creative output. The genesis of *Caritas* was not without its traumas (not least in the casting of the title role) but these will be discussed in a later chapter. For now, we will explore the dramatist's role as he incorporates documents into a play and his play into a libretto.

---

45   Commissioned by BBC TV to be shown on Easter Sunday in conjunction with images of Coventry Cathedral, itself a powerful symbol of resurrection (RS).

Chapter 2
Christine Carpenter:
From Documents to Drama

In the *Author's Note* that prefaced the 1981 edition of *Caritas*,[1] Arnold Wesker formally thanked the touring theatres of Norway and Sweden who, together with *Det Danske Teater* of Denmark, had commissioned the play. He also acknowledged the help of Professor Paul Levitt of the University of Colorado who had urged him to explore the world of anchoresses and, in particular, the 'scant story' of Christine Carpenter. Finally, Wesker appended the briefest of biographical notes about the real-life model for his main character, and mentioned some recently discovered documents that revealed 'that the original Christine was immured [in 1329], broke out three years later and then seems to have been persuaded by the authorities to re-enter her cell'.[2]

As with many theatrical works, the original text of *Caritas* subsequently underwent significant revision during the course of rehearsals. This pre-production version (1981) was further altered during the summer of 1988 after the author had worked on the libretto for Saxton's opera, and the fully revised stage play was published in 1990.[3] The opera libretto itself has been incorporated into various publications, notably the CD booklet that accompanies the commercial recording.[4] As one might anticipate, there are substantial differences between these three published texts – and especially between the libretto and the two editions of the play. These will be analysed during the course of this chapter and the next but, for now, the genesis of Wesker's remarkable drama will be traced from its roots in St James' Church, Shere,[5] through a pathway of several subsidiary sources, via geographical and temporal transposition (and inspired authorial invention) to its final manifestation in operatic form.

---

[1]   Arnold Wesker (1981) *Caritas* (London: Jonathan Cape).

[2]   This statement will be challenged in a later section of this chapter.

[3]   In *Lady Othello and Other Plays* (*Arnold Wesker Plays*, Vol. 6 (London: Penguin Books)). That is, before the premiere of the opera on 21 November 1991, at Wakefield Opera House.

[4]   See the 'Recordings' section of the 'Bibliography'. Wesker's copyright date is given as 1989. The libretto is, of course, present in Saxton's Full and Vocal Scores (Chester Music, 1991 and 1997, respectively), and is also reproduced as Appendix E, by kind permission of the author.

[5]   Where there are still traces of the anchoress's cell once occupied by Christine Carpenter.

To suggest that *Caritas* was founded on fact but crafted by fiction might appear simplistic, if not misleading. Yet close examination of the play shows that, whereas Wesker drew on a number of medieval sources to provide him with liturgical, devotional, political and doctrinal information, his main intention was to weave a narrative that contrived to prove an ideological proposition, largely of his own making. To quote from the preface to the 1990 edition[6] of the play:

> Caritas is about the pursuit of the ideal through dogmas which lead to the destruction of things human.

It would appear that the author regarded Christine's disillusionment and eventual madness as being a direct consequence of the Church's *documented* refusal to release her from her vows, although there is no historical evidence to support this conclusion – as a close reading of the extant letters from the Bishop of Winchester will make clear. As will be seen, the author has taken considerable pains to ensure that his depiction of an anchoress's immurement and daily life in the fourteenth century are as historically accurate as possible; whereas, on the other hand, it would seem that, by choosing to ignore certain details and inventing others, he was prepared to politicize history in support of his declared aims. Not that the story is intrinsically flawed – or that all plays based on history have to be consistent in every detail. As it was, Wesker chose to relocate Christine Carpenter's anchorage from the village of Shere in Surrey to Pulham St Mary in Norfolk and to change the dates of her immurement to coincide with events leading to the Peasants' Uprising in 1381. Wesker (a Londoner by birth)[7] had a particular affinity with East Anglia and, when he made the decision to alter the place and time of Christine's story, he was careful to substitute Bishop John Stratford of Winchester (whose letters are included in the 'documents' referred to above) with Bishop Henry le Despenser of Norwich[8] who, *inter alia*, had played a major role in suppressing the Peasants' Revolt and in defeating the peasants in the Battle of North Walsham in 1381.[9] By the same token Wesker, by association, drew attention (perhaps subliminally) to Julian of Norwich's

---

[6]   But dated 24 October 1981. That is just over two weeks after the first performance of the play on 7 October, 1981, given by the National Theatre Company at the Cottesloe Theatre, London.

[7]   Wesker was born in Stepney in 1932. His links with East Anglia date from c.1952–56 when he was employed in various capacities in Norfolk and met his wife, Doreen (married in 1958). Several of his other plays are set in Norfolk (*Roots*, 1959 and *I'm Talking about Jerusalem*, 1960). He was awarded an Honorary DLitt by the University of East Anglia at Norwich in 1989. In 1991, he wrote the play *William of Norwich* (re-titled *Blood Libel*) commissioned for the opening of the new Norwich Playhouse (world premiere 1995).

[8]   Also known as the 'Fighting Bishop' (1341–1406). Bishop of Norwich from 1370–1406.

[9]   Information from Wikipedia (en.wikipedia.org/wiki/Henry_le_Despenser, accessed 2 August 2010).

Revelation of Love – an account of the Anchoress Julian's visions, now more or less contemporary with Christine's rearranged dates[10] – and he took care to identify (Sir) Mathew de Redeman, her priest and mentor, as Rector of St James' Chapel (a medieval Guild Chapel[11] in Pulham St Mary) since it was the Apostle James[12] who the anonymous author of the thirteenth-century *Ancrene Riwle* recommended should become the patron of anchoresses.[13] In *Caritas* (1981), Mathew refers to his appointment to the parish by Pope Urban himself as 'the Vatican's choice'. Presumably this was Urban V (1362–70), Mathew being 'about thirty' in 1377 (the starting date for the play), rather than Urban VI who was elected on 8 April 1378 and survived throughout the 'Great Schism' until his death in 1389.[14]

Clearly, the main reason for the changes cited above was to synchronize the known and the invented details of Christine's life as an anchoress with the tumultuous incidents surrounding the abortive Peasants' Uprising and the contemporary (Lollard) religious dissidence of John Ball and Wycliffe. By forcing together these events, Wesker intensifies the seemingly irreconcilable extremes of blind faith and the acceptance of established social norms with those of anti-monasticism, anti-clerical thinking and the reforming ideals of Wat Tyler. Wesker's over-riding theme of the 'anti-human quality of dogma'[15] is sharply focused in the year 1381 on the madness of Christine's situation, the (undocumented) death of her ex-fiancé and the madness of social conflict that witnessed the murder of Simon, Archbishop of Canterbury, together with some of his followers in the Tower of London, and the subsequent execution of Wat Tyler and John Ball. Lord Bishop Henry's real-life involvement in the Battle of North Walsham serves to reinforce his 'fictional' obduracy during the play in which he represents the personification of the immense power of the nobility. Mathew de Redeman, however, stands for the more reformist aspect of the established Church and, as the drama unfolds, he grows increasingly critical of his ecclesiastical and temporal superior. His very name might be thought to embody the liberating consequences of literacy and its potentially disruptive effect on established social orders, so fiercely resisted by the Bishop and, paradoxically,

---

[10]   See Julian of Norwich (1986) *Revelation of Love*, ed. Marion Glasscoe (Exeter: University of Exeter), p. vii.

[11]   Established in 1402 by the Guild of Hatters and Milliners as a free-standing chapel away from the parish church dedicated to the Virgin Mary. The likelihood of such a 'secular' chapel supporting an anchorage is uncertain – even allowing for the anachronistic dates.

[12]   James the Less(er): so-called 'brother of Christ' to distinguish him from 'James the Greater', martyr and patron saint of Spain.

[13]   M.B. Salu, trans. and ed. (1955/2001) *Ancrene Riwle* (Guide of Anchoresses) (Exeter: Exeter University Press), p. 4.

[14]   The Schism, of course supplied much ammunition for the reformers such as Wycliffe and Hus. See Geoffrey Baraclough (1968/1975) *Medieval Papacy* (London: Thames and Hudson), pp.165-174.

[15]   Cited in the author's 1990 preface, but dated 24 October 1981.

feared by Christine's mother, Agnes ('Books, I warned against books').[16] It is to Wesker's great credit that his decision to compress events within such a momentous period of British history should be matched with carefully researched details such as those already mentioned – and, even more-so, those now to be discussed.

Documents

The 'Winchester' Letters

A pamphlet, dated 1986, published by St James' Church, Shere, provides the main (secondary) source of information about the history of Christine Carpenter's immurement as an anchoress. In addition to the three extant letters written by John Stratford, Bishop of Winchester (1323–33), which are available in various other sources,[17] it contains a brief account of the discovery of the letters and an extract from the Shere Parish Magazine (October 1972) that helps to locate the home of the Carpenter family in what are now known as Ash and Willow Cottages in Lower Street. In this case, the archival source is recorded as being the 'Bray Papers' held at Guildford Muniment Room and, from its entries, Christine's father is identified as William (Carpenter) who was granted 'Stiles' (as the property was then known) by Richard FitzGeoffrey, son of the Lord Lieutenant of Ireland who was given the 'two acres and a messuage [house]' by Henry III.

Although it is commonly stated that there are but three letters recorded in the Winchester Register of 1329,[18] close inspection of the (three) entries reveals that a correspondence of at least seven letters took place.

Letter (i) [*First Entry*]   From Bishop John of Winchester to the (Officials of the) Archdeacon of Surrey refers to **letter (ii)** received from Christine, daughter of William Carpenter, in which she requests permission to be enclosed 'in a narrow place in the churchyard adjoining the parish church … to enable her to serve Almighty God the more worthily'. His reply advises the officials of the Archdeacon that she should be brought to the church 'in person' and to be questioned to find out if she 'is of such good life and conversation that she is likely to make a success of

---

[16]   Act 1, scene I.

[17]   The letters are included in the booklet provided with Chris Newby's (1993) film *Anchoress* (black and white; London: British Film Institute) and several internet websites on 'Shere' and 'Anchoress'. I am indebted to Professor Paul Moorcraft (author of *Anchoress of Shere* (2002, Scottsdale, USA: Poison Pen Press) for sharing his knowledge of Christine Carpenter and providing me with copies of the extant letters and other information about St James' Church, Shere.

[18]   Egerton MSS, British Library. Episcopal Register of John Stratford (Bishop of Winchester, 1332–33).

[her] proposal for a more saintly life'. It must also be ascertained 'whether she is free or espoused to anyone or joined in marriage'. All being satisfactory, she would be allowed to become an anchoress and 'sworn formally by law' – this last point being crucial to any subsequent request to be released from her vows. The Bishop's letter, written at Farnham[19] is dated 11 July 1329.

Letter (iii) [*Second Entry*]   Again from the Bishop but is more a legal document than letter (i). He refers to letter (ii) and records that the proper investigations have been made and that no cause was found for deciding 'that the said Christine should not be permitted to be enclosed'. The Bishop mentions the 'consent also given by Sir Matthew [sic] the present Rector of the church of Schire [sic] and 'the parishioners, thereof'. The document is sealed and dated 14 August 1329, at Waleton.[20] A period of some three years now elapses before a third (and final) letter (iv) is written by the Bishop of Winchester. It is clear, that at some time, Christine left her cell without permission (as a result of which she would probably have been excommunicated), but there appears to be no recorded reason for her action – nor, indeed, does Wesker suggest one since there is no corresponding break in the action of his play.[21]

Letter (iv) [*Third Entry*]   Addressed to the Dean of Guildford and dated 10 November 1332, at Farnham. The opening paragraph states that Christine had approached him on 8 October 1332 (**Letter (v)**), having withdrawn previously from her cell – 'as we have been informed'. Bishop John then quotes a letter sent to himself from Brother John of Wrotham, Primarius of the Lord Pope, dated 6 August 1332, at Avignon (**Letter (vi)**). In turn this letter (which strongly advocates that Christine should be permitted to re-enclose) refers to a further **letter (vii),** sent by Christine to the Pope in which she humbly confesses her sins and petitions for mercy and re-admission to her anchorage at Shere. Bishop John concludes letter (iv) by commanding the Dean of Guildford that Christine 'shall be thrust back into the said re-enclosure and that with suitable solicitude and competent vigilance you shall take care to guard her ... that she may learn at your discretion how nefarious was her committed sin ... thereafter dedicating herself worthily to God'.

On the evidence of Wesker's note to the 1981 edition of *Caritas*, it seems certain that he was aware of the contents of these entries, even if he had not read them in

---

[19]   Farnham Castle was used by the Bishop as a 'half-way' lodging between Winchester and London.

[20]   Most likely Walton-on-Thames, another possible lodging place for the Bishop of Winchester, near Guildford.

[21]   Although there is an additional year added to the timescale of the documents (i.e. July 1329, to November 1332, becomes July 1377 to June 1381). For some reason one year and four months elapse between Act 1, scene IX and scene XI in the stage-play.

person. However, although he adopted the proper names mentioned in the letters,[22] he chose to ignore the evidence of Christine leaving her (door-less) cell and also the 'salutory penance in proportion with her sin' specified by the Pope.[23] There have been a number of speculations about the reason(s) for Christine's 'escape',[24] but suffice to say that Wesker makes no reference to this event in his play, preferring instead to concentrate on the anchoress's expectations of a 'showing', perhaps inspired by Julian of Norwich's vision of divine love, and Christine's (speculative) disillusionment and loss of faith.

The Office for the Enclosing of Anchorites

After the opening stage directions to Act 1 in both editions of the stage play *Caritas* the author inserts the following note:

> What follows is based on the recorded ceremony for enclosing anchoresses. Poetic licence is taken. But Scene I must be performed in full, as a real church service, so that an audience is saturated in an intense religious atmosphere and feels itself witness to the ceremony of immurement … .

The liturgy referred to by Wesker is taken from the *Use of Sarum*[25] – possibly the copy included in the standard history of Hermits and Anchorites by Rotha Mary Clay.[26] It would be counter-productive to list details of all of the borrowings here, but the author extracts at least fifteen passages – literal quotations of Proper Psalms (Psalms 6 and 131),[27] Prayers and Vows – for use in the first version of his play. As he makes clear in the above note, the work starts with a substantial liturgical ceremony that forms the basis of Christine's story and provides the audience with an authentic taste of the ritual of enclosure, into which Wesker interpolates moments of domestic commentary and rather sceptical support from Christine's parents

---

[22]   Christine and William Carpenter and (Sir) Matthew [Mathew] de Redeman.

[23]   Pope John XXII (Pope from 1316 to 1334 at Avignon).

[24]   Notably by Paul Moorcraft in his novel *Anchoress of Shere.*

[25]   *Manuale ad Usum Sarum – Servitium Includendorum* (Surtees Society, 63) pp. 37-43. This being the Salisbury Rite, commonly used in England in the Middle Ages, rather than the Roman Rite.

[26]   Rotha Mary Clay, *The Hermits and Anchorites of England* (London: Methuen, 1914), Appendix A, pp.193–8. An obvious reference book for anyone planning to write about this subject.

[27]   However, it seems that Wesker has mistakenly used the *Old Testament* Psalm 131 rather than the *Vulgate/Sarum* Psalm131 (= *132 Old Testament*), which is specified in the Immurement Rubric and is far better suited to both ceremony and play. The opportunity to revise/correct this by omitting both Psalms 6 and 131 (*OT*) in the libretto, and the omission of Psalm 131 (*OT*) in the 1990 edition of *Caritas*, appears to be fortuitous. Psalm 6 has the same numbering in both Latin and Hebrew systems and is retained in the 1990 publication.

and ex-fiancé. As well as psalms (which would have been intoned by the cantor or priest and *schola cantorum*), the *Sarum* rubric instructs that, after the anchorite has been clad in their new habit, the great Pentecostal Hymn *Veni, Creator Spiritus* should be sung by the Bishop or priest – indeed, it seems possible that Wesker might have originally planned for this to be sung again at the end of the play (as a sort of cyclical refrain) since it is printed after the conclusion of the final scene of Act 2 in the 1981 edition. Understandably, the transformation of the play into a libretto necessitated some reduction of the liturgical text – and much of this 'thinning-down' is retained in the 1990 edition as well. There is, however, one significant change in the liturgy specified for the libretto and preserved in the 1990 edition of the stage play: an additional chant *Alleluia. Te martyrum candidatus* (from the Mass for the Common of Two or More Martyrs)[28] is inserted at the very start of Act 1 (scene I) with the *Alleluia* recapitulated as Christine is walled-up into her cell. This departure from the *Sarum* ceremony would seem to support the thesis that Wesker intended to emphasize Christine's role as a 'broken victim' of the dogmatic ecclesiastical regime, in line with his overall theme, rather than that of a 'potential saint', more commonly associated with the status of a devotional recluse.

Otherwise, the first scene of Wesker's play is faithful to most of the relevant liturgy and also contains a number of exchanges that demonstrate his absorption of the smallest details of anchorites' daily life and their few belongings. For example, Clay[29] describes how in 'early days' it was customary for hermits and anchorites to be buried in their cells or oratories. Some had tombs prepared in advance and the 'tenant' was 'bidden ... to meditate on death' – a reference that helps to clarify Robert's seemingly macabre statement: 'Suppose we must be thankful she didn't ask for a coffin to sleep in.'[30] As Wesker's dramatic structure takes shape, such factual details are woven into the sequence of sixteen short scenes that make up Act 1 with its alternation of interior and exterior life; its interplay of religious and secular events. Immediately after Christine's immurement (albeit some months later in real time), scene II exposes a totally different side of Bishop Henry's character as he sanctions the public branding of Richard Lonle (father of Christine's ex-fiancé), one of his serfs – a villain or bondsman[31] who had been convicted of absconding from his place of work and home. Lonle refers to the law that allowed men of his station to gain freedom by escaping to a city and living there for a year or more. He had failed by three days. The usual penalty would have been loss of land and livelihood – or

---

[28]   *The Liber Usualis* (1961), ed. The Benedictines of Solesmes (Tournai and New York: Desclee), p. 1171. Also Nick Sandon, ed. (1984–99), *The Use of Salisbury* (Vol. 2, 1986; Newton Abbot: Antico), where it is specified for the Feast of [the Martyrdom of the] Holy Innocents.

[29]   Clay, *Hermits and Anchorites of England*, pp. 113–15.

[30]   Act 1, scene I (1981), p. 17.

[31]   See *Caritas* (1981), p. 21 for details of the conditions of his rental.

worse[32] – but labour would have been in short supply after the ravages of the Black Death[33] and Lonle was branded on his forehead, no doubt as a warning to others as well as to himself.

During the sixteen scenes that constitute Act 1, the years from 1377 to 1381 are summarised as if in a series of snapshots or photographic slides in a scholarly lecture. The stage set is simple:

> a composite set to include: the wall, altar and circular window of the chapel; part of the anchored cell wall and its grill window; a carpenter's workshop

Nearly two years elapse between scene I (dated July 1377) and scene IX (dated February 1379); sixteen months separate scene IX and scene XI (dated May 1381); scene XIII (dated 17 June 1381) follows one month later; scenes XIV–XVI take place in the immediate aftermath of the failed Peasants' Uprising and death of Wat Tyler. In addition to the psalms and hymn referred to above, scene I (1981) also includes the recommended Gospel Reading from Luke,[34] which tells of Jesus visiting Martha and Mary. Several scenes contain virtual re-enactments of historical events (for example, a close paraphrase of John Ball's sermon based on the Book of Joel, in scene XIII). Others contain accounts of the Lives of Saints (scenes V, VIII and XII), and of taxation demands (scenes IV, IX, and XI). All of these provide either specific insights into the daily discipline of anchoresses or else contextual information that illustrates the increasing tensions of socio-political life away from Christine's cell.

Table 2.1 shows the major content of the Act 1 scenes and will provide a basic reference tool when the creation of the libretto is discussed. Although some of the scenes are quite short, the interlocking nature of their sequence results in strong structural coherence and an effective sense of temporal progression. Equally, the refrain-like questioning of the children's chorus intensifies Christine's increasing frustration as she awaits the vision that she hopes will confirm her union with Christ: 'There was a oneness time. I search that'.[35]

---

[32]   Bishop: 'They wanted him hung but I wasn't having any blood-letting because we're short of labour.'

[33]   Wesker makes no direct reference to the Black Death, which decimated the population of England in 1348/49 and 1361/62 and is believed to have been a major factor in the shortage of labour and the social unrest leading up to the Peasants Uprising. Perhaps this would have confused issues as the original Christine 'story' took place *before* the epidemic arrived in England.

[34]   Luke 10: 38–42.

[35]   Act 1, scene V.

Table 2.1   *Caritas*: Act 1 structure (1981 version)

Scene	Action	Cast	Location
I	Immurement Ritual [July 1377]	All*	Church
II	Branding of Richard [some months later]	B/MR/L	Outside
III	Christine and Robert	C/R*	Cell (in/out)
IV	Tax Collector (i)	T/W/R	Workshop
V	Christine and Matilde (i)	C/M	Cell (in/out)
VI	Christine's Confession	C/MR*	Church/Cell
VII	Family Discussion	W/A/R/MR/(C)	Workshop
VIII	Christine and Matilde (ii)	C/M	Cell (in/out)
IX	Tax Collector (ii) [Feb. 1379]	T/W/A/R	Workshop
X	Christine at Prayer	C/MR*	Church/Cell
XI	Tax Discussion [May 1381]	W/A/R/MR	Workshop
XII	Christine and Matilde (iii)	C/M	Cell (in/out)
XIII	Sermon [17 June 1381]	P/B/(C)	Church
XIV	Debate and Petition	B/MR/W/A/R/(C)*	Church
XV	Report on Uprising	P/A/(C)	Workshop
XVI	Bishop's Refusal	B/MR/(W)*	Church

Note: C = Christine Carpenter; W = William Carpenter; A = Agnes Carpenter; B = Bishop Henry; MR = Mathew Redeman; L = Richard Lonle; R = Robert Lonle; M – Matilde; T = Tax Collector; P = Priest; * = Children's Chorus

The Ancrene Riwle

One of the sources most frequently quoted in Clay[36] is the thirteenth-century 'practical guide for female recluses', known as *The Ancrene Riwle* (or *Ancrene Wisse*). Although it is addressed to 'three young sisters of gentle birth who were admitted to a convent to live each in an individual cell',[37] it is evident that it was widely read and consulted in the Middle Ages and beyond. There are many recommended devotional practices that find their way into *Caritas* and a number of references in the play that could be misconstrued if one were unaware of their origins in this or a similar manual. Mention has already been made of the author's advice to anchoresses that they should adopt St James as their patron and mentor because of his great holiness. He goes on to explain that James defined two forms of

---

[36]   Clay, *Hermits and Anchorites of England*.

[37]   Quoted from the Preface to Yoko Wada, ed. (2003/2010) *A Companion to Ancrene Wisse* (Woodbridge: Boydell & Brewer). This volume lists the extant copies of the Middle English versions of this treatise and provides invaluable commentaries on its authorship, readership, and application.

religious practice[38] – one that is followed in the outside world 'visiting the fatherless and widows in their tribulation' and the other followed by recluses who should 'keep themselves unspotted from the world'. He continues, saying that anchoresses (because of their seclusion) do not need to belong to either the Black [Dominicans] or the White [Carmelite] Orders as do those living in convents, where uniformity of habits and cowls might be a helpful indicator of their common purpose. The apparent opposites of black and white can also refer to external 'uncomeliness' and internal beauty, respectively, – or, conversely, to St Matthew's condemnation of the Scribes and Pharisees who 'make clean the outside of the cup and of the dish, but within … are full of uncleanliness, like to whited sepulchres.'[39] This seemingly paradoxical reasoning clearly baffles Robert Lonle (and seems to be only partially assimilated by Christine) in scene III of *Caritas* as he tries to understand Christine's decision to choose a life of isolation over one of marriage with him:

> You explain this an' you explain that, but your words is wind an' mist, an' black meanin' white an' white meanin' black!

Equally, there are exchanges between Christine and Matilde (the 60-year-old 'busybody' who visits her cell window in scenes V, VIII and XII) that show Wesker's familiarity with medieval devotional practices, set out in *Ancrene Riwle*. Making the sign of the Cross and genuflecting are just two of the 'signings' that are recommended as a form of self-discipline to assist the recluse to preserve her 'unspotted' state – especially on the rare occasions when she might meet (through the grill in the outside wall of her cell) those from the secular world seeking her advice or ministry. Matilde invariably greets the young anchoress by checking that she has carried out the disciplines set out in Part 2 of the 'Guide' (*The Custody of the Senses*):

> First of all, when you go to your … . window, find out … . who it is that has come …
> and when you really must go *make the sign of the cross on your mouth, ears and
> eyes, and also on your breast*, thinking of what you are doing, and then go forward
> in fear of God.

It is indicative of Christine's weakening resolve that, at the start of Matilde's third visit (scene XII), she satirizes the old woman's questions ('Crossed your mouth? Good! An' your eyes – ?' and so on) by repeating them in a mocking manner. However, Matilde's main purpose in visiting is to recite examples of saintliness (*Vitae*), such as would have been routinely read aloud in monastic institutions. She appears to have picked up these stories from a series of odd sources ('tell me by a smithy who heard it from a nun who heard it on a pilgrimage to Rome which

---

[38]   James 1: 27.
[39]   Matthew 23: 25, 27.

is how I get all my stories being a collector of stories 'bout saints which is what you'll be one day if you work hard at it'). But, whatever the origins of the tales, the examples of the 'Belgie saint called Yvetta',[40] Saint Veridiana of Sienna,[41] and Saint Christiana (another 'Belgie')[42] ring true and are narrated with a rough naturalness that contrasts with the mixture of pragmatic and spiritual speech found elsewhere in the play and vividly evokes the external village world that Christine has rejected but not completely erased from her memory.

Ancrene Riwle disseminates warnings and advice about an enormous range of subjects, cautioning the reader about the dangers of heresy, gluttony, gossip, evil talk, flattery and lying, while praising the virtues of silence, prudence, continence, confession and prayer. Indeed, it is the regularity and repetitiveness of prayer that forms the corner-stone of life as a recluse, and Christine's own more private moments draw heavily on the formulae of traditional liturgy – for example, her prayers in scene X commence with the recommended *Five Greetings in Memory of God's Five Wounds* before breaking off into her supposed 'showing':

> We adore thee, O Christ, an' we bless thee because of thy holy cross. Thou hast redeemed the world. We adore Thy cross, O Lord. We commemorate Thy glorious passion. Have mercy on us, Thou who didst suffer for us. Hail, O holy cross, worthy tree, whose precious wood bore the ransom of the world. Hail O –

Part 1 of *Ancrene Riwle* (from which the above quotation is derived)[43] lists the daily prayers and intercessions that solitaries are required to recite during the course of the Seven [monastic] Hours, the significance of numbering being an integral part of this discipline that also includes the *Seven Penitential Psalms*, the *Fifteen Gradual Psalms*, the *Ten Commandments*, and *Six Pater nosters and a versicle* in memory of the *Six Works of Mercy*, and so on.[44] Clearly, Christine cannot be seen to observe the full monastic ritual on stage but her mother, Agnes, describes her attempts until, progressively, she loses concentration and lapses into a state of slothful self-neglect.[45] Even as she declines into total disillusionment in Act 2, it is instructive to note how she attempts to recite three Hail Mary's and Hail O Cross before breaking off into heretical fantasies of Manichaean dualism – 'a God of Love and a God of

---

[40]   Probably St, Yvette of Huy (1158–1228).

[41]   Probably St. Veridiana (1182–1242).

[42]   Possibly St Christina the Astonishing (1150–1224).

[43]   *Ancrene Riwle*, pp. 7–8.

[44]   Ibid, p. 9 *et seq*. For more information on Number Symbolism, see: Vincent Foster Hopper (1938/2000) *Medieval Number Symbolism – Its Sources, Meaning, and Influence on Thought and Expression* (New York: Columbia University; reprint New York: Dover Publications). It is noteworthy that Wesker also draws on this medieval use of symbolic number patterns. See comments on the pages that follow.

[45]   Act 1, scene XI.

Hate'.[46] Indeed, it is the obsession with the Virgin Mary and Christ's Crucifixion that manifests itself in Christine's final fantasies as, cradling the crucifix in her arms, she sings a lullaby and begs to be nailed herself through hands and feet.

The theme of opposites that dominates *Ancrene Riwle* and Christine's own life as an anchoress is expressed by Wesker in a wide range of contrasting areas. The juxtaposition of sacred and secular life in Act 1, scene I, for example, is heard in music (liturgical chant and Christine's 'song' *I will forsake all that I see*); it is present in status (the Lord Bishop and the Carpenter); it is visible (in Church and Workshop) and it is created (as 'the old woman' of Christine is transformed into the 'new woman' – the anchoress who exchanges her external life and secular love for divine union with God). Even as the Bishop declares this, the 'Congregation continue[s] in subdued tones to chant the hymn of Pentecost in Latin'– *Veni, Creator Spiritus*, the self-same hymn recommended for recluses to greet each morning as they commence their daily Offices. In its second stanza, Rabanus Maurus (the hymn's ninth-century author) addresses the Paraclete[47] ('O Comforter, to thee we cry') as *fons vivus, ignis, caritas* ('fount of life and fire of love'). The *caritas* of which Maurus speaks is the 'charity' referred to in *The Author's Introduction to His Rule*;[48] the 'charity' of Paul's Epistle to the Ephesians;[49] the *Interior*, rather than *Exterior Rule* that anchoresses must follow; and the title of Wesker's play:

> charity, that is love, humility and patience, fidelity and the keeping of the ten ancient Commandments, Confession and penance, and other such matters, some belonging to the Old Law, some to the New.[50]

In passing, it is worthy of note that, when planning the libretto, Wesker utilized generic groupings (of 'jubilations', 'doubts', 'laments', and so on) that are comparable to the numerical grouping of prayers and intercessions that are recommended in Part 1 ('Devotions') of *Ancrene Riwle*[51] in what he terms 'strands in the weave' of the opera's action.[52] As well as the more obvious *three* Matilde stories and *nine* appearances of the children's voices (in the original play), he listed *nine* 'Jubilations', *eight* 'Unrests', *eight* 'Doubts', *eight* 'Laments', and *five* 'Prayers and Reasonings'. Needless to say, subsequent changes in editing and the ordering of events inevitably

---

[46]   This ongoing obsession with opposites culminates in Act 2, Part 8: 'The remedy for lust is mortification of the flesh.'

[47]   The Holy Spirit. See John 14: 16, 26.

[48]   *Ancrene Riwle*, p. 1.

[49]   Ephesians 2: 4.

[50]   *Ancrene Riwle*, p. 3.

[51]   For example, the 'Seven Penitential Psalms', the 'Five Joys of Mary', 'Five Greetings in Memory of Christ's Five Wounds', the 'Seven Gifts of the Holy Ghost', and so on.

[52]   I am indebted to Robert Saxton for providing me with access to his pre-compositional material, from which this information has been gleaned.

impacted onto Wesker's original scheme so that, for example, the appearances of the taunting children were reduced to *eight* and Matilde's hagiographic citations were severely pruned in substance.

Although there is no absolute distinction between *caritas* (sacred love) and *amor* (secular love) in medieval biblical Latin,[53] it seems very likely that Wesker's *Caritas* (the noun more frequently found than *amor* in the Vulgate Bible) is intended to imply the love that Christine felt for Christ and the Love defined in the penultimate part of *Ancrene Riwle,* as opposed to the amorous emotions still felt by Robert. *Caritas* here signifies the great love demonstrated by God for Man in the crucifixion and sought for by Christine. It is possible that the significance of the earlier Cistercian core-text *Summa Carta Caritatis* (c. 1165) in some way was assimilated into the teachings of *Ancrene Riwle.*[54] The common translation as 'charity' has become embodied in the King James Bible[55] but could be said to fail in communicating the intensity of love such as that experienced by (for example) Julian of Norwich to today's world.

Whereas Act 1 of *Caritas* allows Christine a modicum of privacy and isolation in her cell (the audience is not allowed to see her face during this act), Act 2 is set in the interior of her cell and she is fully visible in all her self-loathing and spiritual disarray. The one continuous scene consists of eleven 'Parts' that follow the stages of her struggle between reality and madness.[56] The director is instructed to use 'puffs of light fading in and out with sufficient darkness in between to allow her to move into a new framed position'. Apart from the taunting Children's Chorus, the unseen girl who seeks 'instruction' and the invisible presence of Bishop Henry and Mathew Redeman in 'Part 7', Christine is alone on stage, moving schizophrenically from one obsession to another, then fixed in suspended animation. An analogy with the *Stations of the Cross* is probably not intended by Wesker but it is tempting, nonetheless, to compare Christine's spiritual decline (from the Bishop's 'Judgement,[57] via the eleven 'framed positions' of Act 2, to her metaphorical crucifixion) with the traditional twelve pictorial images of Christ's agonizing journey to Golgotha. Table 2.2 provides a summary of the main stages and themes in Christine's journey.

One is reminded of Christopher Smart's poem, *Jubilate Agno,* written while he was in an asylum (and wonderfully set to music by Benjamin Britten),[58] which contains the evocative couplet:

---

[53] Indeed, both are used in *Veni, Creator Spiritus* to refer to sacred love or the love of God (lines 7 and 12).

[54] See Constance Hoffman Berman (2000/2010) *The Cistercian Evolution* (Philadelphia & Oxford: University of Pennsylvania Press), pp. 7–9, and elsewhere.

[55] See 1 Corinthians:13, 4-13, for example. The *New Revised Standard Version Bible* (1995) (NRSV; Oxford: Oxford University Press) goes some way to remedying this by translating 'caritas' as 'love'.

[56] 'I'm torn between shame and delirium' (Act 2, part 11).

[57] In Act 1, scene XVI – 'She cannot leave her cell'.

[58] Britten's *Rejoice in the Lamb* (1943) for SATB soloists, chorus and organ.

For I am under the same accusation with my Saviour –
For they said, he is beside himself.

Wesker's preface to the 1990 edition of his play has already been referred to. Within its (dare one say) rather dogmatic statements, he inserts the potent comment that he hopes that through the juxtaposition of the stories of the Peasants Uprising and an anchoress's loss of faith 'the play will make a poetic impact, as a parable does'. As if to reinforce his own views on dogma, the author then adds a copy of a letter from a Chinese lady[59] who describes the extreme behaviour of her sister who was still under the influence of Maoist ideology. Attempting to live by the former Maoist doctrines, the sister wanted to refuse payment for her work (but accepted support from her father); she aspired to train as a teacher but was not interested in culture. When offered watermelon by her father, she feared that he would corrupt her and

Table 2.2   *Caritas*: Act 2 structure (1981)

Part	Christine	Others	Main theme
1	In the corner of her cell, terrified		'I ent narthin' [I am nothing]
2	On her knees before the crucifix		Impassioned personal prayer
3	In the corner of her cell	Children taunting	'I ent narthin'
4	By the quatrefoil		Impassioned personal prayer
5	In the corner of her cell		'I ent narthin'
6	On her bed – sits bolt upright		Two Gods! / Hail Mary
7	Paces up and down her cell	Bishop and Mathew	Vision or Heresy / 'Not fit!'
8	By the window grill / to stool and table / brushes hair / beats breast / urinates	Little girl / Children taunting	Gives advice / Hail O Cross / Hail Mary / 'Not fit!'
9	In the corner of her cell / cradles crucifix, laments and rocks to and fro		Sings to the crucifix: 'The poor wail' / 'Put nails through me'
10	In the corner of her cell / exposes her breasts as she intones: 'The poor wail, the orphan sighs … '		Descends into parody of motherhood / 'Come to me, come to me, come … '
11	By the quatrefoil, back to the wall. Slowly she goes to the grill and sinks her teeth into the hand of one of the taunting children	Children taunting	Impassioned personal prayers / 'Forgive me Father' / 'I am crucified upon the Spring' / 'This is a wall … '

---

[59]   Quoted from David Bonavia (1989) *The Chinese* (London: Penguin).

ran to her room to commit suicide. If this was intended to provide a contemporary equivalent of Christine's story, it succeeds only because the story that Wesker tells about Christine is one that he has modified himself. Both stories could, indeed, be seen as parables of a sort, but what Wesker has created in this play is dramatic literature of the highest order that needs no ideological sign-posts or manifesto. *Caritas* makes its points through its language, its internal dynamics and its thematic parallels. It is true – Christine chose solitude, she was supported by her family, she aspired to live like Christ and to experience divine love. If she failed, perhaps it was because her expectations were too high; because she was human. Madness is not suicide. She was still a part of God's love. Perhaps Christopher Smart was right.

The aim of this chapter has been to provide some background information about (and specific insights into) the construction of Wesker's play out of a fragmentary account of Christine Carpenter's immurement (and re-enclosure) as an anchoress and the more fully documented political history of late fourteenth-century England (which witnessed the early stages in the breakdown of feudal social order). What now follows is a discussion of the commissioning of Robert Saxton's opera and the inevitable changes that needed to be made when translating a stage play into an operatic libretto. This complex process is one that has taxed writers for over four centuries – and has usually required a separate intermediary (the librettist) or else a composer (such as Wagner) who was capable of writing his own text (in his case, based on history or legend).[60] It is not out of disrespect to Beaumarchais that, for example, one refers to *The Marriage of Figaro* as being the work of Mozart and Lorenzo da Ponte. It simply records the difference between writing a novel and contributing a suitable text towards the composition of an opera. Other comparable examples of creative partnerships would include Gluck and Calzabigi, Verdi and Boito, Richard Strauss and Hofmannsthal. A contemporary parallel would be the routine employment of a screenplay writer to transform a novel or stage play into a film. The comparison between Wesker's play and Chris Newby's film *Anchoress* is instructive in this respect (despite the obvious restrictions of Newby's narrative).

---

[60]   In fact, this is a path followed by Saxton in his recent *Wandering Jew* (see Chapter 6).

Chapter 3
Caritas: Towards the Opera

Commission and Making of the Libretto

The opera *Caritas* was commissioned in 1987, jointly by Opera North and the Huddersfield Contemporary Music Festival, with funds provided by Yorkshire Arts and The Arts Council of Great Britain. Although Huddersfield had no suitable venue for opera, Wakefield's beautifully restored opera house was available and its dimensions no doubt conditioned the nature of the commission of a chamber opera.[1] There was to be no chorus (apart from the ensemble provided in the first scene by the whole cast, and the small group of children who taunt Christine throughout the opera); orchestral forces were to be correspondingly reduced. The journalist Norman Lebrecht[2] credited stage-director Michael Rennison with introducing Arnold Wesker to Robert Saxton and setting the project in motion. He also suggested that the composer 'was sucked into *Caritas* against his better instincts' – perhaps 'infected by the enthusiasm of Rennison who praised Wesker's script passionately'.

Bearing in mind that Lebrecht's article was focused on the politics of opera production (the circumstances surrounding the casting and staging of *Caritas* in particular) and set in the context of a domestic meal at Wesker's home, one should, perhaps, not attach too much weight to his comments about the composer's response to the commission. This was to be far more rationally and succinctly expressed in the 'Composer's Note' (printed in the vocal score of the opera) and quoted in full below. It is clear that Wesker *himself* chose to adapt the text of his play into the libretto, rather than employing a third party (as librettist or dramaturge) – indeed, there is anecdotal evidence that he had harboured secret ambitions in this field.[3] To distance himself from his original script (where he had sole responsibility) and to take on a complementary role in a dramatic/musical partnership must have proved an enormous undertaking, although his use of musical items in the play had demonstrated that he was fully aware of the emotional – and emotive – impact of liturgical chant and secular song. Saxton writes as follows:

> In transforming Arnold Wesker's play *Caritas* into an opera, there were three
> central issues in my mind. The first of these was the overall shape; where, in the

---

[1]   Wakefield's Opera House (designed by Frank Matcham) was extensively renovated in the early 1980s. Its seating capacity is a mere 499.

[2]   'A Fight at the Opera', *The Independent Magazine*, 16 November 1991.

[3]   Ibid. However it seems likely that Wesker was more at home with Musicals as a genre.

play, the two Acts to some extent balance one another, for operatic purposes Wesker and I reworked the proportions. We decided to retain the basic structure of Act 1 and to shorten the second Act considerably. Wesker therefore wrote his libretto so that no interval would be required, in order to produce an uninterrupted drama.[4] In the play, Act 2, Christine's long solo scene contained much intoning and verbal repetition. In the opera, this [effect of hypnotic obsession] is largely achieved orchestrally/musically, and, as a result, the original text is cut to a considerable degree, creating a continuous increase in musical-dramatic tension.

This led directly to the second challenge, that of creating a musical continuity and coherence, with the many short scenes of Act 1 experienced as part of a larger whole, and allowing Act 2 to grow from it naturally; this second act is a large-scale Passacaglia symbolising Christine's incarceration. The third issue of importance was to work with a libretto which gave scope for varied vocal characterisation, and which differentiated between verse, prose and conversational modes of expression. Wesker provided a finely crafted text in all of these respects; it is carefully paced and is masterly in its handling of the subtleties of the English language with regard to the requirements of singing and the nature of voices.[5]

It would be naive, of course, to conclude that the composition of libretto and opera proceeded with harmonious accord or that there were no moments of disagreement. Lebrecht writes of 'an initial trial of strength'; of the author baulking 'at Saxton's demands for concision' and then claims that 'by the time they finished, it was Wesker who was urging cuts, and Saxton who was resisting them'. There were inevitably going to be compromises as the two creative writers sought solutions to what they perceived as conflicts of interest – but there seems to be no reason to doubt the veracity of the initial comment by the composer, that he 'saw immediately ... that Caritas would make a superb chamber opera ... . It chimed in with pieces I had written about darkness into light.'[6]

Clearly, there must have been an initial attraction towards Wesker's scenario – a charge of electricity that awakened Saxton's creative energy and stimulated his purely musical imagination. As he mentions in the 'second challenge' (see above), he anticipated that it would be the large number of short scenes (or 'parts') in the original play that might lead to structural problems in the opera – so it is gratifying that the most obvious difference between play and libretto is the compression of sixteen scenes in Act 1 to twelve and the omission of the short breaks between the eleven parts or 'stations' of the drama in Act 2. This allowed the composer to concentrate on the dramatic build-up to Christine's eventual 'nervous breakdown' and to create

---

[4]   In fact, Wesker's original 'Note for directors' (*Caritas*, 1981) specified that 'the first and second Acts [of the stage play] must run together'.

[5]   Robert Saxton (1997) *Caritas*, vocal score (London: Chester Music).

[6]   Lebrecht, 'A Fight at the Opera'.

a coherent musical structure – not just for the final section (now scene 13, the single scene of Act 2) but for the entire opera. At one level, the use of a passacaglia (a progressively more complex set of variations on a repeated 'ground') underpins the dramatic structure of this Act 2 'Mad Scene' while, in parallel with this, the subtle recapitulation of musical items and themes from the earlier scenes (Act 1 of the play – now scenes 1–12 of the libretto) helps to create a more rounded overall structure to the opera than could be achieved with words alone. There are elements of distortion and parody in Act 2 that are analogous to Christine's emotional disorientation, and instances of musical citation (for example, the quotation of *Kyrie De Angelis*,[7] and an inter-textual reference to Marie's *Cradle Song* from Berg's *Wozzeck* in Christine's *Lullaby*),[8] which enmesh sympathetically with Wesker's newly concentrated text where obsessive verbal repetitions and emotional peaks contribute to musical climaxes. In particular, the libretto allows for some of the leading characters from Act 1 of the play to reappear, albeit briefly (and, in one case, posthumously), as invisible commentators on Christine's decline in the final scene.

Regarding Act 1, the changes in the libretto mainly consist of shortening the individual scenes and, in a few cases, altering the sequence of events. The composer has likened the impact of this act to that of 'a kind of theatrical Bayeux Tapestry; a ... potted historical picture-strip; a [coiled] spring to be released in the catastrophe of Act 2'.[9] Table 2.2 (see above) has already demonstrated the interlocking structure of the sixteen original scenes in the play, with the two sets of three scenes, devoted respectively to 'Tax Collection' (IV / IX / XI) and 'Christine with Matilde' (V / VIII / XII), encompassing and framing the more devotional or political events. Clearly, the detailed accounts of three separate saints, provided by Matilde, would have become laboured in an operatic/musical context, as would the separate scene (XI) devoted to rumours about yet another tax. The pruning of Matilde's hagiographic musings and the combining of two taxation scenes into one proved expedient precautions against the possibility of longevity (within an operatic context) – and, together with the compression of scenes XIV, XV and XVI (libretto, scene 12), help to reduce the overall number of dramatic events. Other minor (yet significant) changes include reducing Mathew's presence in scene 1 to that of a silent acolyte[10] and, similarly, Robert becoming a non-speaking/non-singing observer in scene 4. In each case the musical characterization is strengthened.

Table 3.1 provides a summary of the main changes made to Act 1 of *Caritas*, together with an outline of the resulting operatic structure, which involved a significant re-ordering of events in the course of the reduction of the play's first act

---

7 *Liber Usualis*, p. 37. This is labelled (simply as Kyrie Eleison) in bars 40/41 of Act 2 of the opera score, although hinted at earlier. The composer has recently stated that his source for the Kyrie was William Byrd's Five-part Mass.

8 *Caritas*, Act 2, bars 232–250.

9 Communication with the composer (WT).

10 This is partly a consequence of changes made to the sung liturgy. See Table 3.3.

Table 3.1   *Caritas*: From play to libretto (Act 1 summary)

Scene in play	Scene in libretto	Action	Major changes in libretto
I*	1*	Immurement Ritual [July 1377]	Mathew silent/musical items varied (see Table 3.3)/text shortened
II	2	Branding of Richard [some months later]	Mathew seen in sharper contrast to Bishop because of silence in 1/text cut
III*	3*	Christine and Robert	Much as play
IV	4	Tax Collector (i)	Robert silent (until 8)
V	5	Christine and Matilde (i)	St Yvette – much as play
VI*	6	Christine's Confession	Exchanges abbreviated
VII	(6)	Family with Christine	Incorporated into 6
VIII	7*	Christine and Matilde (ii)	All of St Veridiana story omitted
IX	8	Tax Collector (ii) [February 1379]	Abbreviated text
X*	9*	Christine at Prayer	Much as play
XI	(8)	Tax Discussion [May 1381]	Incorporated into 8
XII	11	Christine and Matilde (iii)	All of St Christiana story omitted/focus on Christine's parody of 'crossing'
XIII	10	Sermon [17 June 1381]	Out of sequence
XIV*	12*	Debate and Petition	Text much abbreviated/trio of William, Agnes and Robert becomes central to the scene/Robert's death reported over Ricercar (pseudo Funeral March?)
XV	(12)	Report on Uprising	Declaimed over Ricercar out of sequence at the end of 12/recapitulation of Christine's scene 1 song omitted
XVI*	(12)	Bishop's Refusal	Incorporated into 12 (Refusal out of sequence – before Report on Uprising)

* = Children's Chorus

text from sixteen scenes to twelve. This yields a revised sequence of operatic scenes as expressed in Table 3.2. It is neither possible nor desirable to examine every point of difference between play and libretto at this point since many detailed variants (for example, the removal of a single word) have no direct impact on the sense of the libretto or the opera itself (of which a more detailed analysis will follow in Chapter 4). However, it *is* worth noting the number of *musical items* that Wesker

Table 3.2   Act 1: New sequence of libretto/opera scenes

Libretto numbering	Action	Former play numbering
1	Immurement Ritual [July 1377]	I
2	Branding of Richard [some months later]	II
3	Christine and Robert	III
4	Tax Collector (i)	IV
5	Christine and Matilde (i)	V
6	Christine's Confession/Family with Christine	VI and VII
7	Christine and Matilde (ii)	VIII
8	Tax Collector (ii)/Tax Discussion (iii) [February 1379]	IX and XI
9	Christine at Prayer	X
10	Sermon [17 June 1381]	XIII
11	Christine and Matilde (iii)	XII
12	Debate and Petition Bishop's Refusal Report on Uprising and Robert's Death (declaimed over Ricercar)	XIV/XVI/XV

himself specifies, especially in Act 1, scene I, of the play. Some of these items were omitted from the libretto and replaced by others, with important implications for the focus of the opera and the musical material that the composer clearly derived from the liturgical items throughout the work. It has already been observed that the introduction of the Alleluia for the Common of Two or More Martyrs (*Alleluia. Te martyrum*)[11] was specified by Wesker in place of the two selected psalms from the Office for the Enclosing of Anchorites,[12] thus re-focusing the ceremony towards the concept of eventual martyrdom rather than the prospect of sanctification as intimated by Matilde in both versions of the play:

being a collector of stories 'bout saints *which you'll be one day if you work hard at it* [author's italics].[13]

---

[11]   *Alleluia, alleluia. To thee, Lord, the white robed host of martyrs give glory. Alleluia* (LU, p.1171). From the Common of the Mass for Two or More Martyrs (Mass III). Also included in the Sarum Proper Use for the Feast of Holy Innocents on 28 December. See Nicholas Sandon, ed. (1984–99) *The Use of Salisbury* (Newton Abbot: Antico Edition), LCM2 (1986).

[12]   See Chapter 2, n. 27.

[13]   *Caritas* (1981), Act I, Scene V.

Significantly, this particular phrase is omitted in the libretto, as is the biblical reading about Christ visiting the home of Mary and Martha (specified for the Sarum Immurement Ritual).[14] It seems very likely that the opportunity to revise the text for vocal setting also allowed Wesker to reconsider the musico-liturgical pitch of his original play. What had been abstracted from a liturgical Office and built around psalms, a hymn, a reading, prayers, vows and a litany, now becomes dominated by an element of the Mass, with the melismatic Alleluia, its verse and repetition framing the prayers and vows and accompanying the procession as Christine is led by the clergy to be enclosed in her tiny cell. The hymn (*Veni, Creator Spiritus*) still retains its Pentecostal significance, enhanced perhaps by its new location in the restructured scene. Table 3.3 lists these items as they appear in the three versions of the dramatic text.

Table 3.3   Musical items specified in *Caritas*: Act 1, scene 1

Play (1981)	Libretto (1988)	Play (1990)
	Alleluia. Te martyrum	*Alleluia. Te martyrum*
Psalms 6 and 131 (OT) with Gloria		Psalm 6 [only] with Gloria
Veni Creator Spiritus – in Latin (6 verses + Gloria/Amen)	*Veni Creator Spiritus* (Verse 1 in Latin + Gloria/Amen in English)	*Veni Creator Spiritus* (as 1981 edition)
A Litany (unspecified)		A Litany: Invocation to Christ
Responsorium for St James	*Alleluia* (repeated)	*Alleluia* (repeated)
Christine's Song: 'I will forsake all that I see …'	Christine's Song	Christine's Song

One should not be surprised by the extent of the liturgical and religious 'borrowings' that are found in *Caritas*, bearing in mind the nature of the core story. As well as those discussed above, the libretto of Act 1 retains scenes devoted to formal and personal prayer, confession, recitation of hagiography, and a sermon, in addition to accusations of blasphemy. By comparison with the play, Act 2 of the libretto also introduces a new liturgical item, albeit in instrumental guise. As Christine confronts her loneliness and her fears, and Saxton commences the orchestral passacaglia that propels forward the terrible catastrophe of the 'Mad Scene', he introduces a setting

---

[14]   Luke 10: 38–42. Martha complains to Christ that her sister Mary leaves her to carry the main burden of household chores – to which Christ replies that 'Mary hath chosen that good part [listening to His words], which shall not be taken from her.' This reading has obvious relevance for the Immurement Ceremony since the anchorite's seclusion provides the ideal environment for the contemplation of Christ's teachings (albeit at the expense of fulfilling the traditional obligations of assisting with household chores).

of the Kyrie eleison (*Kyrie De Angelis*)[15] in a sort of fugal exposition for oboe, clarinet and flute above the initial statement of the 'Ground'. This wordless quotation nonetheless carries with it the prayer implicit in its melody – 'Lord have mercy, Christ have mercy' – an intercession at the very heart of the drama that is punctuated throughout the act by Christine's outbursts of 'Hail Mary' and 'Hail O Cross' as set out in Table 3.4. This table also highlights a new, purely musical, pattern marked by a series of dynamic climaxes (and secondary climaxes), that is synchronized with Christine's impassioned outbursts as she appeals for release ('Break down its walls!'), as she confronts her intense feelings of unworthiness ('I am NOT FIT!'), and as she seeks redemption through her hysterical demands for crucifixion ('Put nails through me!'/'I am crucified upon the spring'). More attention will be given to the technical devices employed by the composer in the course of subsequent analysis, but the composer's response to the libretto of Act 2 (as printed) is a testimony to Saxton's own artistic vision as well as to Wesker's concept of spiritual decline, expressed in agonizingly beautiful language. Saxton, it would seem, has transformed the author's original 'frozen moments' into a sustained musical narrative that preserves, yet energizes, the author's literary depiction of the anchoress's descent into madness. Not that the scene lacks periods of contemplation or reflection, however, because Saxton has created poignant solo arias (Christine's *Lullaby*, for example) and ensembles (the various off-stage intercessions of William, Agnes, Robert and Bishop Henry) that introduce potent flashes of earlier times as Christine oscillates between her delicately balanced sanity and absolute derangement. As will be explained, the overall impact of this scene is as much dependent on the composer's use of allusion, quotation, recapitulation and distortion as on a mere setting of words to music – however skilful this might be. If the changes to Act 1, scene 1, appear to steer its focus towards the liturgy of the Mass, then perhaps Act 2 is its parody (in both the satirical and musicological senses) – the theme of opposites writ large.

Characterization

Even as the libretto was being finalized, Saxton would, no doubt, have been considering, *inter alia*, the sort of singer that ideally he would choose for each part as well as the constitution of his (necessarily small) chamber orchestra and the role that instruments might play in establishing mood, supporting narrative or contributing to characterization. His thoughts quite likely turned as well towards the inherent challenge of reconciling vocal specifications – timbre, pitch and dynamic range, voice-production and experience – with the age and profession of the members of cast as dictated by Wesker. In this respect, the author had been quite precise in his theatrical depictions: in descending age, Matilde is an old woman in her sixties (a contralto,

---

15   *Liber Usualis*, p. 37. (Kyrie of the Angels), from the Ordinary of the Mass (subsequently identified as being derived from the Kyrie of Byrd's Five Part Mass).

Table 3.4   *Caritas*: Act 2 opera structure

Bars	Contents	Equivalent part in play
1–39	Introduction to Passacaglia/Christine's Soliloquy: 'I am nothing, I know nothing, I desire nothing save the love of Jesus'/Children taunt Christine	Parts 1 – 4/5
40–56	Passacaglia starts [2 x Ground on D]/*Kyrie De Angelis* (in orchestra)/Christine: 'There's not one God but two!'	Parts 5 (cont.) – 6
57–65	Christine: **Hail Mary, full of grace** (intoned)/'That's a blasphemous thought' (*sprechstimme*)/[Ground on A and E]	Part 6 (cont.)
66–96	Bishop: 'That's heresy'/Christine: 'Let C go/Not fit!'/Bishop, Mathew (unseen) and C debate/C: 'You have hell anchored to your church, father. Break down its walls!' [Ground returns to D + transpositions] **First Climax**	Part 7
97–124	Christine talks to Little Girl: 'When you are dead …'/ Children taunt Christine	Part 8
125–90	Christine: **Hail O Cross**/(agitated, talks to herself): 'They think you're mad'/talks to Little Girl again: 'There's no meaning … The purpose is to love' / (Secondary Climax) 'There, Christine, Mad?'	Part 8 (cont.)
191–220	[Ground returns to D]/Christine: **Hail Mary, full of grace**/'The remedy for pride is humility … Mortification of the FLESH! … I am NOT FIT!' (E/B♭ tritone) **Second Climax**	Part 8 (conclusion)
221–255	Christine: 'The poor wail …'/Lullaby: 'I've loved him from the cradle-time … They nail him now. My own flesh and blood …' (Secondary Climax)	Part 9
256–272	Christine: 'Did I feed … for this?'/C. with Robert (offstage): 'Did we look at blue skies …?'/Agnes and William (off): 'She give our Lord three precious years'/Bishop (off): 'May God put off from thee the old woman'	Not in Act 2 of Play (recap. from Act 1, scenes 1 and 12 of Opera)
273–336	Christine: 'Put nails through me! Pierce my hands, pierce my feet!' (B♭/E tritone) **Sustained Third Climax**	Part 11
337–373	Christine: 'I am crucified upon the spring!'/Children taunt/ *Alleluia* (both distorted on tape) **Fourth Climax on Pedal E**	Part 11 (conclusion)
	Diminuendo to recapitulation of C's Act 1 Song (on oboe)/'This is a wall, and this is wall' (monotone)	

perhaps), Bishop Henry is around fifty (a portly bass might be appropriate), William and Agnes are both in their early forties (baritone and mezzo soprano, possibly), whereas Mathew, at about thirty, could well be cast as a tenor to provide contrast with his older ecclesiastical colleague. Equally, Richard and Robert Lonle (father and son) could be baritone and tenor respectively to signify their relative experience and youth; Christine (as heroine/protagonist) must certainly be a dramatic soprano, able to sustain the emotional peaks and troughs of her extraordinary spiritual journey and possessing the power and maturity to convey her mood-swings as expressed in wide-ranging vocal lines that bear comparison with other famous operatic 'mad-scenes' such as that in *Lucia di Lammermoor* (staged by Opera North in 1988–89, shortly after *Caritas* was commissioned).

Herein lay the problem: for various reasons, Christine had been cast in the play as a young, idealistic girl of between sixteen and twenty-one. She had been promised in marriage to Robert, an apprentice carpenter, and was prepared to abandon him for a sincerely felt 'calling' that was to be severely tested (and apparently found wanting). In spite of possessing a degree of literacy, she nonetheless signed the documents of immurement by making the mark of a cross, thereby casting some doubt onto the extent of her education and, hence her capacity fully to understand her commitment. Even at the conclusion of her immurement ceremony, she demonstrates a child-like innocence, not to say naivety, as she sings the beautifully calculated lines 'I will forsake all that I see Father and friend and follow thee'. During the rest of the opera, however, she is required to interpret an increasingly complex role as, disillusioned by the absence of a personal revelation of divine love, she runs the whole gamut of emotional extremes as she exchanges apparent innocence for frustration, fantasies of self-abuse and insanity. Leaving aside the unfortunate politics of Opera North's decision to over-rule the composer's choice of singer (and the relish with which it was reported in the national press),[16] it is far more likely that an experienced opera singer with the requisite vocal and dramatic qualities would be able to act a more youthful part than that a singer of Christine's theatrical age would possess the power and stamina to perform the role *as conceived by the composer*. Further consideration of the outcome of this dilemma will be provided when the reception of *Caritas* is considered in Chapter 5, but it is quite clear from Saxton's writing that he had a particular sort of dramatic soprano voice (and dramatic actress) in mind when he commenced the opera – and especially so because of the considerable vocal demands made in the final scene.

On a purely practical level, Saxton decided to use nine singers to cover ten (vocal) roles, whereas the play called for ten actors to play thirteen.[17] Of course,

---

[16]   See Lebrecht, 'A Fight at the Opera'.

[17]   Both editions of the play specify doubling roles for (1) The Villager/Travelling Priest/ Bailiff and (2) The Bishop's Clerk/Tax Collector. In the opera there is no Bishop's Clerk in the Cast List and one singer covers Richard Lonle (who appears only in Act 1, scene 2) and The Travelling Priest (Act 1, scene 10). However, there are a few anomalies in that the opera

there could be limitations to the doubling of roles when singers (rather than actors) are concerned, but Richard Lonle and the Travelling Priest are both strong parts, each calling for a mature voice of bass-baritone pitch, and, as they do not appear together in the opera, it made economic sense for them to be taken by the same singer. In addition, the composer chose to make the Travelling Priest a spoken role who declaims his revolutionary sermon in rhythmically notated *sprechgesang* in scene 10, and such a hybrid role undoubtedly benefits from the part being taken by a trained singer. In fact, all of scene 10 is played out in a sort of hysterical 'speech-song' as the Priest and Bishop exchange insults before Christine's first scream of dread 'I do not have the vocation! Release me!' In scene 12, the Priest merely speaks his report on the Peasants' Uprising in approximate synchronization with the orchestra – an appropriately named example of melodrama where information is transmitted above a supportive (yet independent) musical narrative, in this case the polyphonic Ricercar that serves as a transition between the two acts. Chapter 4 will provide an opportunity to explore the way in which Saxton derived most of the musical motifs used to identify the main characters from the plainsong chants introduced into the first scene (at the suggestion of the playwright).

Orchestration

As has been mentioned, Saxton's commission for a chamber opera created restrictive conditions for the staging, casting (use of chorus, especially) and the size of the orchestra (because of the limited orchestral and auditorium space in Wakefield's Opera House). In selecting a basic 'chamber orchestra' of single woodwind, (flute, doubling piccolo; oboe, doubling cor anglais; clarinet, doubling bass clarinet; and bassoon), two brass (trumpet and French horn) and a quintet of solo strings (vln.1/vln.2/viola/cello/d.bass), the composer followed a fairly common precedent of using a 'skeleton' symphony orchestra – perhaps with the long-term intention of increasing orchestra numbers in subsequent performances in larger auditoriums.[18] His chosen ensemble also draws a little on the sort of chamber ensemble favoured by Schoenberg in *Pierrot lunaire*, where five performers play eight instruments.[19]

---

rubrics (one taken directly from the play) indicate the presence of a Villager and Bishop's Clerk at the start of Act 1, scene 1, and (later) Two Villagers who slowly block up the entrance to Christine's cell (something done by Mathew and the Clerk in the corresponding section of the play). Clearly, (non-singing) Extras could be used in this scene as it is unlikely that the singer taking the role of Richard would be able to double so close to his trial and branding in the second scene.

[18] However, the composer has since denied that he would authorise instrumental doubling, preferring rather to maintain the existing balance between voices and accompaniment.

[19] Piano; flute (doubling piccolo); clarinet (doubling bass clarinet); violin (doubling viola); and cello. This was subsequently adopted as a (variable) model by Peter Maxwell

However, Saxton must have been aware of the enormous demand that would be made on his limited resources as the drama reached its tragic climax, so he added a large percussion group[20] to his basic ensemble together with five pedal timpani (one player) – in all, an orchestra of just thirteen players performing on a range of twenty-five instruments. In addition, he availed himself of modern 'instrumental' technology by using electronic distortion to 'distress' the recapitulated plainsong and children's chorus during the final scene.

If this ensemble is compared with those used by Britten (in *Curlew River*), by MacMillan (in *Visitatio Sepulchri*) or Harvey (in *Passion and Resurrection*), for example,[21] an extremely wide variation of orchestral/instrumental groupings in contemporary music-theatre is revealed. Whereas MacMillan comes closest to Saxton's instrumentation,[22] his 'chamber' orchestra is substantially larger and, *inter alia*, is used to create an impressive prelude before the entry of the Three Marys, as well as being coloured by the Scottish *pibroch*.[23] Harvey's orchestra is even bigger – at one stage (the final *Resurrection* section) calling for a 'Male' group of tuba, two trombones and two double basses, and a 'Female' group of trumpet, seven solo violins and viola, in addition to other symphonic forces as employed elsewhere in the work – whereas Britten merely asks for seven instrumentalists in total (flute/horn/viola/d. bass/harp/percussion/organ). As Peter Evans[24] has pointed out, Britten uses the instruments more as 'a range of discrete sonorities' than as a miniature orchestra. The flute and percussion (bells, especially) seem to convey something of the 'exoticism' of Noh plays and the flute also creates characteristic 'duets' with the Madwoman, as does the horn with the Ferryman. There would be limited opportunities for such vocal/instrumental associations in *Caritas* but shades of this duetting can be seen in Christine's scene 1song and its '*obbligato*' oboe accompaniment.[25]

What one learns from these comparisons is that 'universal norms' no longer functioned in music-theatre in the late twentieth century. The vast palette of sonorities contained within a 'standard' symphony orchestra would now need to

---

Davies, amongst others, for his *Fires of London* repertoire.

[20] This consists of a large tam-tam; large suspended cymbal; five tom-toms; large bass drum; snare drum; crotales (two octave chromatic set); vibraphone (without motor); tubular bells and glockenspiel – all played by one percussionist.

[21] See discussion in Chapter 1.

[22] He employs double woodwind (all doubling their smaller or larger relations), double brass (trombone 2 doubling bass), a much bigger string section (minimum 8/6/4/4/2), timpani; large percussion section; and *pibroch* (bagpipe family).

[23] The *pibroch* is a form of Scottish art music (theme and variations) featuring the Great Highland bagpipe.

[24] Peter Evans (1976/2002) *The Music of Benjamin Britten* (Oxford: Clarendon Press), pp. 467–80.

[25] Act 1, scene 1, bars 180–183.

be pre-selected since the luxuries of space and finance that permit such resources existed in only the best endowed companies. Where space and acoustics allow – in Winchester Cathedral (for *Passion and Resurrection*) or Glasgow's *Tramway* theatre-in-the-round (for *Visitatio Sepulchri*) – it is not unreasonable to extend or enlarge basic ensembles (if funds are available). Who would *not* wish to write for Winchester's organ or to exploit its vast open spaces? No doubt Britten had the Suffolk churches of Orford, Blythborough or Aldburgh in mind when he composed his *Church Parables* and his unique and economic scoring seems inextricably linked to their bright (but not cavernous) acoustics and the atmosphere of intimacy and dignity found in such locations.

Although, at first sight, it might appear that the orchestra's main role in opera is either to support the singers or to provide telling moments of tranquillity or excitement (through entr'actes or overtures), the function of instruments in music-theatre has traditionally been much more sophisticated – particularly in works since the classical period. Even in early operas one often finds time-honoured associations of instrumental sonorities with pastoral, regal, military or funereal scenes. For example, one need look no further than the formidable list of instruments used in the premiere of Monteveri's *Orfeo* at Mantua in 1607[26] and the explicit scoring indicated in many sections of the work to appreciate that arias, choruses and dances could attain an additional dimension when coloured with suitable instruments that effectively 'costume' the music into the desired mood, location and/or genre. The use of *obbligato* instruments is especially telling in the hands of Mozart,[27] as is the introduction of wind-band ensembles and 'local colour' (such as fashionable 'Turkish' marches), or overtures that anticipate material used later in the opera.[28]

There are hints of such features in Saxton's score[29] but no overture or even an orchestral prelude to establish a religious atmosphere in advance of the action. Rather, the opera opens with the Immurement Ceremony itself.[30] The audience is taken straight into the church service as the plainsong liturgy is chanted against a pulsating background of low strings, bassoon and timpani. Occasional flashes of light punctuate this predominantly dark texture as flute, oboe and crotales insert *sforzando* octaves – each responding to a stage direction as, first, light falls on Christine and, then, on her father's workshop before (with the entrance of French horn and trumpet) the Bishop raises up Christine from her prone position to begin the prayers for her safety and God's protection as she prepares for the life of a recluse.

---

[26]   This can be found on the second page of the printed score (Venice, 1609) and most modern editions.

[27]   *The Magic Flute* being an obvious example.

[28]   As in the Overture to *Don Giovanni*, for example.

[29]   As has already been referred to in the use of an oboe *obbligato* to accompany Christine's song (Act 1, scene 1).

[30]   One is reminded of Robert Browning's dramatic poetry, for example the line 'That's my last Duchess painted on the wall', which opens his dramatic monologue *My Last Duchess*.

The first great dynamic climax of the opera marks the significance of this moment with the almost filmic clanging of tubular bells. Even at this stage in the work, it is obvious that the orchestra is to be used to supply an auditory context, working in parallel with stage and lighting directions, as well as providing a pivotal harmonic role (a pedal E) within a global tonal plan that eventually sees the music return to this pitch in its final moments. As the score becomes increasingly chromatic from Bishop Henry's prayer (and the concluding 'Amen' from the male cast), wind, lower strings and vibraphone chords direct the scene towards Christine's first words, announced again by an orchestral *tutti* that is as harmonically complex as the previous climax had been unambiguously affirmative. Table 3.5 sets out a simple analysis of the orchestral sonorities used in Act 1, scene 1, of the opera.

Clearly, it would be impossible (given the constraints of publishing space) to provide similar summaries of the orchestration for each section of the drama. Such information will in future will be subsumed into the detailed analysis of the two acts in the following chapter. However, there is an overall compositional strategy that can be identified, even at this early stage in the commentary on the opera,[31] and that is that the orchestra's predominantly accompanimental role throughout the first eleven scenes changes radically from the orchestral transition that precedes the Ricercar at the end of scene 12[32] – as the main narrative moves from the vocal lines into the orchestra; as the role of the orchestra changes from providing colourful support to carrying the main burden of musical story-telling; as the drama's momentum moves from short-term text-led information to musical form-led structures that contain their own argument and logic, as exemplified in the Act 2 Passacaglia.

Musical Language and Techniques

Finally, in this preliminary exploration of some of the main parameters in the evolution of *Caritas* from play to opera, Saxton's musical language and compositional techniques will be examined with particular (but not exclusive) attention to the works cited by Paul Griffiths in his 1986 article[33] – which itself followed on from an interview with the composer, published in *New Sounds and New Personalities*.[34] In this seven-page transcript of his conversation with Griffiths, Saxton bravely responded to direct questioning about his influences, his compositional processes and his artistic development. In reply to a probing enquiry

---

[31] As has been hinted at in the 'Composer's Note' (see n. 5 above).

[32] Bars 1077–1150.

[33] See Chapter 1, n. 1.

[34] This was probably the first major interview/article on Saxton, with the sub-title *British Composers of the 1980s* (Paul Griffiths (1985) *New Sounds; New Personalities*. London: Faber and Faber). Chapter 7 of the present volume continues this tradition of composer interviews.

Table 3.5   *Caritas*: Orchestral strategies – Act 1, scene 1

Bars	Action/musical landmarks	Orchestration
1–70 CD track 1	Start of Immurement Ceremony *Alleluia. Te martyrum*	Very slow – dark textures Low Strings + bassoon + timps. – sustained Pedal E/ chords from flute/oboe + crotales (bb. 8/13/17) = shafts of light/*crescendo* + 'scalic' patterns from horn/trumpet and w.wind (bb. 25–31 lead to -
	b. 32: Bishop raises Christine up *Amen* b. 49: Christine's vows	Full orch. + tubular bells (*ffff*) unison E *diminuendo* then (b. 44) *cresc./accel.* + vibraphone chords (bb. 45–49) Full orch. (*ff*)/chord based on tritones, sustained alternately by strings/w.wind (*mp*)/b. 60 horn quavers marked 'bell-like'/strings drop out (b. 61)
	b. 63: Bishop's Prayer *Amen*	*Subito p*/sustained wind only (organ-like?)/*crescendo* to –
71– 116	Family Comments b. 71: Robert/William/ Agnes b. 86: Christine + above cast	Agitated Strings *tremolo* over progressive bass (E♭–A–E–B♭– F–B, etc.), leading to – Vibraphone chords (86/93/98)/Strings alternating sustained (88–89), *tremolo* (90–92), sustained (93–95), and *tremolo* (96–99)
	b.100: Agnes/William/ Robert	Strings syncopated with horn/w.wind 'flurry' (104–107)/strings return to *tremolo* (cf. 71–86) over tritones in bass-line (E/B♭; F/B; F♯/C, leading to –
117– 135	Table, Chair and Bed completed *Veni Creator Spiritus* (v. 1) *Gloria* (127) *Amen*	Sustained E♭ pedal (strings + w.wind) + vibraphone E♭ (marked 'bell-like') Tubular bells (A–F–G–E♭ quavers)/tritone A/E♭/ timps. C♯ (133) *accelerando* to –
136– 147	Family Comment (cont.) William/Robert ('she won't forget')	Moving on String *tremolo* (*ff*) (cf. 71–85) + 'dislocated' wind chords punctuated by tubular bells and DB *pizzicato*, giving 'carillon' effect
148– 178	Bishop and Congregation Prayers b. 157: Christine enters cell *In nomine patris* *Alleluia* (164–5)	Full orch. (*mf*) A/E♭ chord on tubular bells/sustained by wind and strings (*p*)/crescendo to – Full orch. A Major chord + timps. and bells (ff) sustained and *diminuendo* b. drum and timps. Enter (165) as A Major cedes gradually to A/E♭ tritone/strings/w.wind slow and fading as b. drum dominates texture, leading to –
179– 194	*Christine's Song* b. 186: Children	Accompanied by horn (pedal D) and *obbligato* oboe only Vibraphone D♭/B♭ accompanies children's 'canon'/ wind support lower strings/*accelerando* into scene 2

about [direct] influences,[35] his 'knee-jerk' 'No' was immediately followed by a long list of works and composers that he admired, some of whom 'if I'm honest I still have as models in the back of my mind'.[36] He went on to specify the influences, initially of Britten and Lutyens, and, more recently, Carter who 'could make big gestures that are really quite simple, the way Berg could, and yet the details are all complex and their interactions complex'. In general, however, Saxton stressed that he hoped to have assimilated such musical memories,[37] following Schoenberg's dictum that 'one must learn from the masters, but then take the essence and create something new. One must not imitate.' Like Schoenberg, he has never denigrated the methodical study of earlier musical languages and techniques and, despite Lutyens' promise that she would not ram serialism down his throat, he clearly benefited from her expertise in this field and has applied some of the principles of Schoenberg's practice (but, thankfully, *not* its dogma) into pre-*Caritas* works, especially. Similar points could be made with regard to his insights into Renaissance polyphony and later tonal practice: the beauty and flexibility of musical lines in more recent works and the great single-pitch dominated climaxes of works such as *In the Beginning* attest to the composer's increasing penchant for sustained melody (as opposed to gestural figuration) and his use of large-scale structures built upon/around pillars of sustained pitches – but not (as he emphasized) tonal structures in the classical sense. Indeed, *Caritas* was destined to be a landmark in this development.

Overall, the abiding impression given in Paul Griffiths' interview is of a composer who was unafraid to acknowledge his debt to the past, but equally determined to explore new avenues of creativity. To the couple of examples offered in response to Griffiths' question on influences (of Bach in the trumpet part of the Concerto for Orchestra and *The Ring of Eternity*; of Stravinsky's *Soldier's Tale* in the violin solos of *Processions and Dances*), one could now add that of Berg's *Wozzeck* (Marie's *Cradle Song*) on Christine's *Lullaby* in Act 2 of *Caritas* – but such instances are few and far between, and the latter, surely, is an inter-textual allusion rather than an 'influence' in the accepted sense. What is retained from the interview are little more than hints that Saxton admitted to his pre-1979 music being 'very decorative and somewhat static' (he was moving towards writing music that 'was more dynamic in the technical sense'); that he had assimilated serial as well as tonal techniques; and (perhaps more significantly) that he now (1985) started to compose against:

> [a] background [which] might be some elaborate sort of passacaglia, though not with a thematic bass, because the harmony these days might not be working from the bass upwards. Then the details come intuitively … .

---

[35]   'Are you influenced by other composers when you're expanding your repertory?' (ibid., p. 180).

[36]   The list includes Mahler, Schumann, Bach, Stravinsky, Berg and Bartók, as well as his teachers, Britten and Elisabeth Lutyens.

[37]   'Hopefully, one's absorbed these things a bit earlier [before composing]' (ibid.).

This quotation is of the utmost importance in tracing Saxton's use of baroque techniques and polyphonic forms from his early works up to *Caritas* (and beyond) and will provide the starting point for a consideration, later in the book, of the function of the passacaglia in Act 2 of the opera. In passing, it should be noted that at least two related movements were composed during the period from 1981 to 1988 – the Chaconne for Double Choir (1981) and the Chacony for Solo Piano (1988), both of which will be discussed in Chapter 4.

Whereas the above interview, taken in conjunction with Griffiths's 1986 article, provides a fairly well-balanced introduction to Saxton's works of the early 1980s, the composer's own published account of his composition process[38] is far more revealing, possibly because it was written almost a decade later (for the 1994 Colston Symposium at Bristol University). What was initially put together as a conference paper has been refined into an elegant and compelling self-analysis, with invaluable insights into the composition of two seminal works – *The Ring of Eternity* (1982–83) and *The Circles of Light* (1985). In the case of the former, Saxton demonstrates how an initial idea of a hexachord, comprising two symmetrical trichords, was developed towards chromatic saturation over a timescale of about fourteen minutes until this 'is ended by a deafening tam-tam crescendo – the equivalent of white noise, or light so bright that it is aurally blinding'. Saxton's fascination with hexachords is relatively well documented and requires no further discussion here, although it will be central to the analysis of the opera itself. *The Ring of Eternity*, of course, takes its inspiration from a poem by Henry Vaughan,[39] which Saxton admits to having set for voice on two previous occasions before deciding to compose a purely orchestral piece based on lines that had haunted him for seventeen years. The combination of rational and instinctive processes and his awareness of the inter-relationship between background and foreground activity owe something to his training in serialism and classical tonality respectively, but, as he points out 'the premise is extremely limited'. 'The foreground/background issue that I have mentioned here is not the same as in tonal practice.' What one does learn from studying scores such as *The Circles of Light* and *Music to Celebrate the Resurrection* (1988), however, is that, although Saxton may use traditional (or well-established) compositional techniques (such as complex

---

[38]   Saxton (1998) 'The Process of Composition from Detection to Confection' in *Composition, Performance, Reception: Studies in the Creative Process in Music*, ed. Wyndham Thomas (Aldershot: Ashgate), pp. 1–16. An earlier version was published in *The Musical Times* as 'Where do I Begin?' (October 1994).

[39]   *The World*, published in Vaughan (1896) *The Poems of Henry Vaughan, Silurist*, Vol. 1, ed. E.K. Chambers (London: Lawrence & Bullen), pp. 150–52.Saxton created the new title by abstracting key words from lines 1 and 2: 'I saw Eternity the other night, Like a great Ring of pure and endless Light.'

rhythmic canons,[40] long harmonic pedals,[41] or quasi-fugal build-ups[42]), the listener is not conscious of cerebral activity so much as of experiencing substantial paragraphs of musical narrative or debate that progress from a well-defined starting point (or proposition) to an equally well-calculated conclusion. Although there is an obvious difference between Saxton's use of sustained 'landmark' pitches and traditional (triadic) tonal practice, in which chords/keys have functions that co-exist on both a short-term and large-scale basis, there are occasions when the relationship between Saxton's big 'structural chords' begins to suggest a pseudo-tonal scheme. This is true, not necessarily in a traditional Tonic – Dominant – Tonic way, but in a manner more reminiscent of the favoured tritone relationships of Bartók whose *Music for Strings Percussion and Celesta* (first movement) abounds in such large-scale and compressed relationships between A and E♭ (bars 1, 56, 76 and 82) and F♯ and C (bars 27 and 65). Comparable moments in Saxton's works would include the B♭ pedal at the start of *Music to Celebrate the Resurrection* and its counterpole of E (bar 205) that crescendos to the brilliant E major climax at the end – itself recalling the great E Major chord that announces the opening of the fifth door in Bartók's opera, *Duke Bluebeard's Castle*. One could also include the E to B♭ opening of *Caritas* with its climactic sustained E marking Christine's 're-birth' as she prepares to take her vows – but that's another story (Chapter 4).

If there is a single composition before *Caritas,* that stands out as a technical and structural 'rehearsal' for the opera it is the Genesis-inspired *In the Beginning,*[43] composed between June and November 1987. Indeed, it would not come as a surprise if one were to learn that work on this composition overlapped with the preliminary sketching of *Caritas*. Starting with a low E, marked 'Slow, sustained and mysterious' the opening is scored for double basses, timpani, large tam-tam and bass drum – for all the world like the opening of the opera (but without the plainsong that transforms the *Caritas* 'E' into the major mode). Even as the brass enters, shifting from E to the adjacent F and back before reaching up to B♭, the atmosphere is one of expectancy, leading to a strengthening of the tritone relationship at bars 56 and 82. Although, thereafter, the work progresses into two successive dance-like movements (the first [Movement 2] still based on the E/B♭ axis), the final part of Movement 3 culminates in a much slower, sustained section that starts with a thunderous return to a unison E before recalling the 'anguished' mood of the first few bars. In his short CD booklet description of this work,[44] the composer suggests that the piece might be interpreted in two ways:

---

[40]   In the slow movement of *The Circles of Light*, for example.

[41]   In *Music to Celebrate the Resurrection*, for example.

[42]   Also in *Music to Celebrate the Resurrection,* bars 24–42, for example.

[43]   Commissioned by the London Symphony Orchestra (LSO), with funds provided by the David Cohen Family Trust.

[44]   NMC D102 (Disc 1).

First, it can refer to the opening of Genesis, with its depiction of Creation and the birth of Order and Light. Secondly, it might suggest the idea of growth and re-birth, and both of these concepts were in my mind as I worked on the score.

Symbolically, the familiar concept of Darkness moving into Light ('Creation and the birth of Order') has been extended to embrace the concept of Re-birth (or Resurrection), a fundamentally New Testament counterpart (or counterpoint, even) to the Genesis account – unsurprisingly, perhaps, bearing in mind Saxton's BBC commission for *Music to Celebrate the Resurrection* on which he was certainly working (in 1988) at the time of the premiere of *In the Beginning*.[45] He had also just received the Opera North commission for *Caritas* and was no doubt considering the apparent problem of composing a work that seemed to reverse his usual emotional journey. Without becoming too embroiled in theological speculation, it is possible to argue that Saxton's musical solution shifts the balance of Christine's madness ever so slightly from what Wesker saw as idealism destroyed by dogma, towards her (ultimate) redemption via a metaphorical crucifixion and resurrection. The opera's 'tonal' structure seems to suggest a return to the opening situation (that is, from E at the start of scene 1 to E at the end of scene 13, by way of a coherent and not completely *un*traditional key structure). Crucially, the recapitulation of Christine's (scene 1) song (by the oboe) could be viewed as a renewal – a fresh start, rather like the circular implications of Berg's *Wozzeck*, perhaps (although *that* carries slightly negative overtones). This will be argued in greater detail in the chapters that follow, but might it be significant that, when Wesker specified a repeat of Christine's song, it was at the end of Act 1, scene XV of the stage play (marked 'but sadly now') immediately before Bishop Henry announces the decision that forces her into a spiritual decline?

The purpose of this short survey, has been to describe the early stages in the transformation of one art form into another by examining individually some of the decisions, regarding libretto, characterization, orchestration, musical language and overall structural design, made by the composer (and/or his librettist) from the moment of commission up to the eventual transmission of the new work to performers and audience. This complex process necessarily involves reconsideration of the original play and its theatrical conventions while developing a purely *operatic strategy* (how best to incorporate musical elements into a hitherto spoken drama). Obviously, there is more to composing an opera than merely setting words to music. A survey such as this cannot hope to be comprehensive. The following chapter will adopt a more structured approach to musical commentary, addressing the opera's thirteen scenes individually as well as collectively, and analysing the musical processes employed by Saxton during the course of his retelling of the original play's narratives.

---

[45]   At London's Barbican Centre on 31 January 1988, by the LSO, conducted by Jeffrey Tate.

Chapter 4
Caritas: The Opera

Overview

Concepts of Time

Readers of the previous chapter will have gleaned some basic information about the way in which Arnold Wesker's stage play was adapted for musical setting – and, it is hoped, will be aware of most (if not all) of the dramatic incidents that contribute to the 'plot' of *Caritas*, the opera. As Tables 3.1 and 3.2 make clear, the action is spread over a period of some four or more years[1] with 17 June 1381 providing a focal point for both strands of the interlinked narratives of Christine Carpenter's life as an anchoress and England's social unrest as embodied in the Peasants' Uprising. Clearly, it is a common characteristic of historical dramas that the unities of time and place are rarely observed in production – although the approximate proportions of historical time may be reflected in real time (that is the duration of the corresponding sections of dramatic action). At first sight, the obvious imbalance between the lengths of the two acts of the opera might appear to suggest that this has not been achieved in *Caritas*, but it is important to recall the *Composer's Note*[2] in which Saxton effectively describes Act 2 as a final scene without a separating interval – shortened 'in order to create an uninterrupted drama'. In fact, this concluding scene (scene 13), when combined with the preceding scenes (scenes 10–12) that also take place notionally in 1381, results in a total duration that counterbalances the first seven scenes of Act 1[3] (those that take place in 1377–78) as Table 4.1 demonstrates. Furthermore, the two remaining scenes (scenes 8 and 9), which take place in 1379–80, can be identified as central turning points in the conjoined dramas, with scene 8 (dated February 1379)[4] containing debates in the Carpenter household about yet more taxes, the state of the country, issues of literacy and their observations on Christine's declining self-

---

[1]   The exact dates cited in the score are July 1377; Feb. 1379; and 17 June 1381 – a total of just under four years – although Act 2 continues for an unspecified period afterwards. This notwithstanding, Agnes pleads for her daughter's 'release' by claiming that 'She [Christine] give our Lord three precious years' (Act 1, bars 981–982).

[2]   Quoted in Chapter 3, page 00.

[3]   Scenes 10–13 have a combined duration of 34′41; scenes 1–7 have a combined duration of 34′18.

[4]   The second section of scene 8 (the family debate) is dated May 1381 in the stage play only (as scene XI).

esteem – whereas, by contrast, scene 9 (undated) concentrates on Christine herself, as she oscillates between devotion, imagined visions and a growing awareness of the hopelessness of her situation within the narrow confines of her (now filthy) cell.

Such an overview, therefore, provides convincing evidence that Saxton has striven to create a real-time structure that is both symmetrically pleasing and reflects the passage of historical time insofar as this is possible, bearing in mind the open-ended nature of the period(s) in question. Exact equivalents (of historical and real time), of course, are rarely practicable – and should not be expected, since it is the sum of the dramatic incidents (the action) that is measured and not the invisible weeks and months that intervene. What Table 4.1 does demonstrate most convincingly is that the opera pivots on a central axis marked by the return of the opening 'tonality' (the pedal Es) in scene 8 and (in scene 9) its dominant (B) – a fateful pitch whose use here bears comparison with a similar emphasis in *Wozzeck*, Act 3, scene 2.[5] It is perhaps significant that the start of scene 9 of *Caritas* marks the exact half-way point (in real time) of the entire opera[6] – a true crisis-point in terms of Christine's delicate balance between religious zeal and disillusionment.

With the benefit of hindsight, *Caritas* might more accurately have been cast as a one-act opera, perhaps, rather than retaining the (two-act) structure of Wesker's play, especially since the time needed to readjust the set (to reveal the interior of Christine's cell and to bring *her* into centre stage) is already provided by the extended orchestral transition and Ricercar that separate scenes 12 and 13.[7] These sections have other functions, of course, and, together with the opera's large-scale tonal structure and Saxton's use of motivic cross-references, will be explored in later sections of this overview. However, the use of much shorter transitional passages elsewhere in the opera is also worthy of note – as is the direct juxtaposition of scenes (without specific transitions), since both of these strategies affect the dramatic impact of consecutive incidents. The composer takes great care to mark the start and conclusion of each scene in the score so it is possible to identify the occasions when he plans to introduce a 'breathing point' into the drama and, conversely, where he intends to plunge straight into the new action. For example, the sudden movement from the children's questioning of Christine at the end of scene1 into the 'trial'[8] and branding of Richard Lonle in scene 2 emphasizes the dual roles of Bishop Henry as religious

---

[5]   Compare *Caritas* Act 1, scene 9, bar 788, with *Wozzeck* Act 3, scene 2, bar 109. See later detailed commentary. Berg's focus on B is clearly associated with the murder of Marie and Wozzeck's moment of madness; Saxton's inter-textual reference no doubt aims to relate the (now) inevitable 'spiritual death' of Christine with such an operatic memory.

[6]   Within a margin of 8 seconds: Scenes 1–8 total 39'11; Scenes 9–13 total 39'03 – see published CD track timings and Appendix A.

[7]   In fact, this change is specified in the opera score (during the Ricercar) between bars 1128 and 1232.

[8]   More the continuing debate between Richard Lonle and the Bishop than the legal judgement, of course.

Table 4.1   *Caritas* the opera: Historical and real time schemes

	Act 1			Act 2
Year	1377–	1379–	138 –	1379–
Scenes	1–7	8–9	10–12	13
Main themes	Parallel exposition of two dramas: Christine's transition from secular to recluse (and her expectations as an anchoress), and the political (and religious) impact of the Peasants' Uprising. / Character development through juxtaposed groupings (separated by short orchestral transitions) and the use of thematic motifs.	Growing sense of crisis in both dramas	Sermon marks the interaction between the crises in the country and in Christine's personal world. / Significant orchestral transition, which marks climax of social rebellion.	Christine's descent into chaos. The interior of her cell is now the centre of the action as she oscillates between religious ecstasy and madness. / Brief reminiscences of earlier times. / The orchestral passacaglia sustains the musico-dramatic 'argument' instigated by the ricercar that concludes the previous scene.
Real time	12'06/5'09/3'15/2'29/ 4'11/5'16/1'52	4'53 /4'22	2'32/1'02/11'33	19'34
Total duration	34'18	9'15	34'41	19'34

and secular Lord as well as both the similarity and disparity between the conventions and justice-systems of the two societies that he governs. Although the stage rubric records that the punishment of Richard is separated from Christine's immurement by several months (of historical time), the violent juxtaposition of the two scenes (accompanied by the tritone leap from D to A♭ pedals) thrusts the two worlds (and the two associated dramas) into the sharpest of perspectives. By comparison, the short transition between scenes 2 and 3[9] allows the Bishop's passionate outbursts ('Fervours! Tantrums and fervours!') to subside before the more intimate (though no less impassioned) complaint of Richard's son, Robert, as he accuses Christine of abandoning the real world – and, by implication, his physical love – for 'a devil of your own'.[10] Table 4.2 summarizes Saxton's beautifully calculated use of orchestral transitions within Act 1 of the opera.

As will be seen, there is no fixed pattern of scenes and transitions, although in general the 'outside' world of the workshop is separated from the 'interior' world of the church by short instrumental interludes. Occasionally, the composer also inserts an extended orchestral passage to suggest the passing of time between two or more incidents in the same scene,[11] whereas, after the relatively dense, uninterrupted sequence of four scenes (9–12) at the end of Act 1, the lengthy orchestral section between bars 1015 and 1090 (Transition 7) both reflects the expressionistic intensity of the action and effects a smooth transition into the relative calm of the Ricercar. By comparison, Act 2 (or scene 13 as it should more accurately be termed) would appear to adopt a quite different temporal conceit that approximates more closely to real time than does the sequence of historical 'snapshots' that constitutes the previous act. By concentrating Wesker's original eleven 'framed poses' of Act 2 into a continuous stream of contemplative, devotional and reactive gestures, Saxton not only emphasizes Christine's mental and emotional instability but allows it to develop into a complex and uncontrollable passion that overwhelms her and the witnesses of her decline alike. The resulting 'mad scene' is all the more terrifying because of its rigorous control through the hypnotic rotations of a passacaglia theme and its variants – despite occasional moments of relative stasis as the woodwind intone the *Kyrie eleison* in a textless prayer for mercy; as Christine speaks tenderly to the young girl (her *alter ego?*) or sings the heartbreaking lullaby to her imagined child. Ultimately, it is the memory of her idealized ambitions that completes her decline. The final disembodied intercessions of her family remain unanswered and the distorted echoes of the *Alleluia* overwhelm the slender promise inherent in the return of the opening 'heartbeat' pedal on E. Even the gentle pathos of Christine's

---

9   Act 1, bars 298–312.

10   In passing, it is worth mentioning that a pedal B accompanies this accusation. See above and later references to the crisis-pitch of scene 9.

11   In scene 8, for example, between the rather coarse comments on the Tax Collector's exit and the preparing of a meal, during which the Carpenter family discuss social and personal issues (bars 685–701).

'I will forsake all that I see' (recalled by solo oboe) is darkened by her barely articulate muttering 'This is a wall and this is a wall …'. There is a real paradox in all of this in that the final scene is both contained in time and seems timeless. Because everything that is depicted *could* have happened in an approximately 20-minute period, the action possesses a quality of urgency – even destiny – that makes it an overwhelmingly tragic conclusion to an otherwise episodic preamble (if that is not too casual a description of Act 1). The prospect of the madness being permanent is terrifying – unthinkable, even, in a Christian context.

Table 4.2   Transitions in *Caritas*, Act 1

Scene	Summary of place and action
1	**Church**: Christine's Immurement Ceremony* [July 1377]
2	**Outside**: Branding of Richard Lonle [some months later]
Transition (1)	Bars 298–312
3	**Outside Christine's Cell**: Christine and Robert*
Transition (2)	Bars 363–371
4	**Workshop**: Tax Collector with William
5	**Outside Christine's Cell**: Christine with Matilde (i)
Transition (3)	Bars 524–532
6	**Church**: Mathew hears Christine's Confession
Transition (4)	Bars 623–627
7	**Cell**: Christine's Soliloquy 'Rumours'*
Transition (5)	Bars 667–670
8	**Workshop**: Carpenter Family discuss Taxes, Country and Christine's Decline [February 1379]
Transition (6)	Bars 768–775
9	**Church/Cell**: Mathew and Christine at Prayer/A Showing?*
10	**Church**: Sermon and Bishop's Response [17 June 1381]
11	**Outside Cell**: Christine and Matilde (ii) / Christine's Screams
12	**Church**: Family Petition (Trio) and Bishop's Refusal* / Christine and Robert: 'Break them down!'
Transition (7)	Bars 1015–1090 (Representation of off-stage battle)
Ricercar	**Workshop** (Bars 1091–1150): Report on the Uprising spoken over orchestra / Robert's body is carried in and a Funeral Procession is formed / The wall revolves slowly, revealing the cell and Christine / The Procession disappears / Act 2 (scene 13) follows without a break

* = Children's Chorus

Concepts of Tonality

Reference has already been made to the use of harmonic pedals in scenes 8 and 9 of
Caritas[12] and elsewhere in the opera. As has previously been observed, Table 3.5
above combines information about orchestral strategies in the long and varied first
scene of Act 1 with details of the sequence of sustained pitches that punctuate the
main liturgical items or dramatic incidents, thereby creating pillars of stasis from
the opening E of *Alleluia. Te martyrum candidatus* (in its transposed version)[13]
to the sustained E♭ of *Veni Creator Spiritus* (via the tritone-relationships of E/B♭
and A/E♭), to the radiant A major chord that illuminates Christine's entrance
into her cell (via A/E♭ again), and to the pedal D that accompanies her song
('I will forsake all that I see'). In between these tonal landmarks other members
of the Carpenter family (together with Robert, her former betrothed) intersperse
comments and criticisms supported by generally more rapid harmonic movement,
often built around bass sequences of tritones, perfect fourths/fifths, or whole-tone
scales. This richer, more flowing, chromatic vocabulary reflects the reservations
and unresolved anxieties about the contemplative path chosen by Christine. Such
a tonal methodology is not new to Saxton – nor is it uncommon in large-scale
twentieth-century dramatic structures such as opera or symphony. A number
of Saxton's earlier orchestral works have already been cited in this respect (in
Chapter 3), as has Bartók's use of the 'primary colours' of triadic harmonies to
characterize the contents of Duke Bluebeard's secret rooms. Whether described
as progressive tonality, extended tonality, or even tonality based on the axis-
relationships of all twelve notes,[14] it cannot be denied that such practices move
well beyond the boundaries of classical major/minor tonality and (appropriately
managed) can considerably enrich the harmonic palette and the overall architecture
of compositions that, like *Caritas*, enjoy substantial temporal dimensions.

It is clear from the above description that the tonal pathway of scene 1 leads
the cast and audience into a new environment – from the reassuring liturgy of the
church into the unfamiliar seclusion of the Anchoress's cell; from the known to the
unknown – or, in terms of musical pitch, from E to D. In essence, the composer
has introduced an element of uncertainty into a story whose frail stability is to be
further threatened by the sudden (and tonally distant) leap from Christine's hoped-
for tranquillity into a primitive punishment ritual as Richard Lonle is branded on his
forehead and the music plunges onto A♭. And yet scene 2 does not follow the pattern
of its predecessor by moving to ever-more-distant territories. It has a rounded form,
starting and ending in the same tonality, albeit enclosing brief excursions into more
remote regions. As Bishop Henry and Mathew move into the church, they discuss

---

[12]   See nn. 4 and 9 above.

[13]   The original pitch in *Liber Usualis* (p. 1171) is on C.

[14]   As set out in Ernö Lendvai's stimulating (if contentious) (1971) thesis, *Béla Bartók –
an Analysis of his Music* (London: Kahn and Averill).

the chaos associated in Henry's mind with Wycliffe's teaching and he confesses his fundamental lack of sympathy for Christine's calling. A basic structural plan of the scene reveals that it falls into seven short sections with the vigorous momentum of the opening A♭ *ostinato* returning on two occasions to punctuate more rational passages, during which the ubiquitous pitch (of A♭) is partially obscured by eight- and nine-note cluster-chords, interlocking hexachords, bass-line chains of tritones and perfect fifths, and the use of percussion of indeterminate pitch. It would be difficult to imagine a more disruptive (not to say more disillusioning) contrast than that created between these two scenes. They establish beyond doubt the duality of the plot; the religious and political control exercised by a privileged elite; and the apparent hopelessness of self-determination in a society governed by those with inherited wealth or those who they appoint to positions of power. As subsequent scenes unfold, it becomes increasingly obvious that the composer is constructing a large-scale tonal scheme that will support and identify a rich sequence of scenarios and that allows him to create meaningful pitch cross-references that are analogous to classical practice but without its rather restrictive conventions.

Thus, the first transition (bars 298–312) moves from A♭ to B (perhaps intentionally outlining a triadic relationship between the first three scenes (E–A♭ (G♯)–B) before setting up a strong tritone relationship with F, whence the second transition (bars 363–371) moves by way of a persistent bass drum beat that culminates in the pulsatile pedal A that helps to propel forward scene 4 (containing the Tax Collector's first visit to William's workshop). Although it might appear simplistic to imply that this progression represents a long-term cadence,[15] there can be little doubt that, the further the opera unfolds, the more the composer's target 'tonalities' can be seen to have macrocosmic structural significance. Additionally, some of his quasi-modulatory techniques can be likened to certain classical principles – as, for example, in the two counterbalancing chromatic bass-lines that accompany the Tax Collector's reflections on his profession – 'full of sins and shames' (a rising semitone line from B♭ to E in bars 390–401) – and then his mechanical cataloguing of the Carpenter's possessions (a descending chromatic bass from E to F♯ in bars 412 to 420) – thus setting up the next pitch polarity of F♯/C in scene 5).

Scenes 6 and 7 continue this pattern of tonalities a third apart (scenes 4 and 5: A–F♯/C; scenes 6 and 7: B♭–G) before the already identified return of the opening pedal E that leads into scene 8. This strong impression of tonal recapitulation is further enhanced by the orchestral passage that separates the two main elements of scene 8 (bars 701–714), during which the chain of tritone and perfect fourth steps in the cello and double bass provides a direct reference to a similar passage in scene 1 (bars 108–116) when the Carpenter family first gave voice to their

---

[15]   In this context, a perfect cadence (V–1) – an implied dominant (E major chord) to Tonic (A).

doubts about Christine's calling.[16] There are numerous other tonal correspondences between scenes on either side of the temporal axis of scene 9 (and its tonal focus of B, mentioned above), not least the sequence of tritones and perfect fourths that underpins the start of the sermon in scene 10,[17] the strong Ab orientation of scene 11 and scene 12, and the blazing A major triad (bars 990–997) that marks the climax of the Trio of intercession ('Let her go'), also in scene 12. This is subsequently distilled to a single step from A to Eb as Bishop Henry makes his decision ('She cannot leave her cell') but then returns as a march-like pedal A that initiates the orchestral transition into the Ricercar by way of a sustained minor third (G/Bb) that allows the martial tones of the distant uprising to dissipate into a contrapuntal movement of supreme dignity and logic. The tonal relationships between scenes 1 and 2 have been not so much reversed as rearranged to allow the Ricercar to sustain its D tonality (albeit with a pronounced D/Ab axis) to an extent that would have been impossible earlier, given the dramatic necessities of the start of the opera. This movement itself represents a dramatic imperative. It enables the two parallel narratives to be punctuated, if not resolved. It simultaneously exercises control over the temporal and the tonal elements of the opera by marking the climax of England's social unrest and the culmination of Christine's doubts. Decisions have been reached and time is required to come to terms with their implications. By creating a passage such as the Ricercar, Saxton has introduced an extended tonal oasis; a necessary *plateau* in the action; a much-needed *fermata* that provides an appropriate backcloth for the factual report on the failure of the Peasants' Uprising – all of which help to prepare for the ensuing acceleration of Christine's descent into madness. The final building-block in the opera's overall tonal structure is the lengthy journey from D back to E in the Passacaglia of Act 2 – and this will be the subject of the last section of this chapter.

Table 4.3 summarizes the main tonal landmarks of the opera as discussed above. For reasons of clarity, this is necessarily a simplified plan; fuller details will be introduced into the scene-by-scene commentary that follows later. For the moment, however, it would be timely to analyse the composer's use of characteristic motifs

Table 4.3   Main tonal landmarks in *Caritas*

Scene	1	2	3	4	5	6	7	8	9	10	11	12	13
Main tonalities	E	Ab	B-F	A	F#/C	Bb	G	E	B	G–	Ab	Ab	D
	Eb									C/F#		A	
	A											D/	
	D											Ab	E

---

[16]   The bass sequence in scene 1 is E–Bb, F–B, F#–C, G–Db, Ab–D, A–[Eb]. That in scene 8 is F–B, F#–C, G–C# (Db), G# (Ab)–D, A–Eb, Bb–E. The violin/viola *tremolando* is similar in each passage.

[17]   Bars 845–852: G–C#, F#–C, F–B, E–Bb, Eb–A, D–Ab, Db–G.

(*leitmotifs* in all but name) that are either derived from liturgical quotations, newly invented, or borrowed from his own and other works.

Melody and Musical Motifs

As the opera opens, the assembled cast/congregation sings the plainsong *Alleluia. Te martyrum candidatus laudat exercitus, Domine*,[18] as specified by the author/librettist. It has been transposed into E major from the original Ionian Mode (on C) but, otherwise, the version used in *Caritas* differs only in small details from medieval sources.[19] Example 4.1 reproduces the version used in the opera and has been annotated to show the main intervallic groupings that subsequently provide the composer with some of his most frequently used melodic motifs. As can be seen, the chant is rich in linear (stepwise) movement but also contains characteristic plainsong intervals of fourths, fifths and thirds (often in two- or three-fold sequences). It is these groupings, together with similar features found in the hymn *Veni Creator Spiritus* (see Example 4.2) that Saxton develops into a strongly characterized musical language that identifies individual members of the cast, draws them together in a common vocabulary as they converse, and distinguishes between them when they dispute.

However, the composer is not restricted by the relatively limited interval groupings found in his plainsong material. One of the main sources of harmonic tension found in *Caritas* is the tritone (E/B♭, especially) and this is also employed melodically (together with the related whole-tone scale) to extend and intensify episodes that are associated with Christine's calling. In particular, it is the vocal lines assigned to Christine, Robert and Bishop Henry that draw most obviously on the interval groupings highlighted in Examples 4.1 and 4.2. As has been hinted already (and will be further developed in later analysis), the Bishop first introduces an element of tension into the Ceremony of Immurement as he commences his prayer (in bar 34) on B♭, a tritone above the orchestra's sustained Es, before evolving lines based on a blend of whole-tone segments and sequences of thirds. Christine's reply (bars 52–60) echoes this pattern, albeit starting with an emphatic major third (A–C♯) which foreshadows the A major chord that later announces her entry into her cell (bars 157–165). During the domestic debate (bars 71–116) that follows her declaration and admission to her new life as Anchoress, the fragmentary interjections of her family elicit ever-stronger responses from Christine herself (based on chains of thirds) and provoke Robert to articulate his deeply felt resentment at being rejected in favour of divine love. His dramatic outburst ('And me! She were betrothed to me, she renounced me') has an assertive, almost fanfare-like quality as it draws heavily

---

[18]   *Alleluia. To thee, Lord, the white robed host of martyrs give glory.* Capitalization of the Latin texts is inconsistent in the various sources consulted. In the interest of consistency, this volume adopts the capitalization used in the vocal and orchestral scores of *Caritas*.

[19]   Compare with *Liber Usualis*, p. 1171, and N. Sandon, ed. (1986) *The Use of Salisbury* (Newton Abbot: Antico Edition), p. 68.

Example 4.1   Congregation: Act 1, scene 1, bars 2–26

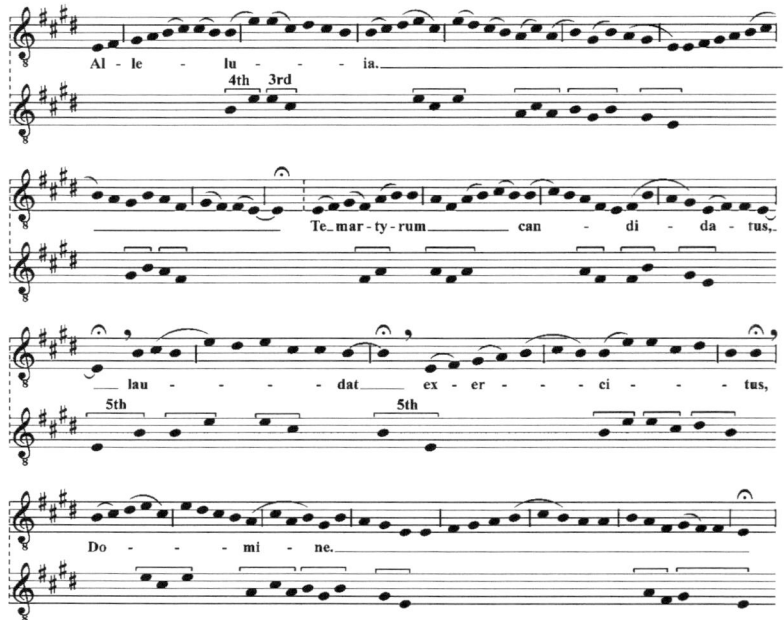

Example 4.2   Congregation: Act 1, scene 1, bars 117–126

on the fifths and fourths found in the plainsong sources (see Example 4.3). Christine, in turn, crowns her protestations with a wonderfully concentrated line of descending major thirds ('Heaven! Heaven! The truth is revealed in heaven'), a passage that outlines two interlocking whole-tone scales (see Example 4.4).

As the first verse of the hymn *Veni Creator Spiritus* is sung, Christine's family continue to comment on her new life. Robert's indignant outburst is now reluctantly

Example 4.3   Robert: Act 1, scene 1, bars 90–92

Example 4.4   Christine: Act 1, scene 1, bars 98–100

Example 4.5   Robert: Act 1, scene 1, bars 119–120

reduced into a passing remark ('I suppose we must be thankful she didn't ask for a coffin to sleep in')[20] – although its motivic content is little changed (see Example 4.5). However, when he recollects the carefree times that they had spent together as a couple, his musical line subtly incorporates Christine's characteristic chain of thirds into his own 'fanfare' before rising to a climax of great passion (see Example 4.6).[21] Then it is the Bishop's turn to paraphrase Christine's motif of thirds as he leads her to her cell. The plainsong *Alleluia* returns (in A major) and Christine is left to sing her farewell to the secular world in a melody (supported by a pedal D and an oboe counterpoint) that combines her characteristic thirds with whole-tone contours (see Example 4.7a).

Finally, the Children's Chorus takes up the pattern of falling thirds and scalic phrases that vary between chromatic and whole-tone identity. This closely entwined three-part writing – reminiscent of a children's round or singing-game in its combination of innocence and persistence[22] – is destined to return in varied forms many times during the course of the opera as a constant reminder of Christine's frustrated wish for a divine vision (see Example 4.8).

---

[20]   The significance of this comment is explained in Chapter 2, p. 19.

[21]   Example 4.6 contains a notable use of a palindrome (centring on the triplet D♯/C♯/D♯ on 'skies'). The reversing of the previous short phrase with the text 'she won't forget' reveals an extremely subtle *aide-memoire*.

[22]   One is reminded of the children's chants in *Albert Herring* or the slightly sinister 'Malo, malo' in Britten's *The Turn of the Screw*, perhaps?

Example 4.6   Robert: Act 1, scene 1, bars 141–146

Example 4.7a   Christine: Act 1, scene 1, bars 180–186

Example 4.7b   Chacony for Piano Left Hand, bars 1–8

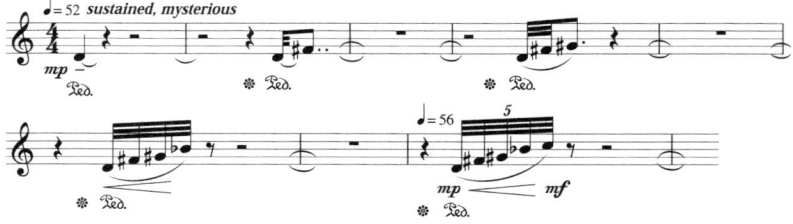

Example 4.8   Children's voices: Act 1, scene 1, bars 186–194

Although it is entirely plausible that Christine's song (Example 4.7a) is derived *directly* from previous motifs in scene 1 (as suggested above), its melody nonetheless bears a striking resemblance to the opening of the theme from Saxton's *Chacony for Piano Left Hand*, commissioned by the Aldeburgh Foundation in 1988[23] (see Example 4.7b). This was composed shortly after Saxton received the *Caritas* commission in 1987 but, as with similarities mentioned in Chapter 3,[24] such a likeness should not necessarily be interpreted as anything more significant than the sort of unconscious self-quotation or generic self-reference that occurs periodically in many composers' outputs – especially when work on several commissions takes place concurrently or within a few years of each other. However, the varied references to the song during the course of *Caritas* might in some small way be an outcome of the composer's use of variation techniques in the original *Chacony* and there are more obvious structural links with the Passacaglia in scene 13, as will be explained. Additionally,

---

[23]   First performed on 18 June, 1988, at the forty-first Aldeburgh Festival by Leon Fleisher and recorded by him on Sony Classical SK48081.

[24]   Between the opera, *Caritas*, and *Music to Celebrate the Resurrection* or *In the Beginning*.

the (probably subliminal) punning reference to 'left-hand' or 'sinister'[25] might have carried some weight with the composer, particularly in view of the theological duality identified by Christine later in the opera.[26] What is indisputable is that both librettist and composer have captured the essential idealism and child-like simplicity of Christine's character in this short set-piece (more akin to folk-song than an aria in the operatic sense). The beautifully balanced alliteration of Wesker's verse and the descending cadences of Saxton's melody combine to define the Anchoress's naive faith at the outset of what proves to be an immensely harrowing spiritual journey.

A comparable blend of unaffected language and melody can also be found in Christine's *Lullaby* in scene 13,[27] although the analogy here with the crucifixion makes this an altogether more poignant item than the earlier song. In one sense, the *Lullaby* represents the counter-pole of Christine's original innocence. Wesker's poetic imagery recalls the rough humanity of medieval Marian verse (the Virgin Mother's complaint about the thorns in her son's brow)[28] and Saxton's oblique reference to Marie's lullaby in *Wozzeck* reinforces the expressionistic dichotomy of love and suffering, of innocence and death, that constantly plays on Christine's mind in the final scene. In another sense, one might interpret this episode as a Freudian manifestation of her frustrated maternal instincts. Her conscious choice of divine over secular love (now being questioned) leads her to contemplate the unthinkable – that her devotion to Christ is, in fact, based on very human, physical emotions. As she reaches out in her delusion to comfort Christ and to share his pain, she confesses that she imagines herself naked, with the sun on her breasts, lying on grass with the scents of hawthorn and wild mint in the wind. She is transported back to the times spent with Robert (ironically, now sacrificed in the cause of social idealism), to the 'blue skies, the mare mating, the lamb sucking [and] sun setting'. Indeed, Robert can be identified motivically within the *Lullaby's* melody as his characteristic intervals of fourths and fifths are woven into Christine's chains of thirds (see Example 4.9). The climax of this passionate (and erotic) outburst is the realization that nature and spring are not forms of the Devil but are God-given. Christine's revelation, presumably, is too late – she is 'crucified upon the spring' as the tide of distorted *Alleluias* overwhelms her.

Of the numerous references to the motifs described above, perhaps the most intriguing is the recapitulation of Christine's song of farewell (Act 1, scene 1) on the last page of the opera. As described in Chapter 3 (p. 46), it provides a clue that

---

[25] 'Sinister' (as opposed to 'dexter') carries associations of left-handedness in medieval heraldry as well as the more common associations of evil or harm – perverse or ambiguous). The left-hand side of the brain is believed to be associated with linear or analytical thought (*Concise Oxford English Dictionary*).

[26] See Act 2, bars 51–56 (Example 4.15).

[27] Act 2, bars 232–250 – see introductory note about misplaced title and incorrect bar numbering in *Caritas* scores.

[28] For example, see 'Mary complains to other mothers' in R.T. Davies, ed. (1963) *Medieval English Lyrics* (London: Faber and Faber), p. 210.

Example 4.9   Christine's *Lullaby*: Act 2, bars 232–237

Example 4.10   Oboe solo: Act 2, bars 366–370

might be interpreted as implying a spiritual resurrection that follows the simulated crucifixion of the youthful anchoress during the 'Mad Scene'. Certainly, the impact of this (unsung) restatement of Christine's farewell 'to Father and friend' is more potent (and more ironic) than it would have been if placed at the conclusion of Act 1, as Wesker originally intended.[29] Some of the alternative readings of the opera's conclusion will be explored in the analytical commentary that follows later in this chapter but there is one audible (and visible notational) clue that should not be overlooked, especially in the transposed version of the song (from D to E) that enables it to match the overall tonal plan of *Caritas* (see Table 4.3). Example 4.10 makes this clear. The first phrase of 'I will forsake all that I see' comprises an ascending major third (E–A♭ [G♯]), followed by a rising whole-tone scale (A♭–B♭–C–D) and, then, the motif (D–C♯–B–C–B♭), which is recognizable as the main theme of the Ricercar (see Example 4.11). Significantly, the main interval of imitation in the Ricercar is the tritone (D/A♭), thus mirroring the juxtaposition of these two pitches between scenes 1 and 2 and the many other tritone polarities of the first act.

If this motivic paper-trail is followed to its logical conclusion (albeit in a sort of reverse gear), it is possible to argue that the Ricercar itself represents an extended fugal meditation on the phrase 'all that I see' (which concludes Act 1), and that the

---

29   In both editions of the stage-play, the repeat of Christine's 'I will forsake thee …' song comes at the end of scene XV (opera, scene 10) after the Travelling Priest has announced the failure of the Peasants' Uprising and the death of Robert. Clearly, the restructuring of this portion of the play in the libretto makes this less suitable, although the Ricercar does dwell on the song's text ('all that I see' / 'Ev'ry day of darkness, Lord') as explained elsewhere.

Example 4.11   Violin 1: Act 1, Ricercar, bars 1094–1095

orchestral accompaniment at the start of the following scene (which constitutes Act 2 and is based on the same musical material, and at the same pitch) serves to punctuate Christine's awareness of her total insignificance as she prays for comfort, deliverance and mercy. At this point she 'sees it all'. She has moved from the idealized state of being the 'chosen one' – the community star – to being a terrified, self-neglecting victim of her own ambition and pride. Her song of farewell has become a lament for life (Example 4.12).

Example 4.12   Act 2 start: Orchestral reduction

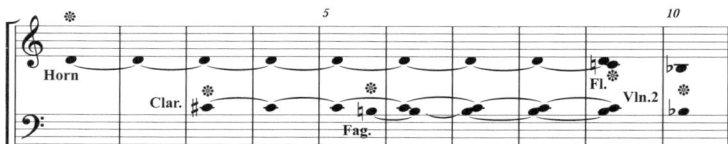

At this stage, Saxton introduces two more musical motifs into the score. Although they appear together, they have contrasting, yet complementary functions. One, clearly labelled in the score (*Kyrie eleison* – 'Lord have mercy'), is obviously a response to Christine's prayer for deliverance and is based (as far as can be ascertained) on the plainchant, *Kyrie De Angelis*.[30] The original plainsong has been lightly paraphrased by the composer, the first note (F) omitted (see Example 4.13), and the resulting motif is presented three times in a quasi-fugal exposition (on A, E, and B) by oboe, clarinet and flute.[31] Simultaneously, the bassoon plays the passacaglia theme (Example 4.14), which forms the structural basis of the final scene through its relentless repetition and variation. The two motifs share some superficial melodic characteristics – notably the sequence of a semitone followed by a series of tones (a common enough scalic pattern, although associated in particular with the Phrygian mode). One might speculate that these two themes have a common origin (although their rhythms and pace are quite different) and this would not be beyond the limits of possibility, bearing in mind that the orchestral transition between scene 12 and the Ricercar contains several pre-echoes of the above formula (see Examples

---

[30]   Kyrie of the Angels: *Liber Usualis*, p. 37. However, the composer has recently identified his source as the Kyrie of William Byrd's Five-part Mass (which itself appears to have used Kyrie *De Angelis* as a model).

[31]   Scene 13, bars 40–43.

4.13 and 4.14). Indeed, as the transition merges into the Ricercar through sequences of falling fifths and rising fourths, the orchestra appears to spell out a cryptic prayer for Christine[32] and all that she has experienced and is experiencing. As has been mentioned, the orchestra briefly muses on the Ricercar theme (itself a loose inversion of the later *Kyrie*) at the start of Act 2, while Christine cowers in abject solitude. Momentarily, the polyphonic *Kyrie eleison* reintroduces the ecclesiastical tone of the first scene – aided, perhaps, by the pseudo-*Alleluia* contours of the passacaglia theme – before a direct reference to Christine's song of farewell (at its original pitch – see Example 4.15) announces that 'There's not one God, – there's two!' This overt, indeed heretical, statement sets in motion the concluding stages of her madness during which the tritone (*diabolus in musica*[33]) is prominent and, increasingly, merges into disjunct vocal lines and *sprechstimme* screams of frustration.

Example 4.13   *Kyrie De Angelis*: Act 2, bars 40–42

Example 4.14   Bassoon: Act 2, Passacaglia theme, bars 40–49

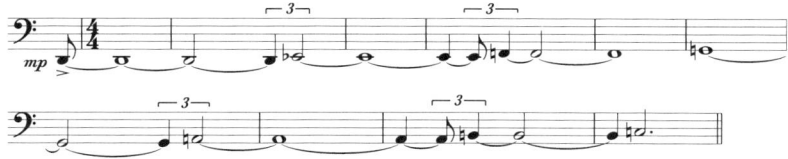

Example 4.15   Christine: Act 2, bars 51–56

---

32   Presumably, Robert is also represented by the fifths and fourths.
33   'The Devil in Music.'

In an opera that is rather light on set-pieces (such as extended arias, choruses and ensembles) it is noteworthy that Saxton has chosen to refer to Act 1 material in Act 2, even when this was not indicated or implied in Wesker's script.[34] Not only does this provide valuable musical and structural cross-references, it serves to heighten the impact of earlier pronouncements and pleas about Christine's declining sanity and illustrates her unconscious as well as conscious re-evaluation of the decision to embark on a life of solitude. In particular, references to her close family demonstrate the fundamental paradox of her situation – that, in pursuit of a better life, she appears to have exchanged release from life's mundanities for imprisonment (in her cell) rather than servitude for enlightenment. In terms of the Bishop's prayer, the 'old woman' has *not* been put off, *nor* entirely forgotten.

Saxton's sophisticated use of characteristic motifs in *Caritas* enables him to construct a compelling musical narrative that convincingly complements Wesker's dramatic and literary story-telling. By blending medieval melody and its modal language with chromatic harmony and baroque techniques, supplemented with contemporary inter-textual allusions – all within an extended tonal structure – the composer creates a seamless musical flow that accommodates the extremes of fourteenth-century liturgy and modernist psychology. The following operatic commentary will further illustrate these contrasting parameters and the consummate technical skill with which Saxton draws the opera to its inevitable climax.

Operatic Commentary

Act 1: Twelve Scenes and a Melodrama
Scene 1 (Track 1): the Interior of the Church of St James – a Carpenter's Workshop – the Window and Part of the Wall of the Anchoress's Cell

Table 4.4   Scene 1 structure

Bars 1–70	**71–116**	**117–135**	**136–156**	**157–178**	**179–194**
Church Ceremony (1)	Domestic Debate	Church Ceremony (2)	Church Ceremony (3)	Christine enters Cell	Christine's Song
Alleluia + *Verse*	Family Ensemble	[Family] *Veni Creator*	Procession through Family	*Alleluia*	Children's Refrain
(E–E/B♭)	(E♭/A)	(E♭)	(E♭/A)	(A)	(D)

---

[34] In addition to instances already cited, Act I material is recalled in Act 2, bars 260–271 as follows: Bishop Henry's 'May God put off from thee the old woman' and Robert's 'She've [sic] seen blue skies' from scene I, and the Trio for Agnes, William and Robert from scene 12.

Much has been written already about the first scene of *Caritas*. In the absence of an overture, the opening plainsong serves as a solemn prelude that establishes devotional mood, liturgical context and general historical period. Not only does this practice comply with the playwright's dramatic intention (to saturate the audience in 'an intense religious atmosphere'),[35] it also allows the composer to introduce subtle (unscripted) hints of later motifs[36] and to reinforce the quoted chant(s) with a highly coloured (at times, bell-like) representation of acoustic reverberation. As has been explained, Wesker's choice of the *Alleluia Verse, Te martyrum candidatus*, carries associations of sacrifice – perhaps, even multiple martyrdom as depicted in the Massacre of the Holy Innocents.[37] At this stage, the significance of the selected chant is unlikely to be fully appreciated but the underlying harmonic uncertainty created by the oscillating E–F–E in the timpani, bassoon and horn proves sufficient to suggest that Christine's immurement will be haunted with self-doubt.[38] Above all, the scene emphasizes the ongoing conflict between the tangible practicalities of everyday (secular) life and the spiritual idealism of the contemplative life of an enclosed anchoress by juxtaposing the church ceremony and the carpenter's workshop, as Christine's family complete the sparse furnishings for her cell and give vent to their misgivings about her calling.

As the *Alleluia* and its *Verse* die away and Christine prostrates herself before the two clergymen, the Bishop imposes his ecclesiastical authority by declaiming the introductory prayer on B♭ (a tritone away from the sustained orchestral pedal E). The relative harmonic clarity of this moment is followed by increased chromaticism in the orchestral accompaniment, culminating in a seven-note *fortissimo* chord[39] (based on superimposed thirds) that gradually distils into the major third (A/C♯) that outlines Christine's response: 'I ... offer and present myself to the goodness of God ...'. Her line echoes the sequence of falling thirds in the Bishop's prayer – both clearly derived from the plainsong (see Example 4.1) – and sets up its own tritone polarity (A/E♭) that will be exploited in the domestic interlude that follows Bishop Henry's pronouncement (once more on B♭): 'May God put off from thee the old woman, and may God clothe thee with the new woman.' After her ritual 'cleansing'[40] Christine, symbolically, is helped on with her rough anchoress's habit and the congregation's

---

[35]   Author's note: *Caritas* (1990) in *Arnold Wesker Plays*, Vol. 6 (London: Penguin Books), Act 1, scene I, p. 69.

[36]   The seeds of *Kyrie De Angelis* and the passacaglia theme (both Act 2) can be traced in the wind parts between bars 24 and 31, perhaps?

[37]   See N. Sandon, *The Use of Salisbury*, p. 68. Feast of the Holy Innocents, celebrated on 28 December.

[38]   It also insinuates the opening semitone of the Phrygian mode that will become such a feature of the passacaglia theme in Act 2.

[39]   See bar 49. There appears to be a misprint in the vocal score where the E♮ (LH) should be D♮, resulting in a chord of superimposed thirds: E♭/G/B/D/F/A/C♯, as in the full score.

[40]   Mathew sprinkles Christine three times with holy water and three times with incense.

modal 'Amen' marks an abrupt division between the dignity of the church service and the agitation of William Carpenter's workshop that follows.

The second major section of scene 1 (bars 71–116, see Table 4.4) focuses attention onto Christine's close family as they 'break away' to complete the table, chair and bed for the Anchoress's cell. Against a background of *tremolando* strings, Robert, Agnes and William question Christine's choice of vocation, pointing out *her* love of fairs, her human passions, and *their* apprehension about books, about too much piety, fasting and suffering, 'which offends the divine spark'. Initially, this communal tirade is underpinned by the Eb/A polarity mentioned above but this is soon extended into a twelve-note bass-line that alternates tritones and perfect fourths,[41] thus providing cumulative momentum to their aggregate of incomprehension. Against a sustained chord of dissonant thirds over a tritone (B/F),[42] Christine responds that it is '*Life* that offends the divine spark'; mere 'good deeds' are not sufficient; she must renounce *life* to marry Christ, whom she truly loves. As Robert intervenes (see Example 4.3), the texture reverts to *tremolando* strings over a twelve-note bass-line,[43] thereby setting up a pattern that continues to the end of this section, with Christine's lines supported by sustained chords,[44] and those of her family predominantly by strings over a gradually accelerating chromatic bass. The final subsection of this domestic ensemble (bars 100–116) increases the rising tension of alternations between parents, daughter and her former betrothed by substituting the earlier bass pattern with a line made up entirely of rising perfect fourths[45] that leads ultimately into a return of the original tritone-plus-perfect-fourth formula and its accompaniment of *tremolando* strings – but this time starting on E and ending on Eb,[46] at which point (bar 117), the third section of the scene commences as the congregation sings the Pentecostal hymn *Veni Creator Spiritus*.

After the emotive exchanges of the previous section, this reinstatement of the more elevated liturgical tone of the Immurement Ceremony (bars 117–135) reverts appropriately to a sustained pedal (on Eb) that slowly opens to include neighbour notes (G, A and F) as the Gloria is sung. The significant tritone polarity (Eb/A) dominates the Gloria, being expressed both harmonically and motivically as this short section merges into the final portion of the domestic debate (bars 136–147) led by William and Robert (who lists the vivid experiences of natural life: 'blue skies … mares mate … lambs skip … she won't forget'). The accompaniment of *tremolando* strings recalls the earlier workshop section but, on this occasion, the church ceremony continues as, in a complex counterpoint of liturgical action and secular commentary, a procession forms and moves through the family towards the

---

41   Bars 71–85: Eb–A–E–Bb–F–B–F♯–C–G–C♯–G♯–D.
42   Bb/D, A/C♯.
43   Bars 90–92: C♯–G–D–Ab–Eb–A–E–Bb–F–B–F♯–C–[G].
44   Bars 93–95: D/Ab/C/E. Bars 98–99: F/A/C/E/G♯.
45   Bars 100–103: A–D–G–C–F–Bb–Eb–Ab–Db–Gb–B–E.
46   Bars 108–116: E–Bb–F–B–F♯–C–G–Db–Ab–D–A–[Eb].

entrance to the Anchoress's cell. Once again, the agitation of the accompaniment culminates in a sustained tritone (A/E♭) as the Bishop and congregation declaim the final vow (the relinquishment of the kingdom of the world for the love of Jesus Christ). Then, to the accompaniment of a *sforzando* A major chord,[47] Bishop Henry commits Christine to her lifelong isolation as Anchoress – his commendation and blessing (*In nomine patris, filii et spiritus sancti*)[48] drawing once more on the pattern of falling thirds associated with Christine and derived from the plainsong *Alleluia* that is then repeated (also in A major). As the congregation sings this final liturgical item, the accompanying harmony is chromatically inflected (with E♭, G, F, and so on) so as to become the dominant of the tonality (D) of the last section of the scene – Christine's song of farewell (bars 179–186) and the questioning refrain of children's voices (bars 186–194 – see Examples 4.7a and 4.8).

The nature and possible origins of Christine's song have already been discussed – and will, no doubt, be referred to again as subsequent allusions are made to its potent symbolism during the course of the drama. Its function in this first scene, however, is simple and clear. Coming after a complex sequence of ceremonial and domestic exchanges, it represents Christine's very first moment of solitude; it shows her in all her spiritual innocence; for this one brief moment her idealism is intact and resolute. Then the children's voices outside her cell's small external window begin to sow their seeds of doubt – the short canonic repetitions commence their insistent interrogation and the nightmare begins.

Scene 2 (Track 2): A Central (outside) Place of Punishment – then the Bishop and Rector move into the Church

Table 4.5   Scene 2 structure

Bars 195–213	214–221	222–237	238–254	255–269	270–286	287–297
A♭ *Ostinato*	Bishop:	Mathew:	A♭ *Ostinato*	Bishop:	Bishop:	A♭ *Ostinato*
Richard/ Bishop: 'Three days!'	'No man's free'	(Sentence passed)	Bishop: 'You think I shouldn't brand a man'	'God's plagues' (John Wycliffe)	'Forgive me Rector' (Christine)	Bishop: 'Fervours! Tantrums!'

Although the primary function of this scene is to provide a shocking juxtaposition of the savage punishment of Richard Lonle and the relative tranquillity of Christine's

---

[47]   Aurally, this has the effect of a brilliant spotlight and marks the start of the fifth section of the scene (bars 157–178).

[48]   'In the name of the Father, Son and Holy Spirit.'

admission to her cell (following, as it does, directly after the overall dignity of the church service), it also supplies the audience with valuable historical and political information that contributes to the (national) context of her life as a recluse and the developing (local) unease about her vocation. The shortage of labour in England after the Black Death[49] had encouraged bondsmen (such as Lonle) to seek freedom by living in towns for a year and a day – but he had been caught and sentenced to be branded on his forehead as a warning to others. Incidents such as this, together with the preaching of Wycliffe and John Ball, in due course helped to instigate the Peasants' Uprising, led by Wat Tyler in 1381 (see commentary on scenes 10–12).

It is also significant that the action of scene 2 takes place outside the church 'in the centre space'[50] and, therefore, could perhaps have been witnessed or overheard from the external cell window through which Christine otherwise offers advice and converses with Robert and Matilde. Even allowing for common dramatic and operatic conventions (which sometimes permit stage deafness), it is important to realize that Christine was already a member of the larger community that was affected by Bishop Henry's characteristic inflexibility – whether it be in his capacity as temporal nobleman or religious Lord. The choice of location accentuates the dominant role played by the princes of the church in the governance of the land during this period, and the seven brief episodes that constitute the action of this scene supply compelling evidence of the Bishop's self-interest, of his fear of change, his suspicion of intellectuals (such as John Wycliffe) and those (like Christine) who, in his opinion, were too demonstrative in their faith. Above all, he claims to value his responsibilities ('duties bind us all') and sees himself as the custodian of the earth and the seasons ('I must attend to what I love'). 'No man is free', he exclaims as he calls on the Rector, Mathew De Redeman, to announce the branding.

Taken as a whole, the scene is tightly organized, with a rondo-like recurrence of material from the first section in episodes 4 and 7 (see Table 4.5). With the exception of the second episode (bars 214–221), the tonality of A♭ is strongly established throughout – either with an emphatic bass-pedal or an inner pedal of sustained A♭s. The seven short sections are characterized by contrasting figurations and speeds – and, of course, by vocal lines that vary between oratorical declamation and the use of motivic patterns derived from the two main types already identified in the first scene. The intervals of a tritone and perfect fourths/fifths are particularly prominent in the Bishop's animated lines as he responds to Richard Lonle's accusation of hypocrisy in the first section of the scene (see Example 4.16), whereas Mathew's indictment of Lonle, in section 3, combines tritones and sequences of thirds with single-pitch

---

[49]   The Black Death accounted for the death of between 30 and 40 percent of the population of England from 1348–50.

[50]   'The/a centre space' is the only information provided about the location of Act I, Scene 2, in the libretto and both editions of the play. Presumably, it separates or is adjacent to the church and workshop. See Figure 5.1 in Chapter 5 for the photographs of Joe Vaněk's set designs.

Example 4.16   Bishop Henry: Act 1, scene 2, bars 207–208

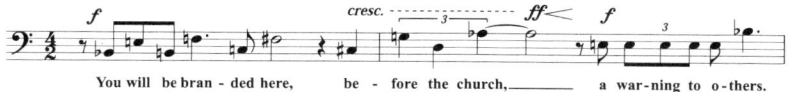

Example 4.17   Mathew: Act 1, scene 2, bars 222–228

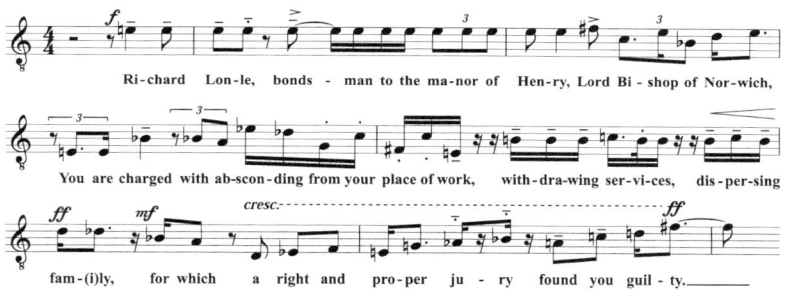

declamation, reminiscent of Peter Grimes's trial in Britten's eponymous opera (see Example 4.17). Occasionally, such vocal patterns are employed as bass-lines (as in the first scene) and provide increased harmonic momentum between passages of more sustained chordal stasis.[51]

The sequence of short episodes also allows for occasional moments of reflective conversation that clarify the contrasting clerical roles of the Bishop and Priest. Compared with Bishop Henry's choleric rage, Mathew's authority appears simulated – 'firm but without the Bishop's dignity'[52] – and the Rector soon reveals that his sympathies lie more with 'free-thinkers' than with the conservatism of the established church ('Times are changing, Lord Bishop'). Such temperamental (and political) incompatibility inevitably comes to a head later in the opera when (at the end of scene 8) Mathew admits his unsuitability for the sort of priesthood identified with Bishop Henry ('For this Church, no!'), although William Carpenter (who provokes this outburst) is not alone in blaming him for encouraging Christine to choose a life of seclusion. 'I always warned – some cannot bear the touch of God' concludes Bishop Henry as he describes his aversion to anchoresses.[53] Whatever may have been

---

[51]   For example, the bass-line of bars 211–213 uses patterns of minor and major thirds; bars 255–259 and bars 270–273 use patterns of tritones and semitones. Such passages are usually twelve-note in aggregate.

[52]   Stage direction in bars 222–223.

[53]   Scene 2, bars 291–294. Agnes also confronts Mathew (in scene 6) thus: 'You thought an anchoress would grace your church'.

Mathew's motivation in supporting Christine's application for immurement,[54] he does appear to provide compassionate guidance during her subsequent confessions and (mistaken) visions, although her response to his counselling proves dismissive and his overall impact on social and political change remains uncertain.

After this remarkable display of violent punishment and outspoken debate, the following scene provides a different sort of confrontation – this time between Robert and Christine, lover and anchoress. Saxton supplies a short transition that slows the orchestral momentum and enables the new tonality and texture to emerge, as if out of an improvised (organ) voluntary, during which the audience metaphorically follows Robert to his place outside the Anchoress's cell.

Scene 3 (Track 3): Outside Christine's Cell

Table 4.6   Scene 3 structure

Bars 313–336	337–362
Robert and Christine: Accusations and Responses	Christine sings a quasi-parable – 'Mother and Son' (overall F tonality with occasional motivic hints of her scene 1 song), followed by the children's refrain: 'Christine, had a revelation yet?' (bars 358–363), a minor third higher than scene 1) as if to provoke the Anchoress anew.
R: 'It is not God you serve' (B-rooted harmony) C: 'In here's the world' (B♭) R: 'Cruelty, unreason, killing …' (G) C: 'Don't taunt me Robert' (G♯) R: 'Black is white and white is black' (E) C: 'I have no other words' (E) R: 'Try village words' (F♯) C: 'Love, Robert, love! I can't say more'	Robert responds by shooing them away. Their singing fades out during the short orchestral transition (bars 363–371) that leads into scene 4.
Oboe (A♭–G) and Flute *obbligato* (based on thirds) leads into second section –	

After the dramatic extremes of idealism and realism experienced in the first two scenes of *Caritas*, the opera embarks on a sequence of more intimate episodes in which Christine is observed in conversation with her former fiancé (Robert), the village gossip (Matilde), and her priest-confessor (Mathew) (Table 4.6). She is also overheard in a short agitated soliloquy ('Rumours, rumours, I hear rumours whispered') that necessarily provides (together with her conversations) fresh insight into her mental state as she adjusts to a new environment (with varying degrees of success) and as she fails to experience the longed-for 'showing'. Bishop Henry, the dominant force in the first two scenes, is absent during these episodes (while

---

[54]   The extant letters (see Chapter 2) suggest that Mathew recommended Christine as an anchorite.

Mathew becomes more influential) and a new character (the Tax Collector) appears in two Workshop scenes[55] that punctuate the series of Christine-centred episodes[56] and continue the socio-historical commentary on external affairs instigated in scene 2.

Scene 3, itself, has its origins in the central sections of the Immurement Ceremony but replaces Robert's complaining third-person outbursts ('She'll miss them fairs!') with direct (second-person) accusatory statements ('He made you for the world, the world for you'). There seems to be no attempt by Robert to persuade Christine of his continuing love – rather he initiates an atmosphere of interrogation. He represents himself as the injured party – a man who has been jilted, rather than an enduring lover. Paradoxically, it is Christine who still radiates love, albeit divine love (*caritas*) for her spiritual Lord. Their respective vocal lines sharpen the contrast between these attitudes: Robert increasingly utilizes jagged chromatic, tritone sequences (sometimes combined with hints of Christine's series of thirds, as in Example 4.18), or patterns of perfect fourths/fifths, whereas Christine recalls motifs from her scene 1 song or indulges in chains of falling and rising thirds (most elegantly expressed in Example 4.19 – 'Love Robert, love. I can't say more; I'm filled with love for him' – after which the flute takes up this pattern as it leads into the next section).[57]

Example 4.18   Robert: Act 1, scene 3, bars 315–316

Structurally, this scene possesses many of the characteristics of a baroque Recitative and Aria in which an introductory proposition or debate is followed by a solo that enlarges upon some aspect of the earlier (more stylized) discussion. In this case, the 'aria' is a relatively short story-cum-parable in which a child leaves his mother's protection (against her advice) to climb a nearby mountain – testing himself against the challenge of the task because 'there were no other way'. Of course, the child represents Christine (the singer); the challenge, to follow her calling. Like parts of scene 1, from which some of its material is derived, scene 3 is constructed over a tritone polarity (B/F as opposed to A/E♭) and creates oscillating semitone *ostinati* that appear in both the 'recitative' and 'aria', thereby helping to unify the two main sections – as the extracts in Example 4.20 demonstrate.

As can be seen in the three short extracts of Example 4.20, the semitone movement takes place on three levels: in the two violin parts (reduced score, treble, bars 313–314 and onwards) as alternating F–G♭–F–G♭ and F–E–F–E, and in the

<hr />

[55]   Scenes 4 and 8.

[56]   Scenes 3, 5, 6, 7 and 9.

[57]   Reminiscent of Christine's 'Heaven! Heaven! The truth is revealed in heaven' (bars 98–99: Example 4.4).

Example 4.19   Christine: Act 1, scene 3, bars 329–334

Example 4.20   Orchestral reduction: Act 1, scene 3

(a) Bars 313–314

(b) Bars 337–338

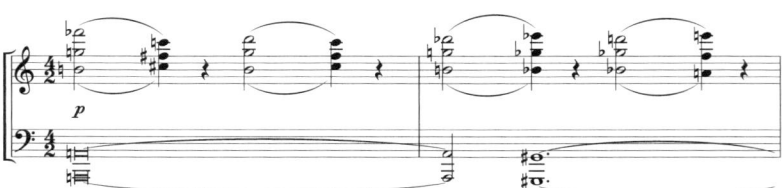

(c) Bar 346

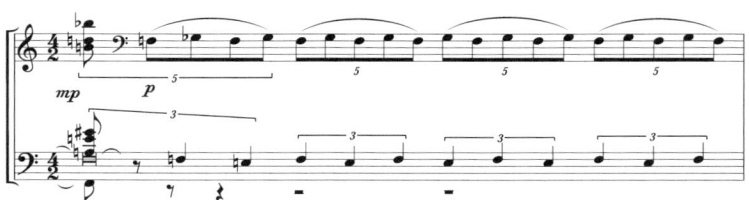

oboe line as A♭–G (reduced score, bars 313–314). Similarly (bars 337–338), during the more chordal texture which marks the start of the 'aria', semitone patterns can be observed in the treble line (D♭–C, G–F♯), and in the bass line (A–G♯). Finally, bar 346 reverts to the oscillation of F–G♭ and F–E found in the 'recitative' (bars 313–319). As the concluding pedal F is reached in bar 358, the children's voices return to taunt Christine and to punctuate the transition into the following workshop taxation-scene. The 'fatalistic' significance of the emphasis on B in scene 9 has already been mentioned and it is noteworthy that a comparable emphasis marks the start of this sequence of episodes (scenes 3–9), which illustrate stages in Christine's life as an anchoress, her mental decline, and the effects of taxation on society. This substantial inner section of Act 1 is, therefore, clearly delineated tonally by these two episodes in B and, rather like a symphonic development, also extends the range of tonal centres (see Table 4.3) until a virtually complete twelve-note spectrum is encompassed.[58] Not that this has any particular serial or doctrinal significance, rather is it indicative of the dimensions of the opera's tonal architecture and the variety of Saxton's chromatic vocabulary within the outer pillars of the work's overall structure (where the 'home tonality' of E is buttressed by substantial excursions to E♭, A and D, and D and A♭ in the outer scenes). As to Christine's almost obsessive references to her scene 1 song, there can be no better example than the start of her short 'aria' where the inherent pentatonicism of the 'song of farewell' appears transposed in two consecutive phrases of the melody (see Example 4.21).

Example 4.21   Christine: Act 1, scene 3, bars 337–341

As the children's voices fade away, the bass-drum introduces a march-like rhythm beneath the widening chromatic oscillations of the brass and (then) the woodwind. The following scene starts with four bars of the new dominant (pedal E) until the lower strings and percussion renew the martial mood with an emphatic pedal on A. The Tax Collector has called on William Carpenter to assess his fiscal dues.

---

[58]   Only C♯/D♭ is missing in this chromatic spectrum of tonal centres. But see also n. 87, below.

Scene 4 (Track 4): The Carpenter's Workshop

Table 4.7   Scene 4 structure

Bars 372–389	390–411	412–419	420–424
Orchestral Introduction	Tax Collector mentions 'The Anchoress' above	Tax Collector asks for information – hints at bribery – above	William lists property above leaping bass
[The external world]	rising chromatic bass (B♭–A–B♭)	falling chromatic bass (E–F)	(F♯–C–B–F–E– B♭–E♭–D♭–
Pedal E–A –E♭			... E♭)

This is the first of two visits by the Tax Collector, the main purpose of which is the regular listing of assets (Table 4.7). The Collector is subtly characterized by Wesker ('arrangements can be made; eyes closed') and Saxton is quick to perceive the satirical potential of this ingratiating state servant, underlining his mock piety and obvious insincerity by giving him slithery chromatic lines to sing (against an exaggerated chromatic bass). He summarizes the Anchoress as 'a chastening rebuke' – 'you [William] must be proud' – although he ('a mortal man') excuses himself from progressing beyond his own 'reverence' because of his lack of self-discipline ('control'). By contrast, William's mechanical cataloguing of his tools, stock and stores is delivered with clock-like precision, as he ignores the proffered opportunity of bribery.

Brief though it is, this scene is an important component in the drama since it maintains interest in the parallel story (which culminates later in the reported failure of the Peasants' Revolt) and provides evidence of the relative insignificance of Christine's life-changing decision in the eyes of the larger world. It also provides a somewhat lighter interlude between the increasingly introspective scenes that trace the Anchoress's desperate search for a 'showing', a divine vision that would sustain her self-belief and justify her decision to reject the everyday world in favour of a life of solitude. Another new character (the village gossip) now emerges to add a hagiographic – not to say comedic – gloss on Christine's situation as she moves between meditative contemplation and demonstrative unease. Matilde is an odd mixture of liturgical acolyte (she assisted Christine at her immurement), collector of *Vitae* (lives of saints), and general busybody who takes it upon herself to check on the Anchoress's genuflection-discipline (see Chapter 2) and to remind her of the sacrifices and sufferings of her predecessors ('she [Yevetta] [sic] were enclosed like you, enclosed').

Scene 5 (Track 5): Christine's Cell

Table 4.8   Scene 5 structure

Bars 425–436	437–454	455–523
Christine sings quietly to herself: 'There was a oneness time – I search [for] that'	Matilde enters – 'You crossed your mouth? Your eyes?'	Matilde: 'a story 'bout a Belgie Saint'; 'and when she die – the birds like summer sang'
($\frac{12}{8}$ – F♯)	($\frac{7}{8}$ – C / F♯)	($\frac{2}{4}$ – C / F♯)

The scene starts with Christine singing tenderly to herself above oscillating woodwind chords (Table 4.8) whose (upper three-part) semitonal movement recalls the opening of scene 3 (see Example 4.21). A developing pattern of alternating woodwind and string textures is then supported by a slower series of falling thirds (D–B/E♭–C/E–C♯/D–F♯),[59] which leads into the F♯/C polarity on which the rest of the scene is based. Christine again draws on the melodic contour of her scene 1 song, but this is soon absorbed into the overall melismatic style of the description of her search for peace – for the perfect balance between body and soul, between God and nature. As if to confound idealism with procedure, Matilde then intrudes into the Anchoress's musings with a deliberately syncopated ($\frac{7}{8}$) metre, above which a parody of Christine's song is played by piccolo, clarinet and glockenspiel. She checks that Christine has observed the recommended discipline of crossing herself (mouth, eyes, ears, breasts), cautions her to beware of the 'lewd eyes' of local boys, and enquires if her mother has brought food, before relating the story of 'a Belgie Saint'.

During her preamble to this tale, Matilde admits that she has collected the lives of saints from rather unorthodox sources ('a smithy, who in turn was told it by a pilgrim nun to Rome'). One can only speculate on the reasons behind Matilde's rather macabre interest in female anchorites and saints ('[you] shouldn't catch me doing that!' she declares) but the net result of her colourful narrative is to provide yet another perspective on the choice of a life of solitude, whether it be designed to warn or to reassure Christine. 'Yvetta' (probably St. Yvette of Huy) is the first of three saints cited by Matilde in the original play[60] and the only one to be retained complete in the libretto. The story (which moves into duple metre) tells of a life of intense suffering (she was a leper) and of self-imposed pain (to keep at bay her 'tempting thoughts of lust'), after which her death was celebrated with unseasonal winter birdsong ('like summer sang'). Clearly, Wesker intended this section to foretell Christine's own demands for chains and haircloth in the following scene ('My body needs the pain

---

59   Strictly speaking, the last third [D–F♯] is a falling sixth.
60   See Chapter 2, p. 23, n. 40.

to help me concentrate on him') – and her eventual desire in (Act 2) to be crucified like her Lord.[61] Sadly, *she* was to be denied the symbolic blessing by Nature that she coveted (and Yvette had been granted).

As, perhaps, might be expected (following the precedents of the earlier scenes), Matilde's delivery of the St Yvette story uses a vocal style dominated by patterns of thirds while introducing tritones or more disjunct leaps of sevenths at crucial references to pain, enclosure or bereavement ('*O she flog* her poor ol' limbs' / 'Then she *were enclosed*' / 'her *husband die and leave her*'). In this way the story is personalized for Christine – just as the tritone (A♭–D) on 'shouldn't catch *me doing that*' embodies Matilde's own reluctance to share Yvette's (or Christine's) self-sacrifice. Delicately balanced between parody and poignancy, Matilde's song provides a perfect foil to the simple sincerity of Christine's earlier heart-searching ('There was a oneness time'). Its conclusion ('and on her face there gleamed a brilliant summer glow. That was a day!') recalls a number of Christine's most ecstatic passages of falling thirds (notably, 'The truth is revealed in heaven')[62] and represents probably the last moment of unadulterated tranquillity in the opera. The short transition (bars 524–532) that separates this scene from Christine's confession reflects something of this peaceful aura although the woodwind's sequence of tritones hints that the Anchoress herself is far from being at peace.

Scene 6 (Track 6): Inside the Church

Table 4.9   Scene 6 structure

Bars 533–544	**545–598**	**599–622**
Christine at Confession: (General) 'O, all you blessed angels and saints of the Lord'	Christine at confession: (Specific) 'I find pleasure in my cell' ... 'I want my chains'	Christine: 'A showing! Give me Lord a showing' (a fervent prayer for the sort of union with God's saints mentioned in the first section of the scene)
	Mathew and Christine argue / Mathew warns of evil beasts	
	C: 'My chains! My haircloth!'	
	Agnes enters and berates Mathew	
(B♭/D sustained)	(E/E♭/B♭)	D/D♭/B♭–(A♭–G)

---

61   Act 2, bars 276–281: 'Put nails through me! Pierce my hands and my feet!'
62   Act 1, scene 1, bars 98–99: Example 4.4.

This scene (together with scenes 3, 5, 7, and part of 8) provides insight into the daily discipline of an anchoress's life, as she disseminates advice, as she prays, confesses and reads (or listens to) instructive writings (*Vitae*) (Table 4.9). There are early signs of Christine's impatience to be given proof of the special quality of her calling; perhaps the very nature of her sacrifice (in abandoning the love of Robert) allows her to anticipate an indication of divine approval?

Mathew is found within the church, hearing Christine's confession through the quatrefoil window that links the Anchoress's cell with the chancel. She begins with a general statement, addressing the 'angels and saints of God' and petitions them for union in their eternal love. This short introductory preface to more specific confessions sits easily with the serene atmosphere created by the climax of St Yvette's story (summarized above) and is sung over an accompaniment of gentle woodwind *ostinati* and a sustained B♭ on cello and D on viola. Thereafter, in a sudden change of mood, Christine demands more severe penances ('I want my chains and my haircloth') and engages with Mathew in an increasingly fractious discussion about the nature of sin and the inherent dangers of the solitary life – into which (the priest warns her) 'creep many evil beasts'. This is the first indication in the drama that the sheer intensity of Christine's desire for a vision has exceeded any rational expectation. The third (and final) section of the scene is devoted to an impassioned pleading for her to witness a special sign of God's grace ('Jesus Christ before me, weep! Gentle crucifix before me bleed' … 'Christine craves a showing'). As the music returns to a B♭ pedal (in bar 616), she re-orders material from her scene 1 song once more. 'Ev'ry day of darkness, Lord! In her cell of darkness, Lord' is sung to motifs made familiar as 'all that I see' and 'I will forsake [all]'. At this moment in time, the beginning, the turning point and the end of Christine's journey are brought together in a form that also, by implication, supplies an additional literary trope to the Ricercar theme ('Ev'ry day of darkness' – see Example 4.22). The resulting referential complexity is enriching at several levels, not the least being the paradox of seeing in darkness – or, as Christine subsequently reverses it, 'the dark in the light'.

Example 4.22   Christine: Act 1, scene 6, bars 616–618

Scene 6 is also noteworthy for its re-working of earlier transitional material – a practice that becomes more common in the scenes that follow. The short section that separates the second and third scenes (bars 298–312) in Act 1 (see Table 4.2) has been described as possessing an improvisatory air, with strings and wind outlining a loose sort of voice-leading in which intervals of tritones, fourths and fifths are mixed with more linear movement to create cumulative chords. This procedure is also reminiscent of continuo-realization (for example, in recitative accompaniment) and proves an effective support to the quasi-debate between Mathew and Christine as her confession becomes more specific (bars 545–562 especially). This is not to say that themes are rigorously developed – as, for example, when the children's voices return in modified or transposed form, or when scene 1 orchestral material is re-used in scene 8 (bars 701–704) – rather, that characteristic gestures from earlier passages are alluded to in order to create structural cross-references and coherent transitions. Another significant example of this can be found at the beginning of the final section of scene 6 as Christine begs for a showing (bars 599–602 closely resemble bars 298–301 in terms of texture, if not pitch).

Overall, the scene is tightly organized tonally (see Table 4.9). The intensity of dispute between Christine and Mathew is presented with expressionistic passion and punctuated with six-note chords that sometimes betray bi-tonal features (for example in bars 563–565).[63] Significantly, prominent timpani strokes on E appear at the climax of the debate[64] as Christine screams for her chains and haircloth – a premonition, perhaps, of the main recapitulation of the opening tonality (and other specific references to scene 1) in scene 8. Finally, as if to frame this demonstration of Christine's wilful demands, the transition into scene 7 draws on Matilde's syncopated accompaniment from the previous scene ('You crossed your mouth?') in a much-abbreviated version of the original play's scene VIII.[65] As in the stage-play, Matilde enters at this point, but (in the opera) merely cards her wool and acts as an observer of Christine's soliloquy before leaving in apparent bewilderment as the children return to taunt Christine once more.

---

[63] Chords in bars 363 are fusions of B♭ major and A major triads; B♭ major and F♯ minor triads; and A minor and an augmented triad on E♭.

[64] Bars 586–588.

[65] Scene VIII of the stage-play contains the story of St Veridiana. This is cut from the opera libretto and it is not made clear that Christine's account of the 'Rumours' of scene 7 (opera) was addressed to a 'young gal [girl]' who approaches the Anchoress's grill, asking about her 'calling'.

Scene 7 (Track 7): *Christine in her Cell; Matilde, Outside Listening*

Table 4.10   Scene 7 structure

Bars 628–644	645–654	655–666
Christine: 'Rumours, I hear rumours whispered'	Christine: 'That were echoes, so I rage and weep and start again'	Matilde: 'Rumours, whispered rumours. Beware echoes' (G)
		Children: 'Christine, had a vision, had a word?'
(G)	(A♭)	(E♭–E)

In the absence of the original context of Matilde's (second) *Vita* and the subsequent question from the 'young gal' (see nn. 65 and 66), Christine's scene 7 soliloquy ('Rumours, I hear rumours') might appear to be, at best, ambiguous or, at worst, ill-calculated (Table 4.10). As with the St Yvetta story, Matilde's choice of St Veridiana (in scene VIII of the stage-play) contained parallels with Christine's own situation and aspirations ('[she] fasted even as a child, an' wore a chain and hairshirt'). During the telling of her story, Matilde became aware of others attempting to speak with the Anchoress and, after failing to chase them away, she acted as an intermediary for a young girl ('You're persistent. What's your question, then?'). She gently chastised Christine for becoming a figure of importance ('Think 'cos you cut yourself off from life you can explain life's mysteries') and explained that 'Your solitary life make [sic] folk uneasy. Your fasting make them feel their greed.' The 'young gal' ('No more'n about twelve') had a simple question: 'Says she wants to know how this life begin for you.'

Christine's soliloquy, therefore, constitutes the *answer to this question*. In describing the internal 'voices' ('the whispered rumours') that suggest 'another kind of knowing', the Anchoress struggles to distinguish between 'the truth' and 'echoes of the truth' (that cause her 'to rage an[d] weep an' have to start again'). Even in the original play, Wesker inserted the direction ('struggling') to qualify Christine's obvious difficulty in delivering such an explanation – a 'response' heard in the opera only by Matilde, who summarizes the soliloquy and leaves, 'shrugging, utterly bewildered'.[66] Taken out of context, this operatic scene represents a slightly nebulous contemplation of metaphysical generalities – perhaps appropriate to a semi-educated novice, but betraying more than a little of the librettist's red pen. Saxton does his best with the skeletal text, composing an affecting vocal line that combines Christine's

---

[66]   Whereas, in the stage-play, Matilde addresses the 'gal' with 'There! You got that? Rumours! Rumours! Wait for the rumours. Beware the echoes, but wait for the rumours'. (Matilde leaves, shrugging, utterly lost.)

characteristic patterns of thirds with a slower bass line of thirds and tritones[67] that, in turn, supports oscillating semiquavers in the woodwind and upper strings. There is a brief change of texture ('That were [sic] echoes ... so I rage and weep') before Matilde leaves and the children's voices conclude this oddly abbreviated scene – and, incidentally, the first time-zone of the opera (see Table 4.1). The two scenes that now follow both take place between February 1379 and 17 June 1381 and represent the growing crises in national politics and Christine's own life.

Scene 8 (Track 8): The Carpenter's Workshop

Table 4.11   Scene 8 structure

Bars 670–684	**685–700**	**701–714**	**715–767**
William's Workshop (Feb.1379):	Orchestral Transition:	Evening:	Mathew joins them:
The Tax Collector returns to raise money for the wars in France	Agnes lays out a meal after the Collector is sent on his way. Spoken dialogue introduces an element of (cathartic) farce	William, Agnes and Robert discuss the events of the day (recalling orchestral material from scene 1 – and, hence, the earlier family debate)	He brings news that the Bishop will not permit Robert to learn to read. Agnes and Mathew describe Christine's declining mental state and the prospect of excommunication, should she forsake her calling
		(Bass: F–B–F♯–C–G – C♯–G♯–D–A–E♭–	
(Pedal E)		B♭– E–B–	(F–)

Like Matilde's visits to the Anchoress's grill, the Tax Collector's arrivals at William's workshop signify a recurring theme that serves to punctuate daily life in Pulham St Mary (whether in church or village) with external opinions or pieces of information that provide a broader context for Christine and her family (Table 4.11). Three bars of repeated Es form a brief transition between the children's refrain in scene 7 and Agnes's complaint that the King had taxed them as recently as two years ago. The drum-beats suggest a martial mood and the theme of 'costly, disastrous, losing [French] wars' is reinforced by the E/B♭ tritone and asymmetric metres (threes against twos) that underpin the scurrying semiquavers in bassoon and cello that accompany Robert's and the Collector's *sprechgesang* and shouting. On hearing that a tax collector in Kent had raped a farmer's girl – and been hanged –

---

[67]   The bass line pattern (bars 628–645) is G–E♭–A–F–B–G–C♯–A–E♭–B–F–D♭–G♭–C– A♭–D–A♭.

the (Norfolk) collector flees, to the accompaniment of laughter and a scatological comment from Agnes.

The following orchestral transition acts as the accompaniment to a domestic pantomime that includes the above, spoken remark ('I do believe the tax collector's shit himself!'),[68] during which, Agnes lays out the family's evening meal. Over their beer and cheese, they discuss the events of the day in an animated manner, predicting the possibility of bloodshed if a third tax were to be imposed. The conspiratorial refrain 'I hear plans, plottings,' helps to counterbalance Christine's (scene 7) 'I hear rumours' and, similarly, has been placed out of context in the libretto (see Tables 3.1 and 3.2 above).[69] During this process, some important (although *not* essential) information was omitted from the opera text, including the plans to set fire to Manor documents at Carrow Priory and Methwold Manor House (drawing, no doubt, on similar recorded incidents during the Peasants' Uprising). As has already been mentioned, orchestral material from scene 1 (bars 71–85) is recycled here (bars 701–714) in a transposed and modified form, thus creating a further link between the opera's start and this crucial mid-way point.

At this stage, Mathew enters with the news that Bishop Henry has refused for Robert to be taught to read ('No grammar for him, says the Bishop'). A characteristic tritone (E♭/A) between voice and bass-line provides appropriate authority for this decision and Robert responds, as in scene 1, with a vocal 'fanfare' of rising perfect fourths and fifths that recalls the sense of injustice inherent in his earlier complaints against Christine's decision to reject his love. As the tonality focuses (briefly) onto the fateful pitch of B, Robert reacts to Mathew's caution that he might be branded like his father (if he were also to leave the Bishop's Manor), by referring to the currently elevated literary state of the English language: 'That were then. But now he [Richard] wants his son to read. The English word is born, the French has died, *and Christine would have been my teacher, guide.*'[70] This reference to the Anchoress is followed by a short instrumental passage, during which the family and Mathew sit in silence (perhaps ruminating on what might have been) before the Rector describes Christine's impatient demands for visions ('At once! When some have waited sixty years and not been graced'). 'She was not made for solitude', he concludes.

Agnes, against a hypnotic background of alternating chords, then supplies fuller details of Christine's pattern of prayer and devotions within the context of increasing filth and misery in her cell. The scene ends with a display of Mathew's anger and frustration as he acknowledges that he is out of harmony with his church. The transition that leads into scene 9 is based again on material from the 'prototype'

---

[68] This comment has been omitted in the Full Score (for no obvious reason).

[69] This section of the libretto (bars 701–767) was scene XI (dated May 1381) in the stage play.

[70] The stage play predicts that English will replace French 'in church and court and school and parliament'. This was the period of Langland's *Piers Plowman* and Chaucer's *Canterbury Tales*, of course.

transition (used between scenes 2 and 3) as the audience once more follows the action from workshop to church.

Scene 9 (Track 9): The Interior of the Church – Mathew in Silent Prayer

Table 4.12   Scene 9 structure

Bars 776–787	788–808	809–824	825–844
Interior of the Church:			
Mathew at silent prayer; Christine heard praying ('We adore Thee, O Christ')	'A showing!' Christine is convinced that she has been given a vision of the pattern of God's creation	Christine: 'That's not an echo, Lord'	Christine: 'The dark in the light?'… 'That were [sic] no showing then?'
		Mathew: 'Beware, Christine, beware the vision'	Mathew: 'Shall I confess you?' Children: 'Christine, had a revelation yet?'
(B)	(B)	(Pedal B)	(B–B♭–A–A♭–G)

As has already been ascertained (in the section 'Concepts of Time', above), this scene marks the temporal centre-piece of the opera and the core of its tragedy (Table 4.12). Over a sustained pedal B and a shifting halo of three-note chords (marked *radiant*), Christine is overheard praying (as recommended in *Ancrene Riwle*):[71] 'We adore Thee O Christ and we bless Thee, because of Thy holy cross, Thou hast redeemed the world.' The devotional emphasis on the Cross and on Crucifixion now assumes over-riding significance as Christine's contemplation of the 'worthy tree whose wood bore the ransom of the world' leads her to experience a (supposed) vision in which technical images of wood-working and carpentry are brought together with age-old theological symbolism to persuade her that she is being shown the secret of creation:

> Shape! Lord Jesus shows me how the world has shape. I see its joins, I see its links, I see what clasps and holds it firm. The hole, the dowel, the dove-tail, mortise, tenon.[72]

---

[71]   Translated M B Salu, *Ancrene Riwle* (see p. 14).

[72]   These are technical terms for carpentry joints in which a 'male' projection is fitted and locked into a 'female' aperture (for example a tenon into a mortise; a dowel into a hole). A dovetail joint (commonly used in drawers) comprises two complementary patterns of projections and apertures that fit together rather like the fingers of two hands interlocking.

As Christine approaches this moment of ecstasy, her prayer rises chromatically through more than an octave before she announces the showing on a sustained B (after a bar of total silence). There is no need to labour the obvious[73] here and Wesker moves on quickly from workshop imagery to poetry in which natural paradoxes stimulate flowing melismatic (musical) lines that are more consistent with transcendental experience ('I hear the flower blossom, Oh I see the harvest grow, know the colour of the wind, the dark in the light'). Even as Christine affirms her belief in the showing ('That's not an echo, Lord'), Mathew, who has overheard all of this, warns her to beware of the vision ('Satan's stratagems delude').This is punctuated with *staccato* octaves and Christine's diction becomes hesitant as she questions her experience. She moves between *sprechgesang* and pitched singing; the omnipresent pedal B slips slowly (chromatically) downward to G as she rejects Mathew's offer of confession; and the children's voices return to question her revelation – and her sanity.

Scene 10 (Track 10): Inside the Church

Table 4.13   Scene 10 structure

Bars 845–889	890–904
Inside the church: a Travelling Priest gives a [spoken] 'sermon' (17 June 1381)	Bishop Henry enters, threatening the Priest. He chases him out of the church
Based on Book of Joel / John Ball in the Peasants' Uprising	Christine screams: 'I do not have the vocation! Release me!'
(G–C/F♯)	(C/F♯–A♭)

With the children's voices still calling Christine's name outside the cell, the interior of the church is taken over by a travelling priest who delivers a ranting 'sermon' to a congregation made up of those members of cast who are on stage (Table 4.13).[74] The date is 17 June 1381 (that is two days *after* the murder of Wat Tyler at Smithfield), but a week before the Battle of North Walsham (25–26 June), during which Bishop Henry (in his well-documented historic role) led the army that suppressed the Norfolk rebellion, and a month or so before the trial and execution of John Ball (15 July). This juxtaposition of Christine's personal crisis (in scene 9) and the 'sermon' describing a national uprising, in which anticlerical (Lollard) sentiments played a significant part, is reminiscent of the dramatic contrast between Christine's immurement and the branding of Richard Lonle (in scenes 1 and 2). Saxton, similarly, employs a bassoon *ostinato* (supported by woodwind and strings) to evoke a sense of martial

---

[73]   Jesus worked as a carpenter, as did William (Christine's father) and Robert.

[74]   The stage directions specifically state that the sermon is *not* to be given to the audience.

unrest during the first section of the 'sermon' together with brass fanfares ('Blow ye the trumpet in Zion') and a twelve-note cello and double-bass line comprised of rising tritones followed by falling perfect fifths (or rising fourths). This texture, constructed initially over a 'fanfare' chord made up of two perfect fourths a tritone apart (G/C and F♯/B), also recalls similar passages in scene 1[75] and enhances the overall cyclic nature of the opera as well as defining the tonal landmarks of the scene, which moves from G to C (at bar 860) and, thence, to a tritone polarity of C/F♯ (bar 894) as the Bishop chases the preacher out of the church.

The text of the 'sermon' (which is shouted from the pulpit rather than sung) is a compilation of quotations from the Old Testament Prophet, Joel (shown in the extract below in **bold**), John Ball's sermon and letters (in *italics*), and comments presumably by the priest himself. It contains a number of important historical citations and, for reasons of clarity, will be quoted in full as follows:

a   **Blow ye the trumpet in Zion, and sound an alarm on my holy mountain!** Thus saith the prophet Joel.

b   Beloved! In our land new sermons: to each man hath God given conscience! Therefore unto your priests say this: one vicar cannot be upon the earth, for each is vicar to himself.

c   **Beat your ploughshares into swords, your pruning hooks to spears: let the weak say, 'I am strong.'** Thus saith the prophet Joel.

d   Wat Tyler leads one hundred thousand men: Canterbury opens up her gates; the manor records burn, and mad John Ball is snatched from jail to sing his lovely sermons to us all.

e   *Good people, goods must be in common held. What right have Lords to Lordship, clothed in velvet, we in rags! When Adam delved and Eve span, who was then the gentleman?*

f   Do you like those songs? They sing them from the coast of Kent to the Wash.

g   **And it shall come to pass that I will pour my spirit on your flesh; and your sons and your daughters shall prophesy, your old men shall dream dreams, and your young men shall see visions.** Thus saith the prophet Joel. And -

[Bishop intervenes]

[Play only: *Help truth and truth shall help you!*]

h   *Now reigneth pride in place [price],*
And covertise is counted wise,
And lechery withouten shame,
And gluttony withouten blame.

---

[75]   Scene 1: bars 71–85; 90–92; and 108–116, for example. The bass line between bar 845 and 852 is G–C♯–F♯–C–F–B–E–B♭–E♭–A–D–A♭–D♭–G–D♭.

[Not used in play or libretto:

Envy reigneth with treason,
And sloth is taken in great reason;]

[Play only: *God do bote, for now is time,*][76] [*Amen*]

The three extracts from the Book of Joel[77] are obviously intended to provide biblical authority to support the rebellion and it would have been easy for fourteenth-century serfs to identify with their sentiments – line c, especially. Equally, old men dreaming dreams (of freedom, perhaps) and young men seeing visions (of a better future) would have empathized with the prophet's promise of intervention – just as Christine herself desired a divine vision as a sign of God's grace. Interspersed amongst these biblical texts, are pieces of information about the progress of the uprising (the burning of manorial records in Canterbury;[78] John Ball being rescued from prison to continue 'singing' his sermons) and interpretative comments from the travelling priest (who attempts to 'almost sing' the much-quoted lines by John Ball (bars 872–881) against a skittish piccolo 'revolutionary marching tune' in the background). With the third of the verses from Joel, the music becomes briefly calmer and more dignified, although an augmented C–F♯ tritone in the bass line gives warning that Bishop Henry is about to enter. He calls for 'the blasphemer' to be expelled from the church and, in reply, is accused (by implication) of indulging in (at least) four of the deadly sins (lines h).[79] To the accompaniment of a terrifying three-octave chromatic descent from woodwind and brass,[80] the Bishop threatens him with execution and hell's flames – at which point, Christine (who would have overheard all of this from the vantage-point of her quatrefoil window) screams 'I do not have the vocation! Release me!'

Wesker had originally planned for this scene (scene XIII in both editions of the play) to be followed by an animated discussion (between Bishop Henry and the Rector) on the implications of the 'sermon', of the consequence of Christine's outburst, and the nature of her vows (that is, scene XIV of the play). However, in an inspired departure from the stage play, the (much abbreviated) *previous* scene (scene XII) was taken from its position *before* the 'sermon' and placed immediately *after* it, thus replacing – or at least delaying – the diatribe against books and reading,

---

[76]   *God do bote* = God provide the remedy. 'Amen' omitted in play and opera.

[77]   In order of appearance (a, c, and g), the sources are Joel 2: 1; Joel 3: 10; and Joel 2: 28.

[78]   Compare this with the details in the play (omitted in the libretto) about the burning of documents at Carrow Priory, Norfolk, cited above.

[79]   Lines h are published in 'The Letter of John Ball' (Stow, *Annales*), in James M. Dean (ed) *Medieval English Political Writings* (Kalamazoo, 1996). The letter/poem refers to six of the seven deadly sins. Wrath is missing.

[80]   Reminiscent, perhaps, of the depiction of the descending scimitar in bars 20–21 of *Enthauptung* (Beheading) in *Pierrot lunaire* (op. 21) by Arnold Schoenberg. Saxton's score, like Schoenberg's movement 13 (bar 21), also culminates on C/F♯/C♯.

together with the Bishop's conclusion ('A vow's a vow!') and the heart-felt plea
for Christine's freedom (from her parents and Robert). The effect of this change
was to create another dramatic juxtaposition, but *not* so much between national and
local events, or between political and personal matters, as between the hysteria of
Christine's religious frustration and the frustration of Matilde's well-intentioned
story-telling by Christine's hysterical intervention.

Scene 11 (Track 11): Outside Christine's Cell

Table 4.14   Scene 11 structure

Bars 910–919	**920–932**
Christine and Matilde (compare with scene 5):	Matilde: 'Now here's a story – she was touched by God ...'
Christine mocks Matilde 'You crossed your mouth?' 'Your mother bring [sic] you food?'	Christine screams three times
Matilde senses something is wrong	Matilde leaves, unable to finish her tale
(A♭)	(A♭)

Scene 11 begins, as does the earlier episode in scene 5 (which contains Matilde's
story about the life of St Yvetta),[81] with an introduction of five syncopated (seven-
eight metre) bars (Table 4.14).[82] However, the strings and woodwind have reversed
roles – perhaps a clue as to the change in tone of Christine's mocking imitation
of Matilde's questions ('You crossed your mouth?' *'You crossed your mouth?'*
'Good! An' your eye?' *'An' your eye?'*). Matilde senses that something is wrong
but continues with her ritual. She starts a tale about St Christiana,[83] 'another Belgie'
(although her name is not mentioned in the opera libretto). The first few lines sung
are punctuated by *sforzando* chords, as though to deny cohesive narrative, and then
Christine (who can contain herself no longer) screams again three times. Matilde
leaves, unable to finish her tale. Even the comic abnormality of her obsessions has

---

[81]   Scene 5, bars 437–441. Compare with the orchestral transition (bars 905–909)
between scenes 10 and 11 (as marked in the full score).

[82]   Bars 905–909.

[83]   Scene XII informs us that St Christiana (possibly St Christina the Astonishing,
1150–1224) was not an anchoress, but 'just holy'. See *Caritas* (1981/1990) scene XII. The
choice of the saint's name would seem to imply a direct analogy with Christine, herself. In
Wesker's original conception of the narrative, Matilde's hagiographic references appear to
come progressively closer to home.

become an intolerable intrusion into Christine's own preoccupations and frustrated expectations.

Thereafter, over an insistent semiquaver A♭ pedal, scene 12 (scene XIV of the play) commences, albeit much shortened (like the previous scene).

Scene 12 (Track 12): Inside the Church, Away from the Cell Wall

Table 4.15   Scene 12 structure

Bars 933–946	**947–1002**	**1003–1014**	**1015–1090**
Inside the church: Bishop and Mathew, Agnes, William and Robert	TRIO: Agnes, William and Robert plead for Christine to be released	Bishop delivers his judgement: She cannot leave her cell (A–E♭)	Orchestral Transition: The Peasants' Revolt
Books and reading: Bishop rules that 'A vow's a vow'	A sequence of major thirds in the orchestra: (E♭/G–A/C♯–D/ F♯–G/B– C♯/E♯– F♯/A♯)	Children's voices Christine: 'Not fit. You have hell anchored in your church – break down the walls!'	(A/E♭–E–A–C♯–A– E♭–G/B♭– premonition of *Kyrie*? Chain of descending whole-tone scales leads into the Ricercar
(A♭)	Climax on A major	(A/E♭–A♭/B♭)	(G♯/A♭–D)

The church now becomes the setting for an enquiry – or informal court of appeal – as Christine's parents and Robert are brought in to speak on behalf of the Anchoress (Table 4.15). Initially, the Bishop addresses Robert alone in an attempt to explain his decision to refuse his request to learn how to read (to be taught, presumably, by the rector rather than Christine, as hoped for by her former fiancé). As he speaks, Henry points towards Christine's cell to indicate the consequences of *her* introduction to the written word. The recurrent denunciation of literacy (in the context of a feudal society) seems to have brought together a highly unlikely coalition of high-ranked clergy (Bishop Henry) and manorial tenants (Christine's parents) who, for different reasons, share a deep suspicion of 'learning'. In Agnes's case ('Books, books, I warned against books!'), this bias is, no doubt, founded on an inherited fear of 'rising above one's station', or mastering a skill for which a serf has no obvious, everyday need; whereas the Bishop (being well educated) is able to analyse the problem and to sum up the situation thus:

> See where books and reading lead? To notions which have lives that chain you, grab you, bind, hold you. [In other words: reading books leads to acquiring knowledge and developing aspirations that influence and help determine subsequent needs.]

He then pauses to compose himself before inviting Agnes and William to join in the discussion.

As has been observed on several occasions, *Caritas* contains relatively few set-pieces such as extended arias or choruses. In part, this is a consequence of the actual duration and time-scale of the drama (it is effectively a continuous, one-act opera that lasts for about 78 minutes). Its action constitutes a selective summary of events that take place over a period of four years or so. Also, because of the very nature of the 'plot' (which is constructed out of a large number of short episodes), the libretto does not lend itself easily to the musical extension of individual events or emotions (other than Christine's madness in the final scene). This is not to imply that the result is unduly sectional – the sequence of varied scenes allows for dramatic contrast and a convincing framework of recurring themes. The timescale of the first and final scenes is testimony to the composer's skill in sustaining relatively long periods of ceremonial ritual and a degenerative emotional state (respectively), as is the transition from sung (textual) narrative to (more abstract) orchestral narrative that takes place in the last section of this scene.

The Trio that occupies the second section of scene 12 is an exception, however, to the general rule. It introduces the theme of 'mercy' (which is progressively developed in the rest of the opera) in the form of a petition from those closest to the Anchoress. This is encapsulated in the *Kyrie eleison* that is quoted at the start of Act 2, and is ultimately denied, in spite of Christine's fervent intercessions. The Trio also fulfils another, traditional, purpose in that it brings together some of the principal protagonists to create a climactic ensemble at, or near, the end of the act. Although it does not constitute the actual *finale*, it does serve as a focal point for the collective challenge to the authority of the Church and State that is the ultimate crisis of the first act of the opera – and the connecting point between the two strands of its narrative.

The libretto at this point recalls the domestic interludes in scene 1 as Agnes, William and Robert revert to their individual themes of parenthood, solitary life and physical love. Agnes stresses Christine's uniqueness ('She's our only child'); William, more logically, argues the dubious benefit to the church of accommodating a reluctant solitary; whereas Robert reiterates their promise of marriage ('She were betrothed to me for love of me'), before they combine in their plea to 'Let her go!'. At first the petition is reasoned and relatively tranquil, sung in short phrases over a harmony dominated by sustained major thirds.[84] Then the ensemble gains in urgency ('No sons to help our work … and bring us heirs'; 'You want your folk to take example from your anchoress'; 'There's not a week passed these three years I've not sat with her'). The orchestral accompaniment is still based on sustained thirds,[85] but woodwind quaver-patterns add momentum to a faster and longer section that culminates in a more demanding appeal to 'Let her go!' Finally, for a third time, the

---

[84] E♭/G–A/C♯.

[85] (A/C♯)–D/F♯–G/B–C♯/E♯–F♯/A♯.

trio of family members try their best to persuade the Bishop to relent: 'She give our Lord three precious years' (Agnes); 'No use to God or Church' (William); 'Let her go and we'll be married. You'll hear nothing of us more' (Robert). This is the longest of the three sections and climaxes on a *fortissimo* A major chord that matches that in the first scene (bar 157 onwards), played when Christine is led into her cell – a supremely ironic parallel between the optimism of Christine's first step into her new life and the prayer for her release from its disillusionment.

As the A major chord and its carillon-like counterpoint on vibraphone, woodwind and first violin slowly dissolve onto a single semitone (A/B♭), a tam-tam stroke signals that Bishop Henry is ready to announce his decision. Above the suspended animation of a solitary pedal A, and employing only a characteristic tritone (A/E♭), he declaims: 'We have no power to sanction breaking of a vow. She cannot leave her cell'. Immediately, the chorus of children's voices commences its intrusive interrogation and Christine herself screams out her self-condemnation: 'Not fit, not fit! You have hell anchored to your church, Bishop Henry. Break down its walls. In the name of God, break them down!' In the background, the sound of marching is heard; Robert joins in the refrain ('Break them down!') and, despite William's and Agnes's efforts to restrain him, runs off to enlist in the Peasants' Revolt. The orchestra takes up the narrative with a programmatic depiction of the Uprising which also serves as a transition into the orchestral Ricercar – the melodramatic *finale* of Act 1. The first of these two orchestral passages (the transition: bars 1015–1090) is effectively a short symphonic poem that juxtaposes impressionistic sections, representing battle and the irregular marching rhythms of an untrained army as it proceeds from one encounter to another. Skirmishes with opposing forces are depicted by asymmetrical *staccato* chords[86] and rapidly repeated *ostinati* (sometimes marked *feroce*); the jaunty piccolo tune (heard during the Travelling Priest's 'sermon') makes another appearance (this time over a C♯ pedal)[87]; and there appear to be two allusions to the *Kyrie eleison* theme which is later identified in bars 40–43 of Act 2.[88] The significance of these should not be underestimated since they further extend the pleas for mercy for Christine to include the casualties of the political uprising (among whom Robert will be numbered).

In deciding to conclude Act 1 with a fugal orchestral movement, Saxton momentarily asserts the dominance of musical order over the chaos of dramatic disorder. As if by definition, the Ricercar[89] permits a 'search' or logical 'conversation'

---

[86]   Using rhythmic patterns possibly influenced by Wozzeck's fateful rhythm in Act 3, scenes 2 and 3.

[87]   Bars 1051–1054. This could be the 'missing C♯ tonality' referred to in n. 58 above, although its duration is relatively short.

[88]   In bars 1059–1062 and bars 1077–c.1085, respectively.

[89]   The term, Ricercar, is probably used in the sense defined by Stravinsky – as a composition in canonic style (Cantata programme note, 11 November 1952). The original Italian, Ricercare, means to 'search out'.

(rather than a dramatic 'debate') between themes and keys that is cast within a framework of controlled tonal symmetry (during which the Travelling Priest returns to the stage to announce the outcome of the Revolt). The following structural plan of the Ricercar demonstrates something of the traditional functions of subject and answer, exposition, episodes, middle entries, augmentation and *stretti*, which provide such fugal movements with their characteristic features and disciplines. In addition, Saxton seems to have drawn on contemporary models[90] and, most importantly, incorporated musical ideas from elsewhere in the opera into this most atmospheric *finale*.

Ricercar (Track 12 cont.): The Melodrama is still Inside the Church until the Scene Changes near the End of the Ricercar to Reveal Christine Within her Cell. She is Filthy and Terrified as she Realizes that she will be Imprisoned For Ever

As has already been mentioned,[91] the theme (subject) of the Ricercar is melodically related to the first phrase of Christine's song of farewell (see Examples 4.7a/b, 4.10, 4.11 and 4.22) and is, therefore, associated with its original text ('I will forsake *all that I see*') and with other sentiments that have been matched to its melodic contour during the course of the opera (for example, 'Ev'ry day of darkness, Lord').[92] It has been argued above that the Ricercar might represent a meditation on one or more of its literary tropes, and, on the evidence of Wesker's original (stage) intentions, this would not seem far-fetched.[93] Indeed, to associate the canons with repetitions of the phrase 'all that I see' would be to acknowledge the reality of the horrors of the rebellion (which are described in some detail by the Travelling Priest) as well as to complete the cyclical reference intended by the playwright. By analogy, the text matched to this motif in scene 6 (Example 4.22), together with Christine's related paradox ('The dark in the light') signals for her the prospect of perpetual darkness. Perhaps the canonic repetitions of the Ricercar are, indeed, a premonition of her fate. It is one of the many complex qualities of the medium of music that it can communicate in both abstract and specific terms. Deprived of any associated information (such as its hidden text), the Ricercar is a relatively calm, extremely well-ordered piece – although, perhaps, its essentially repetitive character might be considered obsessive; its dynamic range and added figurations might appear to generate a sense of increasing agitation. With

---

[90]   For example, Stravinsky's Cantata (1951–52) contains celebrated *Ricercari* (canons) in his settings of English medieval texts. Also, *In Memoriam Dylan Thomas*, where antiphonal 'Dirge-Canons' for a quartet of trombones and String Quartet frame a setting of 'Do not go gentle into that good night'.

[91]   See n. 29, above, and Example 4.22, together with numerous earlier references to the Ricercar (see Index for details).

[92]   See n. 29, above.

[93]   Wesker intended the first Act to contain a repeat of Christine's song of farewell at the end of the penultimate scene (XV) – after the Travelling Priest's description of the failure of the Uprising.

Table 4.16   Ricercar structure

Bars	Commentary	Text/Action
1091–1093 (3)	Introduction of rising fourths (Strings): G♯/A♭–C♯- - - - D	–
1094–1101 (8)	Four-part Fugal Exposition on Strings: Subject on D – Answer on A♭	–
1102–1109 (8)	Fugal Episode. Wind: Rising fifths/falling fourths (4 bars) / Strings: Falling fifths/rising fourths (4 bars)	London – the boy king met Wat Tyler at Mile End
1110–1113 (4)	Middle Entry: Horn on D in Augmentation (new countersubject)	Ancient scores …
1114–1117 (4)	Middle Entry: Cello on A♭ in Augmentation (Strings)	Smithfield – second paper of demands
1118–1121 (4)	Middle Entry: Violin 1 on D in Augmentation (Strings)	Mayor kills Wat Tyler
1122–1125 (4)	Middle Entry: Bassoon on A♭ in Augmentation (Strings)	Freedom Charter withdrawn. John Ball to be executed
1126–1133 (8)	Middle Entries: Horn on D♭ (2 bars)/D.B. on G in Double Augmentation (8 bars)	Funeral Procession begins. Dead boy (Robert) carried off
1134–1137 (4)	Pedal A: Timpani play rhythmic statement of Subject. *Crescendo* to *fortissimo* on B♭	Scenery wall revolves to reveal Christine
1138–1142 (5)	Pedal B♭ with sextuplet 'fanfares' in Wind and Brass. B♭ sinks to A (bar 1141)	Christine is dirty, unkempt, terrified
1143–1150 (8)	Closing Stretto: Viola (D)/V2 (A♭)/V1 (D)/Cello (A♭) in Augmentation – cadencing on D (1149–1150) (Strings)	Lights fade on the Funeral Procession

the addition of textual references, remembered words and associated contexts, it could be that it now incorporates a range of possible 'meanings', on which audiences or listeners might draw to supplement the factual information declaimed by the Travelling Priest and, hence, to enrich the counterpoint of music, spoken text and symbolic pageant that brings the events of the first act to a traumatic close. On a purely musical/technical level, Saxton's frequent use of subject-augmentation in the Ricercar (see Table 4.16) represents a highly sensitive complement to the solemnity of the Priest's announcements, and the double-augmentation (on G, between bars 1126 and 1133) is an appropriate indicator of the tragic death of Robert, whose body is carried away in the funeral procession. As the scenery wall rotates to reveal the terrified, unkempt Christine, the timpanist beats out the rhythm only of the Ricercar theme, while the viola struggles to articulate scurrying references to the melody.

Act 2: The Passacaglia as a Dramatic Device

Scene 13 (Track 13): Inside Christine's Cell

As with Saxton's use of the title, Ricercar, to describe the fugal/canonic movement just discussed, the term, Passacaglia, also has baroque overtones and invites comparison with its own close relations – notably the Chaconne. However, this is not the place to indulge in musicological (or etymological) digression. Suffice to say that both genres (Passacaglia and Chaconne) have their origins in dance. Both flourished as instrumental forms during the seventeenth and early eighteenth-centuries before falling out of favour until being revived during the late nineteenth-century and more modern times – notably in the Chaconne finale of Brahms's Fourth Symphony, Webern's Orchestral Passacaglia (opus 1), Britten's *Peter Grimes* (Act Two), Schoenberg's *Pierrot lunaire* (the Passacaglia, *Nacht*), and Berg's *Altenberg Lieder* and *Wozzeck*.[94] That some composers have found the passacaglia useful as a dramatic device is apparent from the operatic examples cited above by Britten and Berg – and there is little doubt that Saxton, too, was attracted at an early stage to the concept of building an entire work (movement or scene) using the principle of a repeated chord sequence or bass-line ('ground-bass') that is subjected to continuous variation. His *Chacony for Piano Left Hand* (1988) has already been mentioned and, to this, one could add the earlier *Chaconne for Double Choir* (1980/81) and the second movement of the *Sonata for Solo Cello* (based on a theme by William Walton), composed for Steven Isserlis in 1999. There is good reason to suspect that Saxton described the first two of these works as Chacony/Chaconne[95] because of the predominantly harmonic nature of the original theme and its subsequent 'working', whereas the solo cello movement (entitled 'Passacaglia') uses a melody, designated by Walton (in 1970) as *Tema per variazioni*.[96] The significance of Walton's *Tema* is that it presented Saxton with a very special kind of challenge – not merely to compose a set of variations on what is an evocative, song-like tune,[97] but to embark

---

[94]   Berg's *Altenberg Lieder* (op. 4, no. 5) and *Wozzeck* (Act 1, scene 4).

[95]   *Chacony* is the traditional English version of the genre.

[96]   'Theme for variations' – there is no evidence of Walton having composed his own variations, however.

[97]   Saxton entitles the final movement of the Sonata, 'Song', in recognition of its ballade-like character and AaB form.

on 'a voyage of discovery in search of Walton's [original] melody'.[98] In the case of Act 2 (or scene 13) of *Caritas*, the Passacaglia also takes the audience on a journey – but, sadly, one that leads to unresolved despair (although it *does* culminate in the restatement of part of Christine's song).

The Method

The nature of the *Caritas* Passacaglia theme is scalic rather than song-like, and its character owes more to the Guidonian 'theoretical' hexachords that served as 'grounds' in William Byrd's or John Bull's keyboard variations,[99] than to predetermined harmonic progressions (although the over-arching tonal structure of the second act is of the utmost importance, as will be demonstrated). Such six-note 'scales' (as the hexachords found in the *Fitzwilliam Virginal Book* fantasias, for example) invariably contain the interval structure of tone-tone-semitone-tone-tone (T-T-S-T-T), as opposed to Saxton's more varied sequences such as S-T-T-S-T or S-T-S-T-T. In fact, it is the variety of interval structures (most versions of Saxton's theme include *two* semitones) and the wide range of modulations that characterise the *Caritas* Passacaglia and allow it to function so successfully as a constantly shifting commentary on Christine's descent into madness, while still providing a regular reminder of the liturgical intercession, *Kyrie eleison* ('Lord, have mercy'), from which the theme draws much of its intervallic identity (see Example 4.13). A close inspection of the composer's Act 2 plan (Figure 4.1) reveals how carefully the sequence of statements of the passacaglia theme is also controlled in terms of speed by a process of tempo modulation, in which a pattern of metronome mark changes (MM) is specified to match the variation in characterisation and intensity of action.[100]

As has already been noted, the second act opens with a short introduction, during which the terrified Christine is seen praying for comfort and mercy. The orchestra slowly outlines the Ricercar theme (see Examples 4.11 and 4.12)[101] as the Anchoress confesses that she has mistaken Satan's voice for God's – and that she 'is nothing': 'I have nothing, I desire nothing, save the love of Jesus only'.[102] The Children's

---

[98]   Quoted from the composer's note at the head of the manuscript of the Sonata. The four stages (movements) in his 'journey' are *Praeludium, Passacaglia, Dance* and *Song*.

[99]   See Bull's Fantasia in the *Fitzwilliam Virginal Book* (ed. J.A Fuller Maitland & W. Barclay Squire, 1894–99, vol. 1, p. 183) for example.

[100]   See the middle column of Figure 4.1 and note the occasional mirror-like symmetry as in the first section up to bar 38. The significant statements of the passacaglia theme at original (D) pitch are clearly labelled.

[101]   In fact, the Ricercar theme is heard three times: D–C♯–B–C–B♭ / B♭–A–G–A♭–G♭/ G♭–F–E♭–E–D/ thus completing a (perpetual) twelve-note set (with internal repetitions).

[102]   Although, in the opera, an indicator of her troubles and loss of faith, this statement is undoubtedly related to the 'three nothings' referred to by Julian of Norwich (*Revelations*

Chorus intrudes again into her misery but she ignores its presence and resolves: 'I must return to the living'! Once more, she dwells on her loneliness and isolation (symbolically in an unaccompanied soliloquy) and, for the first time, she introduces the concept of madness as a possible outcome, if she were not to receive the help that she prays for.[103] The Passacaglia itself begins in bar 38[104] (see Example 4.14 and Figure 4.1), overlapping with the end of Christine's soliloquy, and its first statement is combined with the exposition of the short *Kyrie eleison* canons (see Example 4.13). In its initial form, the passacaglia theme is elongated; it occupies twelve bars of the score and contains seven, rather than six consecutive notes (with a pattern of S–T–T–T–T–S) that leads naturally into a second statement on D, but this time establishing an interval sequence of S–T–T–S–T that allows for smooth upwards modulation by fifths as demonstrated in Example 4.23.

Example 4.23   Passacaglia theme sequence (bars 50–97)

From the viola's version on E (bar 62), the passacaglia pattern settles onto a slightly varied sequence of S-T-S-T-T until, at bar 97, the theme reverts (in a varied form) to its original pitch (D), having moved through the complete 12-note cycle of fifths (see Example 4.23). The return to D at bar 97 is synchronized with the start of an episode involving a little girl, to whom Christine explains that her spiritual destiny is dependent on the quality of her worldly life ('You live like that, my little friend, life without terror, till the end.'). While there is no textual evidence to suggest that this 'little friend' is the same 'young gal' who enquired about Christine's motivation in scene 7,[105] it seems more than likely that the two incidents are related to some degree

---

of Divine Love – Short Text) quoted in Elizabeth Spearing, ed. (2002) *Medieval Writings on Female Spirituality* (London: Penguin Classics), pp. 179–80): '[...] until all that is made seems as nothing, no soul can be at rest'. Christine's soliloquy contains echoes of ritual prayer, therefore.

[103] However, in both editions of the stage-play Agnes Carpenter refers to her daughter as 'mad gal' (Act 1, scene 1) – presumably implying that she had not thought through her idealistic passion for solitude ('She'll die of her own smells, mad [silly or stupid] gal'). This passage is omitted in the libretto.

[104] As labelled in the score. The first note (D) is repeated on this occasion but is not a general feature of the 'ground' thereafter. It is ignored in Example 4.14.

[105] See also n. 65.

– especially since the recollection of Act 1 material plays such a significant role in the Anchoress's mental breakdown during the final scene. Not only is the involvement (or invention) of a third-party a feature of childish play (and childlike behaviour), it is also symptomatic of various illnesses related to identity crisis and provides a convenient mode of self-analysis (or self-description) which facilitates the sort of disjunct speech that characterizes this depiction of Christine (and other, comparable mad-scenes). Table 4.17 attempts to coordinate the action of the final scene with the main transpositions of the Passacaglia theme, just as Table 3.4 above synchronized the main stages in the action with Wesker's original eleven 'Parts' of Act 2.

As will be seen, the total length of the Passacaglia is 299 bars, with an 'Introduction' of 37 bars being counterbalanced by a concluding 37-bar 'Coda', containing distorted references to earlier material (such as the *Alleluia* and the children's voices) over a pedal E that effectively completes the cycle of tonalities on which the opera is constructed. Within the Passacaglia itself, there are three approximately symmetrical tonal 'pillars', which establish and then reinforce the tonality of D (bars 38–56; 97–104; 191–220)[106] before grounds on G♯ (A♭) (bar 223 onwards) and B (bars 256 onwards) assume greater importance in preparing for the return to E by way of continuous scalic momentum.[107] Interspersed amongst these tonal structural points (and, in a few cases, synchronized with them) are three passages of stylized intoned prayer ('Hail Mary'; 'Hail O Cross'; 'Hail Mary') whose ritualistic chanting provides liturgical *fermatas* (emphasizing A, G♭ and E♭, respectively) that frame the rapidly changing passages of mental disintegration as Christine moves from self-disgust to resolution; from remembered love and self-esteem to suspicion and despair; from aspirations of self-sacrifice to physical violence. Also, as though responding to the fluctuating emotional tensions of Christine's mood-changes, there are three extended passages of transposition during which, as mentioned earlier, the ground-bass moves, first, upwards through the full cycle of fifths (bars 57–96), then by way of freer transpositions and variants – as she struggles with the onset of madness (bars 125–190) – and, finally (bars 273–336), downwards by twelve steps from B to G (a tenth below) as she begs to share Christ's pain and suffering ('Put nails through me!'). At this point (bar 279), the composer emphasizes the growing tension in the drama by introducing a rhythmic pattern (mainly in the horn part) that works in conjunction with the passacaglia theme rather as the *talea* might partner the *color* in a medieval motet. Using augmentation and diminution of the rhythmic pattern, Saxton contrives to bring this last section of the passacaglia to a magnificent climax as the main theme is transformed from a grandiose *cantus firmus* into closing

---

[106] See Figure 4.1, although Saxton's 'signposts' separate the two entries at bars 40 and 50, and omit the D entry at bar 97. His plan concentrates on the correlation between stage action and tempo. Figure 4.2 is more helpful in this respect.

[107] From bar 284–332, the ground effectively moves upwards through continuous scales, although the sequence of starting notes actually *falls* by step from B to A to G to F to E♭/D♯ to C♯ to C to B to A to G♯ to G (to E) as set out in Table 4.17.

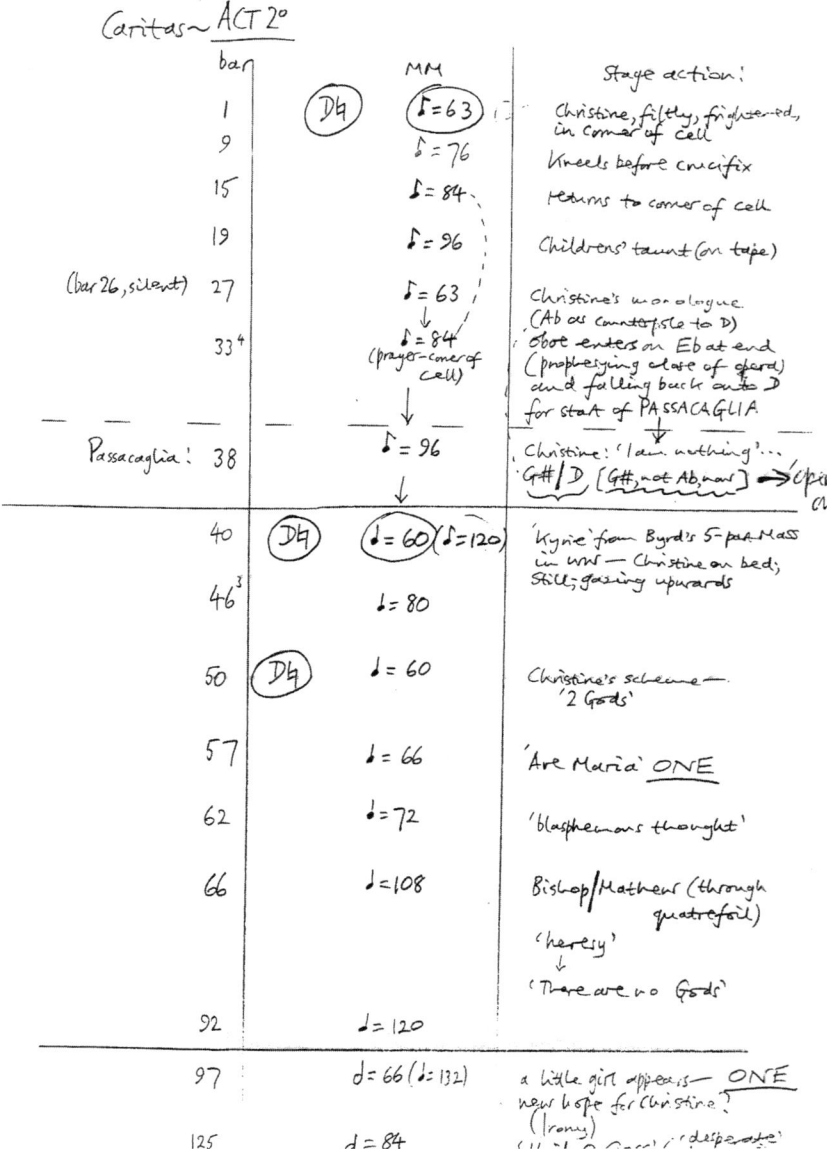

Figure 4.1   Composer's manuscript plan of Act 2 (metronome marks and stage action). By permission of the composer

bar	MM	stage action:
132	♩ = 88	Christine Strikes her breast — tries to keep balance of mind via 'tasks' (self-imposed)
146	♩ = 104	hairbrush search (Combing hair as sign of sanity, neatness, cleanliness — former freedom + 'the running, dancing girl')
166	(moving on) ♩ = 108	2nd attempt to advise little girl TWO
173	♩ = 120	'love'
176	♩=♩ ³ ♩ = 132 ♩ = 88	'Lord Jesus Christ loved you so — he died for you'...
184	♩ = 60	Christine tries to gain stability... ('word will spread'...
191	♩=♩ ³ ♩ = 84	'Ave Maria' TWO
199	(D♮) ♩ = 56 ↓ (♩ = 66)	'Sins' — start of final breakdown 'Mortification of flesh'
221	♩=♩ ♩. = 66	Lullaby with Cross ARIA
251	♪=♪ ♩ = 99	'They nail him now'...

Figure 4.1   *concluded*

Table 4.17   Act 2: Passacaglia structure

Bar Nos	Contents	Tonal centres
1–37	Introduction to Passacaglia / Christine's Soliloquy 'I am nothing, I know nothing, I desire nothing save the love of Jesus' / Children taunt Christine	D – (based on Ricercar theme)
38–56	Passacaglia starts / *Kyrie De Angelis* (canons in orchestra) / Christine: 'There's not one God but two!'	Ground on D × 2
57–65	Christine: **Hail Mary full of grace** (intoned) / 'That's blasphemous thought' (*sprechstimme*)	Ground on A and D
66–96	Bishop: 'That's heresy' / Christine: 'Let Christine go / Not fit!' / Bishop, Mathew (unseen) and Christine debate / C: 'You have hell anchored to your church, father. Break down its walls!' **First climax**	Ground on: B/ F♯/C♯/G♯/D♯/ B♭/F/C/G
97–124	Christine talks to Little Girl: 'When you are dead …' Children taunt Christine	Grounds on D varied/B♭/C♯/F♯/D varied
125–190	Christine: **Hail, O Cross** (agitated, talks to herself) 'They think you're mad' / talks to Little Girl again: 'There's no meaning … The purpose is to love' / (Secondary Climax … 'There, Christine! Mad?')	(Freer use of Ground) D/B/E varied/G♯/D♯/C♯/ G♯/G♯/D♯/A♯ /B/ F♯ (× 3)
191–220	Christine: **Hail Mary full of grace** / 'The remedy for pride is humility … Mortification of the FLESH! … I am NOT FIT!' (E/B♭ tritone) **Second climax**	Grounds on D – some varied and inverted and in diminution
221–255	Christine: 'The poor wail…' / C. Lullaby: 'I've loved him from cradle-time … They nail him now. My own flesh and blood …' (Secondary climax)	(Freer) – concluding with Grounds on G♯ (× 3)
256–272	Christine: 'Did I feed … for this?' / C with Robert (offstage): 'Did we look at blue skies …?' / Agnes and William (off): May God put off from thee the old woman'	Grounds on B (× 3)
273–336	Christine: Put nails through me! Pierce my hands, pierce my feet!' **Sustained third climax** (B♭ / E tritone)	Grounds on B (× 4) / Grounds on A/G/F/D♯/C♯/C/B (inverted)/ B/(A)/ G♯/(G inv.)/
337–373 (end)	Christine: 'I am crucified upon the spring!' / Children taunt / *Alleluia* (both distorted on tape) **Fourth climax** Diminuendo to recap. of Christine's Act 1 Song (on oboe) / 'This is a wall, and this is a wall' (monotone)	Pedal E (E/B♭) [Passacaglia ends]

flourishes that reaffirm the E/B♭ duality that marked the start of the opera. Figure 4.2 contains a summary of the rhythmic plan, commencing at bar 279.

As the tonality of Christine's Immurement Ceremony is re-established by the *fortissimo* pedal E (although immediately undermined by the tritone, E/B♭, as in Bishop Henry's first intercession in bar 34 of the opera), memories of the earlier liturgy and the children's interrogation come tumbling back until the Anchoress, incapable of coherent speech, plunges her teeth into one of the waving (children's) hands. This single act of violence marks the complete disintegration of her sanity and she is reduced to a state of catatonic inertia, capable only of identifying the walls that enclose her. The solo oboe sings her threnody until it, too, fades away on the (remembered) text: 'I will forsake all that I see, Father, friend, *and follow Thee*'. The ending is unresolved – yet exquisitely poised between hope and despair, depending on one's interpretation and beliefs. On the one hand lies the hope of forgiveness and healing – a virtual Resurrection after Christine's metaphorical Crucifixion; on the other, a 'tragic ending' – the almost Faustian destiny of someone who aspired too much to be like God.

Several centuries before the real Christine Carpenter was born in Shere, the great mystic and polymath Hildegard of Bingen[108] described her own vision of *caritas* (the embodiment of divine love) in terms of a beautiful young girl (*puella*) who held the sun and moon in her hands and whose person radiated dazzling light – 'and all creation called her *domina*'.[109] It is tempting to associate this image with the youthful Christine in the first scene of the opera, however far-fetched it might seem to compare such an idealized figure (suggestive of a virgin-bride at Hildegard's aristocratic monastery on the Rupertsberg, perhaps)[110] with the reality of a rustic village girl from Pulham St Mary who had answered the call to serve the Church as an anchoress. Christine, despite her doubts and impatience, is revealed to be a strong and committed character. At her most devout (as in her Immurement Ceremony and at the start of scenes 5 and 9), she, too, radiates an aura of religious zeal. Undoubtedly, she expected to obtain some sort of divine recognition – to be singled out for a special insight (a vision or a showing) as was her close-contemporary Julian of Norwich. Indeed, her expectations sometimes seem to run in parallel with Julian's 'three graces of God's gifts' – these being a vivid perception of Christ's Passion, a bodily sickness, and the 'three wounds of St Cecilia'[111] – and it is conceivable

---

[108] Hildegard of Bingen (1098–1180).

[109] See Peter Dronke (1984) *Women Writers of the Middle Ages: A Critical Study of Texts from Perpetua to Marguerite Porete* (Cambridge: Cambridge University Press), p. 170. 'Domina' in this context carries implications of higher status than merely head of a household – possibly a goddess or royal lady?

[110] Based on Dronke, *Women Writers of the Middle Ages*, p. 170.

[111] See Elizabeth Spearing, *Medieval Writings on Female Spirituality*, pp. 175 et seq. and n. 102, above. Traditionally, St Cecilia is believed to have been beheaded (an execution requiring *three* axe blows). Julian makes it clear that the 'three wounds' that she craves are metaphorical – that is, wounds of contrition, compassion and earnest longing for God.

Figure 4.2   Composer's sketch for Act 2 showing the Passacaglia theme with transpositions and variants. By permission of the composer

that her mental illness could be interpreted in the same way as the physical illness, from which Julian suffered in her thirty-first year.[112] There seems little doubt that Christine's perception of Christ's Passion is as vivid as could be wished for, ranging as it does from personal identification with the Virgin Mary (the Lullaby) to her offer to experience the nails and bleeding of her crucified Saviour. Her compassion, contrition and longing for union with God are also demonstrable during her traumatic spiritual journey. Clearly, she was prepared to exchange the rural life she loved and the near-certainty of a happy marriage with Robert Lonle for her inhospitable cell and the possibility of divine union with her maker.

What is less than clear is the reason for Christine's disillusionment. Wherein lay the seeds of her (supposed) loss of faith? Possibly it was pride. Some have concluded that she was not cut out for solitude.[113] Perhaps she missed the external world more than she had anticipated (as her family suggested), or perhaps she was impatient (as Mathew remarked in scene 8)[114] – so impatient, in fact, that she didn't realize that whatever visions she might receive could only be *part* of a larger commitment to divine love rather than a prelude to some elevated state of grace. What Arnold Wesker understood so well was that expectations, such as Christine's, invariably lead to the most convincing drama *when they are frustrated*. If at times the author tends to politicize his subject, there is no doubt that his dramatic instincts are sure-footed and his insights into the workings of the Catholic Church in the Middle Ages are both well-researched and perceptive. His depiction of Christine's madness is masterly – as is Saxton's response to his libretto and the cadences of his verse. *Caritas*, the opera, stands as a vindication of music's ability to enhance texts and to sustain arguments – and the final scene of *Caritas* is *just that*: a large-scale operatic confrontation between good and evil; between Christine's ambitions and reality; between divine and human love; between idealism and human frailty. By choosing to construct this final scene on the foundations of a passacaglia, Saxton has ensured that the fluctuating sequence of (often conflicting) thoughts and emotions is connected with a thread of purely musical dialectic that is capable of responding to sudden changes in pace and mood – or, occasionally, being temporarily suspended as, for example, when the focus of the action rests for a while on Christine's tender lullaby for her crucified 'child'.

---

[112] Ibid., pp. 176–7. The implication is that, by surviving a near-death illness, Julian shared in Christ's own experience of death and rebirth.

[113] Mathew (scene 8) and other family members.

[114] 'She sits demanding visions. Now! When some have waited sixty years and not been graced' (Mathew, scene 8).

Conclusion

Whereas the reception of the final scene of *Caritas* allows for certain shades of
interpretation (as outlined above), the composer's achievement in creating such a
convincing musical structure for its presentation leaves little scope for criticism. Not
only is the choice of a passacaglia vindicated as a dramatic device, the tonal scheme
that is employed in the final scene effectively reverses that of the opening scene
of Act 1 and completes the large-scale structural conception of the entire opera, in
which relatively simple harmonic progressions are active on both microcosmic and
macrocosmic planes. At its most basic, *Caritas* is founded on a Phrygian Cadence,
in which the tonic (in this case, E) is approached by its flattened supertonic (F) – or,
chordally, by the first inversion of a D minor triad (see Example 4.24). As mentioned
earlier, this Phrygian[115] characteristic is also a feature of the passacaglia theme itself
(although transposed up a tone onto D) and represents the overall tonal scheme of
the final scene (D–E) and (in reverse) the Immurement Ceremony. Saxton allows
himself the freedom to alter the theme's interval structure and its note values from
time to time, of course, and this enables the Passacaglia's continuous variations to
recede from foreground to background and from background to greater prominence,
depending on the nature of the episode being set. Example 4.25 illustrates some of
the permutations used during the final scene.

Example 4.24   Phrygian cadence

Example 4.25   Passacaglia theme variants

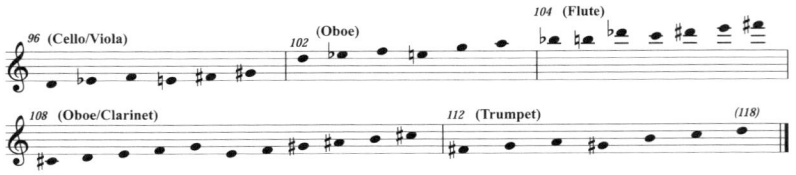

---

[115]   The Phrygian Mode is characterized by having a semitone between its first and second
notes. The 'natural' mode, starting on E, consists entirely of 'white notes' (in pianoforte terms).
Whereas other natural modes utilize a raised seventh note at cadences, the Phrygian mode
uses a 'flattened' seventh degree (D♮). These characteristics are shared with the rarely used
Locrian mode (on B). All modes may be transposed but retain their characteristic sequence
of intervals.

Example 4.26   *Caritas* – tonal symmetries

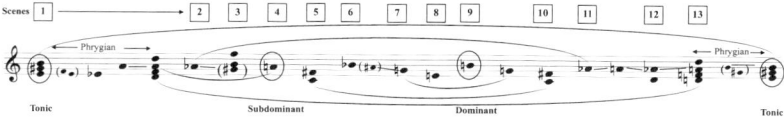

Although an earlier diagram (Table 4.3) provided a working summary of the tonal structure of the entire opera (if somewhat simplified), one final music example (Example 4.26) is offered as a slightly fuller summary of the tonal symmetries that are found in *Caritas*. This also brings into prominence the more traditional roles of subdominant (A) and dominant (B) tonalities within the thirteen scenes and demonstrates the way in which modality and major/minor tonalities are utilized to create such a convincing fusion of medieval and modern principles within the architectonics of this operatic structure.

Chapter 5
Caritas: Performance and Reception

The world premiere performances of Robert Saxton's first opera took place as planned at Wakefield Opera House on 21, 23 and 24 November during the 1991 Huddersfield Festival of Contemporary Music. The members of cast (listed in Appendix B), the children's chorus, from Allerton Grange Middle School, Leeds, and the Chamber Orchestra of Opera North were conducted by Diego Masson. The Director was Patrick Mason; the set was designed by Joe Vaněk, and the lighting by Nick Chelton. The electronic tape used in Act 2 was recorded and edited by Mark Bromwich in Huddersfield University's Electro-Acoustic Studio. Even before the first performances, the casting of the leading role had been the subject of considerable dispute, which was then elaborated (with journalistic flourishes) in the *Independent Magazine*.[1] It is *not* the purpose of this chapter to revisit events that have now been consigned to history. Discussion of performance is based on the commercial compact disc that accompanies this volume, together with documented reports on public productions in Wakefield, London and Cheltenham (see listings in Appendix C).

Despite the conversational tone of Lebrecht's preview of *Caritas*, his article contains some useful background information – such as the 'discernible operatic' potential of Wesker's original play, with its specification of a plainsong hymn, choral responses and 'intense solo monologues'. These components are perhaps *musical* and/or *dramatic* rather than being intrinsically operatic, but they do demonstrate that the playwright was aware of the importance of selecting appropriate liturgical items to create period atmosphere and to draw individual members of the cast into dramatic ensembles – a practice further exploited by Saxton, although subsequent reviews failed to give him credit for incorporating the modal characteristics of medieval chant into his fully chromatic idiom and inventing compatible *leitmotifs* without loss of compositional integrity. Indeed, initial response to the first performances tended to focus on peripheral issues (such as the above-mentioned casting controversy)[2] or the librettist's deep concern about 'the anti-human quality of dogma' (as exemplified in the Bishop's refusal to allow Christine to leave her cell),[3] before addressing the performances themselves. Once such preambles had been delivered, both Malcolm

---

[1]   Norman Lebrecht, 'A Fight at the Opera' – see comments in Chapter 3, p. 37, n. 16.

[2]   For example, Malcolm Hayes (1991) 'Playing safe', *The Daily Telegraph*, 25 November.

[3]   Michael Kennedy (1991) 'All walled up with somewhere to go', *Sunday Telegraph* (Review Supplement), 24 November. One could argue that Wesker's concern is fundamental, of course, but the term 'peripheral' is used here in the context of a *performance* review.

Hayes (MH) and Michael Kennedy (MK) were eloquent in their praise of the high standards of preparation of the performances and of the imaginative production team. Inevitably, Saxton's 'debt' to Britten was examined and comparisons with the Church Parables, *Albert Herring* and *The Turn of the Screw* were duly explored, although both critics emphasized the positive effects of Britten's mentoring rather than implying any slavish imitation: 'Saxton is no Britten clone. He is less sentimental and has a tougher approach to harmony. What he has learned most fruitfully is to move swiftly from climax to climax ...' (MK). 'Saxton's music is free of the dirge-like monotony of pace [found in many new operas] ... intelligently, taking a leaf out of Britten's book, he has realised that transitions between scenes simply can't be too short' (MH). Overall, Saxton was identified as possessing a 'natural sense of theatre' (MK): '[his] fluent and meticulously structured score is much more successful than most recent attempts at chamber opera' (MH) – 'this is an opera which deserves to be taken up widely' (MK).

As for the singers, nearly all were singled out for praise at one time or another and Eirian Davies was commended for her acting as well as her vocal performance, which, however, 'might be tested in a larger theatre' (MK). Kennedy reported that there were 'sympathetic performances by Roger Bryson and Linda Hibberd as Christine's parents. Jonathan Best was the acme of Episcopal pomp, and Brian Cookson and Linda Ormiston turned in pleasing cameos as a tax-collector and village gossip'. Hayes, for his part, noted that Christopher Ventris stood out 'as Christine's bewildered and then rebellious fiancé, as did Jonathan Best as the domineering Bishop of Norwich, and Paul Wilson as the more sympathetic parish priest'.

Whereas the general critical reaction to the first performances (summarized above) was laudatory, Hayes gave voice to a reservation that was to reverberate occasionally in later reviews.[4] It was simply that he found Saxton's sheer technical accomplishment 'an end in itself'. The composer was recommended to 'dare himself the creative equivalent of climbing a mountain in a thunderstorm – and maybe getting struck by lightning'. While it is not unusual for 'academic' composers to be berated for their apparent preoccupation with technique, it is difficult to countenance a risk much greater than composing an operatic *finale* that depicts the accelerating madness of a youthful anchoress who has been denied the freedom to leave her tiny squalid cell. Such a critical caveat as this appears misplaced, coming as it did immediately after a paragraph that praised Saxton's handling of Act 2 in the most fulsome of terms: 'There was a genuine sense here of the music's sweeping paragraphs surging outwards from within, rather than having been pieced superficially together' (MH). Of course, there is a vast difference between the hill-walking of the twelve scenes that make up Act 1 of *Caritas* and the mountaineering of the Mad Scene, just described, but each activity requires mastery of an appropriate technique if travellers are to reach their goal unscathed. This is not to belittle the suggestion that creative artists

---

4   For example Michael White (1992) 'A lifetime's search for the moment', *The Independent*, 5 July.

should take risks, but simply to affirm that Saxton accepted a daunting challenge and carried it off with immense flair and formidable technique. Incidentally, when he was faced with setting Christine's account of a boy who climbed the high mountains near his home, despite his mother's opposition,[5] it was the sheer technical economy of his writing that conveyed the spirit of the mountains and the determination of the youth. He was adored by his mother who experienced 'the helpless ache' (of pain) as she retraced his steps, but 'there were [sic] no other way'.[6]

Perhaps the most coherent and well-balanced review of the premieres is found in a (slightly delayed) report in *Die Welt*.[7] This combines the seemingly obligatory references to Saxton's early teachers, a summary of the opera's plot and Wesker's indictment of the inhumanity of fundamentalists with pithily expressed insights into the nature of the commission and the standard of the performance. It was a 'brilliant occasion', Siegfried Helm writes, 'It was also the embodiment of the current trend in regional theatre to break down the cultural dominance of London in English cultural life.' Christine's Mad Scene is traced back to *Lucia di Lammermoor*, Verdi's *Macbeth*, even to Monteverdi's *Lamento d'Arianna*. 'The disintegration of Christine's personality is presented to us in climaxes of ever-increasing passionate potency. … In this scene of great passion [the Mad Scene], Saxton is stronger than in the twelve often shorter scenes of the first act.'

Helm draws attention to the composer's affinity with Alban Berg, and praises his scoring, albeit with the reservation that the use of percussion at climaxes can lead to them being rather 'one-sided'. In summary, he concludes that '*Caritas* vibrantly articulates for our generation the story of a fourteenth-century recluse and does it with brilliant force and accuracy', although 'a truly great soprano voice is needed' for the main role of Christine (Eirian Davies' convincing characterization and vocal performance notwithstanding).

Two further performance reviews – this time of the Queen Elizabeth Hall production in the 1992 London Opera Festival – merit attention at this point because they refer back to the premieres (and/or the recently released recording).[8] Experiencing a new work for a second time, clearly can sharpen the critic's perception (and his pen). Stephen Johnson[9] took the opportunity to compliment the commissioners of the opera on being presented with the Prudential Award for Services to New Music (on the evidence of this production, 'richly deserved'), before comparing the live performance with the recently issued compact disc. On balance he seems to find

---

[5]   *Caritas*, Act 1, scene 3. This description is an extended metaphor for Christine's own struggle in following her religious vocation.

[6]   See detailed commentary on this scene in Chapter 4, pp. 70–73.

[7]   Siegfried Helm (1991) 'God's Hostage', *Die Welt*, 12 December.

[8]   *Caritas* was staged at the Queen Elizabeth Hall on 1 and 2 July 1992. The recording on Collins Classics (1992), now NMC D102 (2004), was released to coincide with this production.

[9]   Stephen Johnson (1992) 'Charity without Clarity', *The Independent* 3 July. The title appears to ignore the true meaning of *caritas* in the interests of alliteration.

that the 'determined motivation' of the orchestra's 'multi-layered toccatas … still appear[s] on the whole to respond to situations, feelings and ideas in only a broad, generalised way [although] this forward drive can be compelling, and the nervous, claustrophobic atmosphere grows in intensity towards the final climax [the end of Act 2]'. He goes on to comment favourably on the composer's orchestration ('it's remarkable, too, how powerful – how "orchestral" – that writing sounds, despite the smallness of the instrumental forces') and he admits that the effect of the voices hovering uncertainly above the so-called 'torrent of notes' can 'in places [be] undeniably effective'. In summary, the problem he perceives is that the instrumental writing dominates the vocal parts and, he speculates, 'Is this an opera, one wonders, or a play with music?'

In the context of an otherwise well-argued and reasonable *critique*, it is hard to justify so provocative a question. Wesker's stage play, *Caritas*, is a *play with music*; Saxton's *Caritas* is an *opera* – and not just because it says so on the title page and in the programme. The work is musically through-composed; it is sustained by a recognizable *leitmotif* scheme that defines characters on a purely musical level; there are no episodes *without* music; it includes many examples of traditional operatic devices such as recitative, narrative *arioso* and dramatic vocal ensembles; there are sections of extended aria-like song (Christine's Act 2 *Lullaby*, especially); the second act contributes to an established operatic genre; above all, the large-scale tonal structure of the score is symphonic and operatic in a sense that would be have been recognized by Mozart, Berg and Britten. It is true that the work also contains a fine example of melodrama (the Travelling Priest's report on the failed Peasants' Uprising, declaimed against the Ricercar), but so do a great many operas. The declared inability of a critic to discern recurrent vocal characteristics (apart from the difference between baritone speech-song and high soprano) is certainly not evidence of the work being other than operatic.

Like, Johnson, Michael White[10] refers back to an earlier experience of *Caritas* – the Wakefield premiere – which, he felt, 'had diluted rather than enriched the personalities it drew on'. The same cast and production at the Queen Elizabeth Hall had not changed his mind but had made him realize that he had underestimated the stature of the score: 'intense, tightly coherent and especially effective in its use of a Brittenesque repeating ground to wind up the emotions of the short second act'. White then declares *his* reservation – 'the narrative … has two main qualities: it's shocking and it's physical. I want to see these things on stage and hear them in the music, and I don't'. Presumably, the sight of a young anchoress exposing her breasts and urinating on stage is not sufficiently shocking or physical nor, it would seem, is the heroine's hysterical screaming – together with a notated vocal line that alternates rapidly between barely suppressed passion, monotone prayer and paranoid expressionism (not to mention the electronic distortion of sacred chant).

---

[10]   Michael White, 'A lifetime's search for the moment'. The title appears to refer to an earlier section of the review, devoted to the late Stephen Oliver, composer of 40 operas.

In spite of concluding that '*Caritas* is a mature, impressive piece', he adds: 'I wish it stirred my soul'. Presumably, this is an echo of previous caveats that suggested that the composer's technique might be 'an end in itself'. If so, it would be an issue worthy of debate. However, no objective or balanced argument ensues. It is not unreasonable for critics to have reservations about a new work, even after experiencing several performances. One suspects that this kind of unsubstantiated reservation is the ultimate resort of equivocal opera reports; that subjective reaction becomes an acceptable substitute for informed commentary.

Once the commercial recording had been released, a steady stream of reviews appeared in magazines and on websites together with the composer's own CD sleeve notes. It is not surprising that the extremes of critical perception (noted above) gave way to a more adulatory tone – no doubt a consequence of close study of the score and recording, but perhaps calculated to encourage sales as well. Chester/Novello (publisher of the opera) quotes a relevant paragraph from Andrew Clements' review of February 2005,[11] which praises Saxton's 'beautifully crafted [music], with finely drawn instrumental detail and vocal writing, especially for the main character, Christine, that packs a real emotional punch'. Peter Graham Woolf,[12] like others, notes a similarity between the first scene of *Caritas* and the plainsong derivation of Britten's Church Parables, but also identifies the harrowing performance of Eirian Davies as the 'self-deceiving sixteen-year old' (Christine) before providing a neatly expressed summary of the two contrasting acts that itself merits quotation as a representative appraisal of Saxton's technical virtuosity:

> In the first act Saxton's music displays a real opera composer's skill in counterpointing the text so that equal attention is given to both; in the second the orchestra comes to the forefront as Christine becomes more alone and unable to express herself ... the scene has a 'harmonic ground whose incessant cyclic repetitions reflect Christine's mental state'.[13] ... The outcome is a satisfying and unforgettable music drama, perfectly conceived and paced to match the treatment of Arnold Wesker's powerful subject, one that leaves you looking forward to another opera from Robert Saxton, ... now in his prime.[14]

As a later chapter in this book reveals,[15] Saxton had been planning an opera on a quite different subject when the commission for *Caritas* was received in 1987. It is a happy coincidence that that project (a radio opera/fantasy on the legend of the Wandering Jew) should have been completed and performed before the present

---

[11]   Andrew Clements (2005) 'Review of NMC D102', *BBC Music Magazine*, 1 February.

[12]   Peter Grahame Woolf (n.d.) *Review of Robert Saxton's Caritas and other works* on NMC Anchora D102 (www.musicalpointers.co.uk; accessed 18 September 2007).

[13]   This part of the sentence is quoted from the composer's sleeve note.

[14]   Presumably written in 2004 – [just over 50] omitted.

[15]   See Chapter 7, p. 125.

Figure 5.1   Photographs of stage design model (by kind permission of Joe Vaněk)

Christine's world pivoted literally from light into dark and back again. This quasi-medieval world was basically created with three low walls together with a fourth tall mud-daubed wall at the rear, through which the eye of heaven stared balefully down on her anguish.

Two of the three walls were placed up and down stage with tall narrow slits as entrances, whilst the third one (placed centrally) was cantilevered two inches off the stage-deck on a metre-wide revolve, thus enabling us to move in and out of the cell at will. Christine was able to stand on this and, in her final agonizing moments, it was spun at speed by the cast as her world closed in on her.

The cell was sealed manually by the cast with a physical door, black on one side and white on the other. Set into a contrasting wall, it indicated the dark inside or the light outside, and the small square aperture was all that we felt was needed to focus on Christine's sense of entombment.

volume was submitted for publication, since it allows for a brief comparison to be made with its predecessor[16] as well as supplying a welcome response to Woolf's journalistic hint. In one sense, at least, the more recent opera is a relatively optimistic complement to *Caritas*, despite their seemingly irreconcilable choice of media.[17] Perhaps it (or/and its predecessor) could be adapted to create a 'double-bill' of dramatic musical pageants, even if this were to involve sacrificing a little of their original conception in the cause of increasing the opportunities for programming and, thus, enhancing the reception of two remarkable music-dramas. The composer has implied as much in his remarks about concert-performances of opera and the possibility that *The Wandering Jew* might be performed live (although designed for a non-visual medium).[18] The very favourable reception of *Caritas* since its first performances and recordings seems to more than justify a revival of the opera – whether in the theatre or concert-hall, or on radio or television. When critics of the stature of Michael Kennedy state that 'this is an opera that deserves to be taken up widely' perhaps theatre directors and concert promoters should be encouraged to follow this lead and to broaden their planning horizons to create more innovative groupings of scores and dramatic productions such as those that are commonplace in the field of ballet and dance.

Caritas has been welcomed as a significant addition to the operatic repertoire, despite a few critical caveats. In addition to its use of a dramatic masterwork by one of the greatest living playwrights, it has been well served by a director and a conductor of the highest calibre and it benefited from costumes and a truly imaginative set design by Joe Vaněk (see Figure 5.1), whose design statement (quoted below) encapsulates the creative fusion of media that has characterized the best in music-drama since its inception:

> I had never read or seen this play when I was asked to design the opera but I found it immediately compelling, relentless and brutal. Robert Saxton's music seemed to exemplify this and, furthermore (for me), added a frisson to the entire process. Whilst the setting was basically medieval, we chose to cross the centuries in costume and artefacts so as to create a style that suggested an aura of a middle-European world still on the edge of darkness.
>
> Costumes were homespun, rough looking and soiled. The entire performing space was set into a muddy floor that washed up the crudely textured walls. Lighting was harsh and angular, and shafts through the entry-slots assaulted the central wall, conjuring up a world of increasing hysteria as it spun.[19]

---

[16]   See Chapter 6.

[17]   See Chapter 1, p. 2 and Chapter 6, pp. 120–21.

[18]   See the composer's remarks in Chapter 7 and his Record Notes, p. 7, in NMC D170.

[19]   See the designer's captions to the set models on p. 111, which describe how Christine could stand on a revolving cantilevered wall that was spun at speed by the rest of the cast.

With the benefit of hindsight – and especially in the light of his recently completed second opera – *Caritas* can indeed be identified as a landmark in Saxton's output and one of the most significant musical scores of the second half of the twentieth-century.

Chapter 6

The Wandering Jew and Other Works after *Caritas*

As Robert Saxton approaches his sixtieth birthday,[1] one cannot help but affirm the proposition made in the introductory chapter to this book that his two operas occupy strategic positions in his output – symmetrical punctuation marks, perhaps, in a composing career that started in earnest in the 1970s (when he was in his twenties), reached 'a highpoint in terms of public recognition in the [early] 1990s',[2] and attained a new level of intellectual curiosity tempered with more traditionally based modality/tonality in the years that followed. *Caritas* (completed in 1990 and first performed in 1991) can be seen both as the climax of his first and (to date) most prolific period, and as initiating a considered review of various aspects of the composer's style and his approach to structure in previous works – as David Wright has eloquently observed.[3] In addressing some of the issues that might have contributed to the perceived neglect of compositions produced after *Caritas* (in spite of their greater surface accessibility and widely acknowledged quality), Wright suggests that perhaps the very nature of the chosen repertoire (predominantly chamber music and vocal/choral settings) might have been considered as insufficiently 'mainstream' to merit detailed discussion or more widespread dissemination. The fact that some of these works are liturgical or occasional pieces might also be seen to have limited their acceptance somewhat into the fashionable canon of concert programmes – a possibility that could well repay further investigation as this brief survey of works after *Caritas* proceeds.

Wright's spirited defence of Saxton's music of the 1990s was prompted (and enhanced) by the marketing of a fresh compact disc 'anthology' of chamber works, mostly from that decade.[4] Innovative compositions such as *Invocation, Dance and Meditation*, and *A Yardstick to the Stars* became available for repeated listening and study (they had already been published in 1994 and 1995, respectively) and the Fantazia (commissioned as a test piece for the 1994 London International String

---

[1]   Saxton will be sixty in 2013. The relationship between his two operas is mentioned in Chapter 1, p. 2 and elsewhere (Chapters 6 and 7, especially).

[2]   Quoted from David Wright (2001) *Robert Saxton in the 1990s* Tempo: New series, 2–6 (Cambridge: Cambridge University Press).

[3]   Ibid, p. 2.

[4]   Robert Saxton, *A Yardstick to the Stars* and other chamber works (2000) on NMC D065; cited in the opening paragraph of David Wright, ibid.

Quartet Competition) similarly became more widely accessible – although the composer's Second Quartet (*Songs, Dances and Ellipses*) had to wait for another eight years before the release of a recording.[5] The three works on the new disc that are cited above (and there are another four besides these) illustrate several of Saxton's recurrent fascinations, such as early English music (in the Fantazia, where the spirit of Purcell is omnipresent), mathematical and cosmological speculation (*A Yardstick to the Stars*), and his Jewish heritage (*Invocation, Dance and Meditation,* which draws on ancient religious and musical traditions). This latter work shares with the slightly later Sonata for Solo Cello[6] a concluding sequence comprising a (penultimate) dance and a final, more contemplative, lyrical movement that encapsulates the spirit of the whole piece. In the case of the Sonata, the dance (in $\frac{3}{8}$ metre) is reminiscent of those found in baroque cello suites; in the case of *Invocation, Dance and Meditation* (for viola and piano), the corresponding section represents the composer's tribute to the Hassidic custom of praying by dancing oneself into a state of ecstasy. The closing *Meditation* is based on an old Rabbinic prayer, chanted at midnight as a reminder of the destruction of the Temple in Jerusalem in 70 AD, whereas the *Song* that ends the Sonata is Walton's original *Tema per variazioni.* Nor is the spirit of the dance absent in the Fantazia (String Quartet 1), where the third (final) movement follows comparable precedents in Purcell's viol fantasias, although Saxton matches the jaunty syncopated tune (heard mainly in the three upper parts) in more modern fashion with toe-tapping *pizzicati* on the cello.

While none of the above compositions could be said to be lacking in technical artifice, it is the work for String Quartet and Piano (*A Yardstick to the Stars*) that reveals the full extent of Saxton's absorption of the proportional and symmetrical characteristics of medieval and renaissance polyphony – aspects of his style that have already been observed in *Caritas*, albeit in the context of the passacaglia's tempo modulation and the overall structural symmetry of the opera. As the composer makes clear in his programme note,[7] *A Yardstick to the Stars* 'is concerned with proportional time and distance, as related to the heavens; its time-cycle represents the planets' orbital paths, moving like cogwheels ...'. Although sharing the same musical material, the piano and strings progress at different (overlapping) speeds with some sixty-eight bars of the opening music being recapitulated in retrograde in the final section of the fourth movement.[8] Like a large-scale ceremonial motet by Dunstable or Dufay, the composition's four continuous sections are related proportionally

5   *Northern Lights*: String Quartets by John Casken, Robert Saxton and Judith Weir (2008) on Metier msv28507. *Songs, Dances and Ellipses* was composed in 1997 and revised the following year.

6   The Sonata for Solo Cello was composed in 1999 for Steven Isserlis.

7   See the booklet included with CD NMC D065, pp.17/18.

8   This use of a partial or complete palindrome recalls similar processes in Berg's *Lyric Suite, Der Wein* and *Lulu* (amongst other works).

by simple number ratios (6:4:3:6).[9] The miracle is that the metaphorical heavens of Saxton's music can be viewed through the medium of a live performance or a compact disc 'telescope' without necessarily needing to understand the technical processes involved – although, of course, analytical insights can enrich auditory experience, as with comparable works by Schoenberg or Berg.

Interspersed amongst the chamber works of the 1990s is a series of choral compositions that continues a pattern established during the previous decade with pieces such as the *Chaconne* (1981), *Child of Light* (1984), and *I Will Awake the Dawn* (1986–67). *At the Round Earth's Imagin'd Corners*, written for St Paul's Cathedral in London (1992) is an *a cappella* setting of John Donne's metaphysical poem that concludes on a brilliant A major chord, recalling a similar use of this tonality at focal moments in *Caritas*.[10] By contrast, *O Sing unto the Lord a New Song*, composed for the St Cecilia's Day Service at Westminster Cathedral, London on 24 November 1993, juxtaposes and then combines resonant nine-part chordal declamation with *concertante* organ writing as the setting of Psalm 98 builds to *its* climax on D major. Although impressive, and entirely appropriate in celebratory anthems, such blatant use of tonal reference-points could well have become a predictable mannerism (especially within relatively short time-scales) so it is refreshing to find that Saxton's next choral work avoided the temptation to direct harmonic progressions to such an unequivocal form of resolution. *Canticum Luminis* (1994), a cantata on texts by Lucretius and Sir Isaac Newton (in their original Latin), was commissioned by Cambridge University Musical Society in 1994 and dedicated to the memory of the composer's former tutor (and distinguished early church music scholar), Dr Peter le Huray.[11] The texts of the four movements are concerned with the natural phenomenon of sunlight, its structure, effects and refraction – hardly material for the faint-hearted. But this is a work deliberately cast in the form of a philosophical tract, recalling again the more esoteric features of medieval motets that, like *Canticum Luminis*, were either composed for an intellectual élite or designed as musical architecture whose structure and proportional features were as aesthetically gratifying as their surface melodies might be pleasing.[12] David Wright

---

[9]   An obvious point of comparison would be with Dufay's isorhythmic motet, *Nuper rosarum flores*, written for the consecration of Florence Cathedral (1436), which uses the ratios, 6:4:2:3, between its four sections. The proportions of Saxton's composition are calculated using numbers of bars rather than temporal duration (as in *Caritas*). Clearly, such proportions contain harmonic implications – 6:4 and 2:3 representing a perfect fifth; 4:2 [2:1] representing an octave, and so on.

[10]   For example, Christine's entrance into her cell in scene 1 and the climax of her parents' (and Robert's) petition for compassion in the Trio of scene 12.

[11]   *Canticum Luminis*, in four movements, is scored for full orchestra, solo soprano and chorus.

[12]   Further examples of proportion and other arcane features in musical architecture can be found in Wyndham Thomas 'Composing, Arranging and Editing: A Historical Survey' in

makes a comparison with twentieth-century works such as Tippett's *Vision of St Augustine* and Schoenberg's *Jacob's Ladder* and this does, indeed, appear to point to a common area of influence.

However, as with many such comparisons, the essential quality of the original can be obscured by generalizations that attempt to unlock the 'hidden secrets' of art. Even without an initiate's familiarity with Latin texts, the cantata can be heard as a masterly demonstration of choral writing – its dedicatee would no doubt have approved of the inverted points of imitation in the first movement. The second movement introduces the soprano soloist into a dance-like section (which describes the non-stop motion of atoms), and this is followed by a rhetorical slow movement (a setting of Newton's explanation of light rays) that culminates on a *fortissimo* unison A♭ before merging into the final movement, which ends with a glittering nine-note chord on the key word, 'lumina' ('light'). In effect, this is a work that can be appreciated in a number of different ways. On the one hand, the proportions of its four movements (5:6:6:4)[13] and their use of esoteric texts might lead one to conclude that the composition's true home remains in the rarefied atmosphere of King's College Chapel (where it was first performed), but its easily assimilated fugal polyphony and dramatic interaction of soloist and chorus suggest that, like Stravinsky's *Symphony of Psalms*, it has a place in mainstream concert programmes where its subject matter would resonate with a contemporary audience at least as conversant with the science of light as were the intellectual circles of either Lucretius or Newton.

In 1999, Saxton was appointed to a University Lectureship in Music and a Fellowship of Worcester College, Oxford.[14] It was, perhaps, inevitable that he would be drawn even closer to the sphere of choral (chapel) music and this has, indeed, proved to be the case, although commissions have continued to come from *outside* academic circles (Edward Wickham and The Clerks' Group) as well as from within. In particular, he has established a fruitful artistic relationship with Stephen Darlington and the choir of Christ Church Cathedral, Oxford, that has resulted (to date) in evocative settings of W.H. Auden (*O Living Love*), the alternative Evening Canticles (*Cantate Domino* and *Deus Misereatur*), and the *Magnificat* and *Nunc Dimittis*, all of which extend and further enrich the traditions of Christian collegiate worship.[15] Conversely, the two compositions for the Clerks' Group have developed Saxton's ongoing association with Jewish culture and faith. The first of the pieces is an eight-voice *a cappella* cantata (2000) that sets a poem by the sixth-century

---

Thomas, ed. (1998) *Composition – Performance – Reception: Studies in the Creative Process in Music* (Aldershot: Ashgate).

[13]   As with *A Pathway to the Stars*, the ratios are based on bar numbers rather than temporal periods.

[14]   For most of the 1990s Saxton headed the Composition Departments at The Guildhall School of Music (1991–98) and The Royal Academy of Music (1998–99). He is currently Professor of Composition and Fellow of Worcester College, Oxford.

[15]   All of these works date from 2006.

Israeli writer, Eleazar Ben Kallir (*The Dialogue of Zion and God*);[16] the second, commissioned for the 2003 Promenade Concerts, and rather disarmingly entitled *Five Motets for Nine Voices*, is a weightier work that intersperses (and occasionally overlays) Latin texts extracted from the Vulgate Bible with English poems by the composer himself. The overall theme of the motet-cycle is that of journeys, as described in Genesis 12: 1–3, when Abram [sic] travels from Ur to Canaan, and the eventual arrival of his grandson, Jacob, at the point (near Haran) where he receives God's promise to guide and protect him and his descendants forever (the dream of Jacob's Ladder in Genesis 28: 10–13 and 15–17). These two episodes are contained in the two outer motets. The second and fourth are settings of Saxton's poetic commentaries (in English), while the central movement is a choral dance celebrating the singing and dancing of Miriam, sister of Moses and Aaron (Exodus 15: 19–20). Saxton's indebtedness to earlier polyphony has already been mentioned and is maintained in this work through references to the *In Nomine* motif from John Taverner's *Missa Gloria tibi Trinitas*.[17] Additionally, the composer has volunteered the information that the superimposition of Latin and English in the middle (third) motet is his tribute to the thirteenth- and fourteenth-century practice of bi-textual/ bi-lingual motet composition.[18]

Five Motets for Nine Voices is a visionary work that combines many of the best features of the composer's output since *Caritas* and points onwards to the musical language of his second opera. Like *The Wandering Jew* (and, to a certain extent, *Caritas* itself), its main sections are identified by clear tonal centres: Motet 1 progresses from E to A; Motet 2, from A to E♭; Motet 3 is centred on B♭; Motet 4 is in A♭; and Motet 5 returns to E. As in *O Living Love*, the motets introduce key-signatures as though to acknowledge the importance of tonal orientation in his works – and, possibly of greater significance (though not for the first time), Saxton uses his own poetry to comment on and to clarify the narratives that have become so vital to his compositional procedures and structures (whether vocal/choral or purely instrumental).[19]

Although, today, it is possible to identify *The Wandering Jew* as a comparable landmark to *Caritas*, it is important to realize that it is much more than a mere end-point to what may conveniently be described as Saxton's second creative

---

[16]   Little is known of this Jewish poet who wrote in the sixth century of his mourning and yearnings for Zion. Some of his works are used in synagogue services to this day.

[17]   A borrowing, reminiscent perhaps of the derivation of the Kyrie eleison motif from Byrd's Five-Part Mass in *Caritas*, Act 2.

[18]   See Saxton's introduction to the score (probably based on his 'Proms.' programme note for the first performance at the Royal Albert Hall on 5 September 2003).

[19]   *Prayer before Sleep* (1997), dedicated to the memory of the famous Rabbi, Hugo Gryn, contains a setting of Saxton's poem *O wing your way to freedom*.

period.[20] Ever since the composer first read Stefan Heym's politico-satirical version of the ancient legend in 1984,[21] an operatic project based on the subject had been germinating in his mind until it was finally consolidated with the BBC commission for a radio-opera in the 1990s. By the composer's own admission, work on the opera dominated the decade leading up to its premiere.[22] Bearing in mind that an earlier impulse to contemplate the state of eternal searching and wandering can be dated back to Saxton's reading of *The Epic of Gilgamesh* in the mid-1960s, one might conclude that the subject has been virtually a lifelong obsession.[23] Its impact on other works in the first decade of the century has been explicitly set out by Saxton himself in his CD essay:[24]

> I used commissions along the way to create satellite pieces, testing what I was trying to achieve on a larger scale. My music of the past decade – all of it related to the opera – is not only modal, but increasingly tonal in functional terms; technically, it is serial in the sense that interval cycles and pitch groups are heard in specific, but slowly changing, orders. The music is based on a 7-note expanding and contracting set which, symbolically, represents wandering and return, as well as offering the possibility of creating long-range structural unity ... .[25]

With the exception of a couple of obvious references ('wandering and return'), this description could as well apply to the passacaglia in Act 2 of *Caritas* as to *The Wandering Jew*. It is clear that the two operas share many significant stylistic features despite the very pronounced differences between their subject matter, scoring and choice of medium. A basic comparison of the two works has already been rehearsed in Chapter 1 and will be considerably amplified later, although for the moment it requires little further discussion, other than to underline the second opera's concluding spirit of reconciliation in a narrative that has its origins in

---

[20]   *The Wandering Jew* was completed in 2010 and first performed in a BBC Radio 3 broadcast on 7 July 2010. Its place in Saxton's (ever growing) output must remain a matter of speculation despite the critical convenience of judging its completion to be a significant fulfilment of long-standing plans.

[21]   Stefan Heym is one of three pen names used by Helmut Flieg (1913–2001). (The other pen names are Melchior Douglas and Gregor Holm.) His political satire was first written in German as *Ahasver* (1981) and subsequently published in English as *The Wandering Jew* (1984).

[22]   See the composer's stimulating essay, *The Wandering Jew*, in the booklet that accompanies the recording on NMC D170.

[23]   Ibid., p. 4. *The Epic of Gilgamesh* is a Babylonian moral adventure tale written before 2000 BC. Saxton tells us that Rainer Maria Rilke described it as 'the epic about the fear of death'.

[24]   Ibid., p. 8. Gilgamesh has to wander to attain enlightenment; so my own cycle has [also], to some extent, been realized.

[25]   Ibid., p. 6.

medieval anti-Semitic propaganda (as opposed to the final despair of *Caritas*).[26] It is also important to stress the significance of Saxton's dual role as composer and librettist in *The Wandering Jew* and to emphasize the astonishing originality of *his* version of the medieval legend, into which he introduces instances of musical as well as literary/historical time-travelling.[27] Instead of Heym's more continuous, albeit multi-levelled, narrative in twenty-nine short chapters (symbolically, perhaps, twenty-eight [7 x 4] plus one final, un-numbered, episode), the opera concentrates its action into eight scenes [7 + 1] using seven locations. Starting in a Second World War death camp, a flashback to 70 AD[28] describes the Jew being stabbed by a Roman soldier. Because of his 'curse' he does not (cannot) die. The following scenes move forward chronologically (through the desert at night) to eleventh-century Cordoba at Passover, and thenc, via sixteenth-century Leipzig, to a 'wild, bleak terrain' to witness the rite of Odin's rebirth. The protagonist then finds himself in Venice at Carnival-time in the early eighteenth-century, before returning to the Nazi death camp and the desert *in daylight*. During the course of his travels, the Wandering Jew is joined by various historical figures – Faust, Mephistopheles, Kundry (from *Parsifal*) and the legendary wanderer, Odin (immortalised as Wotan in Wagner's *Ring* cycle), as well as by literary archetypes such as a Fortune Teller, a Widowed Mother, a Showman, and a Beggar (who turns out to be Jesus himself).

Perceptive readers of the earlier account of Saxton's compositions during the two decades from 1990 and 2010 will, no doubt, have already made connections between *The Wandering Jew* and texts and dramatic themes found in works such as *Five Motets*, *Canticum Luminis*, and *O Living Love* – as implied by the composer in his essay on his second opera.[29] Not least amongst these are the concepts of light (a recurring theme in works before *Caritas* as well as after) and travel (whether specific as in *Five Motets* or eternal as in *The Wandering Jew*). Equally, one can trace parallels concerning dance (Miriam in *Five Motets* and Kundry in *The Wandering Jew*), angels, and dialogue (*... of Zion and God* and between the Wandering Jew

---

[26] It is interesting and informative to note that, after the joint project of *Caritas*, both Robert Saxton and Arnold Wesker began to focus on works that had their origins in anti-Semitic history. Wesker produced a commissioned play in 1991 for the (re)opening of the Norwich Playhouse and there is an early typescript of this, entitled *William of Norwich*, in Saxton's *Caritas* papers. The subject of the play is the rape and murder of a young boy (William) and the accusation of 'blood libel' (the eventual title of the play) made against the Jewish community in twelfth-century Norwich. A short account of the play and its significance can be found in Appendix D.

[27] Examples of musical 'time-travelling' include references to Berlioz and Mendelssohn, and the use of four Wagner tubas and modern electro-acoustic manipulation. Liturgical texts employed include *Shema Yisrael* ('Hear O Israel'), the psalm, 'By the Waters of Babylon', the *Agnus Dei*, *Nunc Dimittis*, and the Blessing of Aaron.

[28] This being the year of the Destruction of the Temple in Jerusalem.

[29] See the quotation on p. 120 above and nn. 22 and 23.

and Jesus). Saxton's scenario draws both specifically and indirectly on his earlier 'workshop' compositions; it is made up of a complex sequence of symbolic episodes and a multitude of sophisticated cross-references, the full discussion of which would require a book to itself. The Wandering Jew, himself, is employed as both a singing protagonist (identified with the note A below middle C) and as a narrator who speaks his commentaries during the 'real-time' action of a particular scene or transition. Underpinning the entire structure is a well defined tonal scheme, in which succeeding scenes move through a cycle of fifths from the E of the Chorus of Prisoners in Scene 1, part 1, upwards to F at the start of the eighth scene.[30] Key signatures are included for such scenic identification and when incidental modulations occur – within individual episodes as well as during the (mainly) orchestral interludes that separate pairs of scenes.

Inevitably, the non-visual nature of the opera liberates the audience's imagination and facilitates the frequent changes of location and atmosphere. In this respect, the work shares something of the dramatic quality of an oratorio or Passion – and there are individual items in the radio-opera, such as the settings of Psalm 137, *By the Rivers of Babylon*,[31] and the *Agnus Dei*, that are almost chorale-like in function.[32] The presence of a narrator and the use of the chorus as commentators on the action (whether in the guise of Prisoners, Roman Soldiers, Revellers, Spirits, or the anonymous crowd and congregation) also carry associations with traditional Passion features – as do the more lyrical extended solos of the Jew, the Widowed Mother and the Beggar/Jesus. Overall, the sequence of scenes suggests a continuous cycle that starts and ends in the death camp and desert; yet there is a real sense of progression in the opera as the true nature of the Wandering Jew becomes clearer and he and Jesus are reconciled to their mutual dependency: 'We are one, You and I, through all eternity … My pain is your pain', sings Jesus at the end of Scene 7. Symbolically, the final scene is set in bright sunshine in the desert amongst trees and flowers. The Jew sings *Shema Yisrael* ('Hear, O Israel, the Lord our God is One') before wandering off into the distance, towards the horizon.[33]

Greater familiarity with Saxton's *The Wandering Jew* will doubtless lead to the discovery of many more details of literary and musical significance. In particular, a much closer relationship with *Caritas* seems likely, as one is able to identify common themes and procedures – such as the incidence of liturgical items (*Alleluia* and *Kyrie*

---

[30]   The tonal structure is actually more complicated than this as the beginning E is itself reached by a *downward* series of fifths from A (–D–G–C–F–B♭) and a B♭–E cadence. Thereafter, individual scenes contain varying numbers of modulations, before and after the central key has been established.

[31]   Psalm 137, Old Testament numbering.

[32]   In scenes 1 and 6, respectively.

[33]   *Shema Yisrael* are the first two words of a section of the Hebrew Bible that forms the centrepiece of morning and evening prayers. Deuteronomy 6: 4 also encapsulates the essential monotheism of Judaism.

[*Caritas*] / *Nunc Dimittis* and *Agnus Dei* [*The Wandering Jew*]), hymns and psalms (*Veni Creator Spiritus* [*C*] / *By the Rivers of Babylon* [*WJ*]), and ritual prayers (*Hail Mary/Hail O Cross* [*C*] / *Shema Yisrael* and the Blessing of Aaron [*WJ*]) – not to mention the core themes of crucifixion, spring, re-birth and everlasting life (viewed from Christian and Jewish perspectives), and (most importantly, perhaps) the inter-related themes of charity and love (central to *Caritas* and fundamental to the Jewish Passover). The two operas also share a deeply symbolic attitude toward number(s), with potent parallelism between Christine's three screams (of despair) and Odin's three cries of rebirth (as he attempts to lift the runes at the Yggdrasil);[34] between the Christian 'Five Greetings' (based on Christ's five wounds) and Odin's 'Five Answers' (in response to the five questions to which he must successfully respond before he can commence rebirth).[35] One is reminded also of Wesker's number-groupings in the working draft of his libretto where he identifies five 'prayers and reasons', seven 'laments' (both in Act 2), eight 'unrests' (leading to the Peasants' Uprising), nine 'jubilations' and nine appearances of the children's voices – all as components in what he termed the 'strands in the weave' of his text.[36]

One could continue in this vein – but the purpose of the chapter is close to being accomplished. The summary of Saxton's works after *Caritas* makes it clear that many of the compositions produced in the two decades from 1990 to 2010 (and in the second decade, especially) were used to try out procedures and structures that were being developed with *The Wandering Jew* in mind. Saxton's second opera represents a synthesis of such compositional elements – and also of the twin cultures and faiths that constitute his identity and from which he has drawn so much inspiration. The ancient legend is re-told with literary and musical coherence and the remarkable dialogue between the Jew and Jesus that concludes Scene 7 of the work points to a larger reconciliation between faiths, providing an eminently peaceable solution to an age-old issue. It also underlines the composer's own extraordinary sense of compassion and is a timely reminder of the power of forgiveness in an opera that was ultimately commissioned as a millennium project.

A comparison between *The Wandering Jew* and Saxton's first opera, however, reveals a rather less conciliatory view of religion – not surprisingly, perhaps, bearing in mind that the medieval Catholic Church of *Caritas* was under attack from without and within. It certainly lacked the confidence to tolerate dissent and to learn from it. However, there is something intrinsically human about Christine's terrible

---

[34]   Yggdrasil is the 'world ash tree' from which Odin is seen hanging by his hair at the start of scene 5. At his third attempt, Odin succeeds in lifting the runes (stones) and, thereby, achieves a new life (after nine days of 'sacrifice').

[35]   The five questions are on the subjects of death, suffering, the ravens that fly to him, the rock at his feet, and the fountain at the foot of the tree.

[36]   As previously mentioned, some of the final numberings require revision, depending on changes made subsequently to the libretto. However, these are the groupings found in Wesker's 'working draft' in the Saxton papers.

psychological suffering as she discovers that her expectations are unrealistic. As the audience watches her at the lowest ebb of her existence, they (we) probably experience the same sense of loss that Christ's companions felt at his crucifixion. If *Caritas* does not contain the idealistic certainty attained at the conclusion of *The Wandering Jew*, this is not a criticism of either work – or the composer. Rather, it defines the nature of art; each opera asks different questions; neither exists in isolation.

Chapter 7

Reflections and Projections:
An Interview with Robert Saxton

Note: WT = Wyndham Thomas; RS = Robert Saxton.

WT: Regarding the commissioning of *Caritas*, how much can you recall about the negotiations leading up to the genesis of the opera – was it your idea or was it suggested by Opera North and/or the Huddersfield Festival?

RS: Its inception can be traced back to a conversation with Richard Steinitz (Director of the Huddersfield Contemporary Music Festival) who invited me to discuss a possible operatic project with him. At the time (1986), I was working on an education project for the Leeds Festival and Richard was exploring potential cooperative ventures between *his* festival and Opera North. The idea of adapting Arnold Wesker's play as a chamber opera was introduced by Michael Rennison (then at Opera North but also engaged in directing a production of Henze's *Elegy for Young Lovers* at the QEH [Queen Elizabeth Hall, London], featuring my wife Teresa Cahill). I was immediately attracted by the prospect of working with an established dramatist of Arnold's calibre, particularly when he agreed to provide the libretto himself. Nicholas Payne at Opera North gave the proposal his full support. As it happens, I had already formulated some plans to compose an opera although, oddly enough, the subject I had in mind then was *The Wandering Jew*!

WT: Well, it's good to note that this work has recently been performed on BBC Radio 3, and I have introduced it briefly in Chapter 6 of this book. But how did things proceed with the *Caritas* proposal from that point? Had you seen the play in the theatre; were there detailed talks with Wesker or were you simply provided with the libretto?

RS: Of course I knew of Wesker's plays – especially the trilogy of *Chicken Soup with Barley*; *Roots*; and *I'm Talking about Jerusalem* – but Arnold was wonderfully helpful, sending me a typescript of *Caritas* and inviting me around to listen to a tape of the radio broadcast in his kitchen. Yes, there were detailed talks about the sort of script that a composer might need and he proved very accommodating – although I did make a few changes (for which I hope he has now forgiven me!).

WT: I shan't press you for details, but I am intrigued to know when the plainsong *Alleluia* replaced Psalm 6 in the first scene. Was that your decision?

RS: No, *Alleluia. Te martyrum* was in the opera libretto from the beginning. Perhaps you should ask the librettist about that.[1] However, it *was* my decision to omit the repeat of Christine's song ('I will forsake all that I see …') that Arnold had specified at the end of scene XV of the play (1981 edition), and to supply a shorter instrumental version at the end of the second act of the opera. The sung repeat was restored to its original place in the second edition (1990) of the stage play, although Arnold left out the implied second statement of *Veni Creator Spiritus* (printed at the end of Act 2 in the earlier edition of the play, but only used in the very first scene of the opera).

WT: While we're on this subject, I notice that some changes made for the libretto have involved re-ordering the sequence of certain events as well as truncating scenes from the stage play. For example, the 'sermon' given by the travelling priest is placed *before* Matilde's third (much abbreviated) citation of female recluses[2] and the final two scenes of Act 1 are also reversed.[3] Can you remember who made these decisions and similar judgements?

RS: As a composer yourself, you will realize that creative momentum often necessitates a radical re-appraisal of textual or dramatic events, such as those you mention. Smaller changes (word order, even occasional substitution of 'open' vowels for 'tight' sounds) are often made by the composer – in conjunction with the librettist if circumstances permit – whereas other decisions have to be made almost surgically to maintain the pace of composition and to achieve musical as well as dramatic goals. It is possible that I was encouraged to follow my operatic instincts in these instances – but, ultimately, it is the composer who has to accept responsibility for such decisions, even if supported by directors or singers.

WT: At a more general level, would you like to say how you have benefited from working alongside colleagues as eminent as Arnold Wesker, Patrick Mason, Joe Vaněk and Diego Masson?

RS: The simple answer *has to be* that being surrounded by professionalism of the highest calibre is both stimulating and educative. Diego Masson rehearsed and conducted public performances that now form the basis of the

---

[1]   See Table 3.3 in Chapter 3 for details of the liturgical items in the libretto and the 1981 and 1990 editions of the stage play.

[2]   In the stage play, the 'sermon' takes place in Scene XIII and Matilde's third example of saintliness precedes it in scene XII. In the opera, Matilde's scene (11) *follows* the 'sermon' (scene 10).

[3]   Scene XV of the play contains the Travelling Priest's description of the failed Uprising (and the repeat of Christine's song) and scene XVI contains Bishop Henry's refusal for Christine to leave her cell (followed by the children's chorus). These events are reversed in the opera (as a continuation of scene 12) so that the indignation of Robert and Christine leads into the offstage sounds of battle (orchestral transition) and then the orchestral Ricercar (with the Priest's lines spoken above it).

commercial disc of *Caritas*;[4] Patrick Mason brought the score to life through his imaginative staging, which admirably suited Joe Vaněk's intentionally claustrophobic set; Arnold Wesker's libretto was a wonderful blend of strongly characterized prose and evocative poetry. I could go on ...

WT: Yes, I know what you mean about Wesker's language. Various reviewers have commented on his 'beautifully poetic prose' and *Caritas* being written 'at his poetic best'.[5] Elsewhere in this book I have compared the lyrics of the Act 2 *Lullaby* with medieval Marian poems such as *Mary Complains to other Mothers*, and I personally believe that the so-called *Song of Vows* (Song of Farewell), sung by Christine at the end of Act 1, scene 1, is a masterpiece of succinct alliterative verse – naive, in the true sense, as it applies to the idealistic young anchoress. It seems to me that you have exactly matched the tone and intention of this short poem in an almost folk-like setting. Were you ever tempted to expand the song into an aria by repeating words or phrases?

RS: No, I don't recall being tempted in that direction. The simple smallness of the poem is its essence, I feel. To have dwelt on the text (as in an aria) would probably have run the risk of tampering with its intrinsic innocence.

WT: I take your point. However, to return briefly to the lullaby in Act 2 of *Caritas*, is there an intentional inter-textual reference to Marie's *Cradle Song* from *Wozzeck*? My instinct is that *there is*, but I'm rather less sure about the significance of the 'fatalistic' emphasis on the note B that occurs in scene 9 of the first act – especially the *tremolando* on B that accompanies Christine's supposed showing or vision (in bars 788 and 789). Am I imagining Bergian links?

RS: Well, *Wozzeck* was one of the very first operas that I got to know thoroughly when I was young so it's almost inevitable that my mind will make unconscious connections as well as conscious links with it if I'm dealing with comparable subjects. The lullaby definitely *does* carry an intentional reference to Marie's song. Although they are very different characters, Marie and Christine are each cradling a real or simulated child. The deep sadness of 'a woman taken in adultery' seeking solace in serenading her infant, and a profoundly religious recluse adopting an uncharacteristic (and fundamentally unstable) pose with the model of Christ on her crucifix are fused into a combined image of physical and divine maternal love. As far as the pitch emphasis in scene 9 is concerned, I am unaware of any conscious *Wozzeck* reference. As your analysis demonstrates, the emphasis on B is probably a consequence of its function as the dominant pitch in the overall

---

[4] NMC D102 - the disc included in this book - uses recordings made at premiere performances of *Caritas* at Wakefield Opera House on 21, 23 and 24 November 1991.

[5] Just two of the 'review-bites' quoted on the reverse cover of Arnold Wesker (1960) *Lady Othello and Other Plays* in *Arnold Wesker Plays*, Vol. 6 (London: Penguin Books), which contains the revised text of *Caritas*.

tonal scheme of the opera. However, I would not discount some subliminal connection.

WT: Perhaps we could now consider the relationship between the two acts of the opera? Clearly, there is an obvious reversal of location and mood in the second act in that the audience is allowed access into the cell that had shielded Christine from sight during the first act. We had previously seen Christine only briefly as she was prepared for entry into her anchorage. Thereafter, although she had been heard as she prayed and when she conversed with Matilde, Mathew and other members of the cast, she was effectively invisible. Act 2, however, reveals her to have been profoundly changed by her three years of seclusion. Her deep desire to experience a vision has been denied and she has allowed herself to sink into self-neglect.

Robert, in the first place, when did you decide to transform material from the first act into a parody (in the technical, musical sense)[6] of the original, and did you find this an especially taxing transition to accomplish *musically*? And the use of a passacaglia – presumably it was a deliberate policy to follow the text-led structure of Act 1 with the music-led discipline of the final scene?

RS: I seem to remember describing the twelve scenes of Act 1 as a sort of Bayeux Tapestry of events leading up to the crisis of Christine's madness. In this sense, I had little option but to be led by the regular changes of pace, location and characterization provided by the libretto, albeit utilizing musical motifs that I hope help to connect the often disparate episodes into a coherent unit. The comparison with the portrayal of incidents from the celebrated battle of 1066 is, of course, somewhat flawed, but I did see Act 1 as a series of snapshots that culminated in a more sustained second act, during which the musical score was able to provide its own commentary on the action. In answer to your questions, I decided to recall material such as the *Alleluia* and a few key lines from Act 1 (as well as the children's questions which recur throughout the original play) quite early in the composing process. These 'remembered' themes illustrate Christine's own mental battle between internal and external forces, between orthodoxy and heresy, and between faith and doubt. Much of this re-used material is distorted electronically to reflect Christine's troubled mind – a positive/negative transformation, perhaps?

Regarding the circumstances of composition, I have stated elsewhere that I thoroughly re-ordered Act 2 myself, although all of the words are still Wesker's. The pace of writing the opera was fairly evenly sustained over a period of about eleven months. My decision to incorporate a passacaglia into the final scene has many precedents and, I believe allows the soloist's lines to 'fly free' above the incessant cyclic repetitions of the 'ground' (itself

---

[6]   The term *parody*, is used in the sense that Act 2 uses material from Act 1, in the same way as a Renaissance Mass might be based on an existing song or motet. For example, Dufay's Mass on his chanson, 'Se la face ay pale'.

a reflection of Christine's mental state). This was a process that required careful planning and execution – and was draining emotionally – but it doesn't stand out in my mind as being especially taxing. Incidentally, this might be the moment to comment on the Orchestral Transition and Ricercar that conclude scene 12 (and the first act). Because it was so important for the dramatic text to dominate the previous twelve scenes, this was the first real opportunity for the orchestra to participate in the narrative as an equal partner, as it were, with the voices. The Transition effectively acts out the off-stage battle (complete with 'marching-song') before the prayer for mercy (*Kyrie eleison*) is introduced in the strings and the section merges into the more formal, fugal discipline of the Ricercar – which then serves as a counterpoint to the Priest's report on the Peasants' Uprising. When Act 2 starts, the orchestra has been liberated from its purely accompanimental function in preparation for its new 'narrative' role.

WT: Regarding location of performance, *Caritas* was premiered in 1991 in Wakefield Opera House and then taken to the QEH and the Cheltenham Festival. I still have vivid memories of a later concert performance of Act 2 in St George's Brandon Hill, Bristol, with Tessa singing the main role.[7] What do you think about concert-hall performances of opera?

RS: In general, I approve of such performances, which certainly provide significant opportunities for audiences to revisit (or simply to hear) new operas and for composers to reappraise their own work. Otherwise, a great deal of note-learning (by singers) and intensive rehearsal are not fully utilized, such are the economic constraints of opera house productions. Of course, modern recording technology (both sound and video/film) plays an important part in creating permanent production records and I was fortunate that a CD of *Caritas* appeared so soon after its premiere.[8] In addition, the functional design of Joe Vaněk's set has enabled it to be relocated relatively easily.

WT: Sadly we are coming to the end of our allocated space but I have two specific questions to ask you – the first concerns your future compositional plans and the second is about the influence of Benjamin Britten as your teacher/mentor during your schooldays. As I understand it, you sent him some of your music and he encouraged you to continue composing. How long did he correspond with you and did he see a copy of your early opera *Cinderella*, for example?

RS: Britten was extremely helpful with word-setting. I recall one lesson on my setting of Gray's *Elegy* and he also made suggestions as to what I should compose, for example 'character' pieces like Marches, Waltzes, and so on. I also sent him a Woodwind Trio for comments and, yes, he saw a score of

---

[7]   Brunel Ensemble, conducted by Christopher Austin (17 May 1996). The part of Christine was sung by Teresa Cahill, to whom the opera is dedicated.

[8]   CD first produced by Collins Classics (Lambourne Productions Ltd) in 1992; reissued by NMC Recordings Ltd in 2004 as NMC D102.

Cinderella that he retained in his library at Red House, Aldeburgh. We kept in touch from 1963 until his death in 1976. After Britten suggested that I should find a 'regular' teacher, I continued studies with Elisabeth Lutyens from 1970 to 1974, with Robin Holloway during my final undergraduate year at Cambridge, and with Robert Sherlaw Johnson while a postgraduate at Oxford. Britten was very professional himself and emphasized that I should be equally conscientious (I once received quite a stern letter admonishing me for not keeping up with my 'homework').

WT: And now you find yourself in the position of being a distinguished composition tutor. Is this something you welcome?

RS: I strongly believe that composers in my position *should* do their best to help develop the skills of younger composers. In my case, this has involved working with students at the Guildhall School of Music and Drama, the University of Bristol, the Royal Academy of Music and Oxford University where I am now – and, incidentally, I feel that writing for Stephen Darlington and the Choir of Christchurch, Oxford, is also a great privilege.

WT: But, future plans?

RS: At present, I have a commission for a Cycle for the Oxford Lieder Festival (which will add to the little song I wrote for the twenty-fifth anniversary of NMC [NMC Recordings]) but my main ambition is to compose for dance. This would be a full-length ballet – the scenario is complete in my mind. My sister is a ballet teacher and examiner, so I have some idea what to expect! Like most professional composers, I welcome the challenge of commissions that happen to match my current interests and aspirations.

Appendices

Appendix A
Caritas CD Tracks and Timings
(CD: NMC D102)

Track		Timing
Act 1	**Scene**	
1	1	12'06
2	2	5'09
3	3	3'15
4	4	2'29
5	5	4'11
6	6	5'16
7	7	1`52
8	8	4`53
9	9	4'22
10	10	2'32
11	11	1'02
12	12	11'33
Act 2		
13	13	19'34

Appendix B
Caritas: Original Cast List

Characters	Performers
Christine	Eirian Davies (S)
Bishop Henry of Norwich	Jonathan Best (B)
Robert Lonle, Christine's fiancé	Christopher Ventris (T)
Agnes, Christine's mother	Linda Hibberd (M-S)
William, Christine's father	Roger Bryson (B-Bar)
Richard Lonle, Robert's father	David Gwynne (B-Bar)
Mathew, Christine's parish priest	Paul Wilson (T)
Tax collector	Brian Cookson (T)
Matilde, a village gossip	Linda Ormiston (M-S)
Travelling priest	David Gwynne (B-Bar)
Children's Voices	Trebles (in three-parts) from Allerton Grange Middle School, Leeds
Bailiff	(Acting role)
Villager	(Acting role)
Director:	Patrick Mason
Set Designed by:	Joe Vaněk
Lighting:	Nick Chelton

English Northern Philharmonia conducted by Diego Masson

Appendix C
Caritas Performances

Wakefield Opera House	**Opera North (Diego Masson)**
21, 23 and 24 November 1991 (Recorded for BBC and CD)	
Queen Elizabeth Hall London	**Opera North (Diego Masson)**
1, 2 July 1992	
Cheltenham, Everyman Theatre	**Opera North (Diego Masson)**
11 July 1992	
St George's Brandon Hill Bristol	**Brunel Ensemble (Christopher Austin) Teresa Cahill, soprano**
17 May 1996	Act 2 Concert Performance

Appendix D
Wesker after the *Caritas* Libretto

Note 24 in Chapter 6 briefly mentions the 'coincidence' that, after their cooperation on *Caritas*, both Saxton and Wesker began to focus on works that had their origins in anti-Semitic history. In Saxton's case, the subject of the Wandering Jew (which began as a youthful obsession) was subsequently transformed to conclude with a process of reconciliation, and his eponymous second opera has now been discussed in various sections of this volume. Several of his other compositions have also been based on, or been influenced by, Hebrew texts and Jewish culture. Likewise, a number of Wesker's plays have featured historical Jewish archetypes or communities, so it should come as no surprise that he was attracted by Henry Burke's suggestion that he might consider the twelfth-century tale of the murder of William (a young Skinner's apprentice) and the subsequent 'blood libel' accusations directed at the Jewish community in Norwich.[1]

However, a typed draft of *William of Norwich* – this being one of several early 'working- titles' used by Wesker – found its way into Robert Saxton's *Caritas* papers together with a 'compliments' note from the author, dated 26. x [10]. 91 (the actual draft of the play is dated 3 September 1991). In view of the forthcoming premiere of *Caritas*, and the rather cryptic title page of his new play,[2] perhaps it was possible that Wesker (believing Saxton then to be freed from the onerous duties of scoring the opera) hoped that the composer might consider setting the 'Hymn to St William' and supplying what the author described as 'religious music based on traditional church music … for scene-linking, background and ceremonial moments'.

Whatever the validity of such a conjecture, it is clear that Saxton did not become involved in this particular project,[3] although the music specification (outlined above)

---

[1]   Henry Burke was then the Director/Manager of the Norwich Playhouse, which commissioned Wesker (c.1989) to write a new play for the (re)opening of the Professional Repertory Theatre. It was Burke who introduced the playwright to a relevant chapter in a book on the Jews in medieval Norwich (possibly V.D. Lipman (1967), *The Jews of Medieval Norwich* (London: Jewish Historical Society of England), but more likely Augustus Jessop and Montague R. James (trans. and eds) (1896/2011) *The Life and Miracles of St. William of Norwich by Thomas of Monmouth* (Cambridge: Cambridge University Press) – from which a quotation is included in the title-pages).

[2]   The main title page reads: 'BLOOD LIBEL – a play in four parts – *with music needing to be composed* [my italics] …'.

[3]   The music specified was composed by Derek Barnes who is credited thus in the World Premiere programme (1–17 February 1996).

appears to match very closely that required in the stage-play versions of *Caritas* –
and, in some respects, by the opera libretto. Rather, the significance of the play lies in
the information provided by the playwright concerning his choice and treatment of
historic subjects. Wesker's short programme note in the World Premiere Programme
(see n. 3 for dates) is a model of clarity – as is Alan Webster's *Suffering – The Jews
of Norwich and Julian of Norwich* – which (under its subtitle of *The Persistent Lie*)
provides an admirable context for the play and the author's commentary.[4]

Wesker's note is prefaced by a facsimile of page 1 of his first draft (together with the
printed equivalent) and brief extracts from the correspondence between the playwright
and Henry Burke.[5] The draft evidently perpetuates Wesker's indecision about the title
since the manuscript bears the legend (in underlined capitals) – <u>MARTYRS FOR
SALE</u>. In fact, the first scene is a short sermon, very loosely based on Daniel 3, (the
miracle of the burning fiery furnace), and preached (in c.AD 1110) by Bishop Herbert
de Losinga at Norwich. The similarity (and contrast) with the sermon in *Caritas* needs
no further comment, but what does benefit from emphasis is Wesker's description
of the various options that were open to him when dealing with an historic subject.
In summary, he tells the reader and audience that he chose to select material from
the record (of William's rape and murder) written by Thomas of Monmouth and to
comment on its veracity; that his comment would come from three areas: the rape
scene; Prior Elias's personality; and Hethel's dream,[6] in which she was being chased
by Jews. From a further set of options, Wesker then chose to lay out the play as a crime
story and to make a ritual out of the exposition rather than a naturalistic narrative:

> I chose crime and ritual. Naturalistic detail characterises my two other historically
> set plays – *Shylock* and *Caritas*. This time I wanted to make the play an unfolding
> drama involving ritual. Put another way: I wanted to build a drama out of large
> primary blocks rather than minute details – the difference between naturalistic and
> abstract painting, between, say, Constable and Ben Nicholson.[7]

Such declarations might seem to imply that the (opposite) approach adopted in
Caritas had necessarily culminated in a decision to reach a dramatic conclusion (or
solution) to the detailed events that had been included in the play's (naturalistic)
narrative, whereas in *Blood Libel* the events, being set out as a ritual, are permitted
to speak for themselves. That certainly is the impression gained from a reading of
the later play and, conversely, perhaps, a justification for Wesker's use of the story
of Christine to define political attitudes.

---

[4]   Alan Webster (1981) *Suffering – The Jews of Norwich and Julian of Norwich* (London:
St Paul's Lecture).

[5]   Dated 30 June, 5 July and 14 July, 1989.

[6]   Hethel was William's aunt (sister of his mother).

[7]   'Arnold Wesker's Notes on *William of Norwich*' in the Norwich Playhouse programme
for the world premiere of Arnold Wesker's *Blood Libel*, 1 – 17 February 1996.

Appendix E
Caritas Libretto

ACT ONE

SCENE 1

July 1377

The interior of the church of St James in the village of Pulham St Mary, Norfolk; a carpenter's workshop; the window and part of the anchoress's cell anchored in the church wall.

CHRISTINE, daughter of WILLIAM the carpenter, is about to be immured in the cell.

Sound of "Alleluia, Te martyrum". Light slowly touches the opening in the wall. This is the first thing we see. Huge stones alongside, waiting to be put in place.

Light then touches the solitary figure of CHRISTINE, who stands before the altar, her back to us.'

Light next touches the carpenter's workshop where stand three rough but solid pieces of furniture: a small table, a chair, a hard wooden bed. They are for CHRISTINE's cell, made by her father. The bed is not complete. One side is down and needs to be dovetailed to complete the frame, after which the boards must be hammered into position.

HENRY, Lord Bishop of Norwich, enters, followed by MATHEW DE REDEMAN, rector of the church; and then CHRISTINE's parents, WILLIAM and AGNES, followed by CHRISTINE's ex-fiancé, ROBERT LONLE, followed by an old villager, MATILDE, and two others, a VILLAGER and the BISHOP's CLERK. A strong smell of incense is in the air.

During this beginning, AGNES stands before her daughter and begins to unbutton her dress. She is so distressed that she cannot complete the task. Sobbing, she is taken aside by her husband, WILLIAM.

MATILDE, the old villager, takes over and soon the girl is in a white chemise. Another VILLAGER stands by with CHRISTINE's habit in his arms.

CHRISTINE prostrates herself. BISHOP and RECTOR stand before her. BISHOP holds a cross in front of her. MATHEW sprinkles her three times with holy water, then three times with incense. BISHOP raises her up. Two lighted tapers are placed in her hands.

BISHOP
O God who dost cleanse the wicked and willest not the death of a sinner, we humbly beseech Thy majesty that in Thy goodness Thou wilt guard Thy servant, Christine, who trusteth in Thy heavenly aid, that she may ever serve Thee and no trials may part her from Thee. Through our Lord, Jesus Christ.

ALL
Amen.

CHRISTINE moves forward, places her candles before the altar, steps back, reads her profession from a document.

CHRISTINE
I, sister Christine, offer and present myself in the goodness of God to serve in the order of an anchoress, and according to the rule of the order I promise to remain in the service of God through the grace of God and the guidance of the church.

A pen is handed to her. She scratches the sign of the cross. Returns to stand before the altar. She is helped on with her rough habit as the BISHOP intones:

BISHOP
May God put off from thee the old woman, may God clothe thee with the new woman, for you who yearn passionately for union with God are created in righteousness and true holiness.

ALL
Amen.

CHRISTINE prostrates herself before the altar.

AGNES, WILLIAM and ROBERT break away to the workshop. She to finish the last stitch on a tablecloth, they to finish making the bed.

ROBERT
I know her passions. They have more to do with her than heaven.

AGNES
Why? Why? I ask her, she tell me, but I understand nothing.

WILLIAM
And it's just you who should!

AGNES (*Ignoring that*)
"Alright", I say, "You want to retreat? But fasting? Beating? Praying hours on end? Weave!" I tell her. "Collect for the poor, comfort the grieving. Where be the virtue of suffering? The divine spark is offended by suffering".

CHRISTINE
Life offend the divine spark, I must renounce life and good deeds for the divine spark.

ROBERT
And me! She were betrothed to me. She renounced me –

CHRISTINE
– to marry Christ! To marry him I truly loved.

AGNES
Nothing! I understand nothing, nothing!

CHRISTINE
Heaven! Heaven! The truth is revealed in heaven.

AGNES
If heaven is where all truth is revealed, then it must be hell!
(*To* WILLIAM) Books! Books! I warned against books!

WILLIAM
Piety! Too much piety! Who took her from the love of fairs and dancing? Who talked her silly about angels, heaven, hell, the suffering of the Lord!

AGNES
Books, I warned against books!

WILLIAM
Who had a daughter lock herself in tiny rooms for months on end? More passion than a child should take.

AGNES
Books, I warned against books!

ROBERT
She'll miss them fairs.

AGNES

The tumbling and juggling and wrestling, she loved all that.

WILLIAM

There! A table and a chair for I don't know what. And a hard bed to prevent her sleeping too well!

ROBERT

Suppose we must be thankful she didn't ask for a coffin to sleep in.

They place the chair and table on the bed and carry all through the hole in the wall. Soon they return as the intoning of the hymn "Veni Creator Spiritus" comes to an end. The ceremony continues over the prostrate CHRISTINE. MATHEW goes to the altar, plucks up one of CHRISTINE's candles.

ALL

Glory be to the Father, and to the Son, and to the Holy Ghost; as it was in the beginning, is now, and ever shall be, world without end, Amen.

CHRISTINE rises. MATHEW turns, hands the taper to her. The BISHOP takes her hand, the others form a procession behind. They move towards the hole. The procession moves through the family.

WILLIAM

No more games for you, my girl, your running, dancing days are done, all your fleet, sweet, days, sweet daughter.

ROBERT (*Angry*)

She've seen blue skies, she won't forget. She've seen mares mate, she've seen lambs skip, calves suck, the setting sun, the rivers run; and once, she've seen me naked, oh she won't forget.

The BISHOP and CHRISTINE into the cell, saying:

BISHOP

The Kingdom of the world –

ALL

– and all the glory of it have I despised for the love of my Lord Jesus Christ, whom I have seen, whom I have loved, in whom I have believed, whom I have chosen for myself.

CHRISTINE enters.

BISHOP
"Go my people, enter into thy chamber, shut thy doors upon thee, hide thyself a little, for a moment until the indignation pass away".

In nomine patris filii et spiritus sancti.

The **BISHOP** *leads the procession off to the Gregorian chant which began the ceremony: "Alleluia, Te martyrum".* **TWO VILLAGERS** *slowly block up the entrance. It is a chilling sight.*

The cell is walled up.

Empty. Silence. Then – a song is heard. **CHRISTINE** *is singing to herself, very sweetly, calmly.*

CHRISTINE
I will forsake all that I see, father, friend and follow Thee, gold and goods, riches and rent, town and tower and tenement, playing and prosperity, in poverty for to be one with Thee.

Between many of the scenes, like punctuations or comment will be heard – loud or soft, vicious or sympathetic – the chanting of children. Like a street game. Now we hear it tenderly.

CHILDREN'S VOICES
Christine, Christine. Had a vision, had a revelation yet? Had a vision, had a word? Christine, had a revelation yet? Had a vision, had a word?

SCENE 2

Some months later.
A loud scream is heard from a man. **RICHARD LONLE** *is dragged into the centre space by a* **BAILIFF**. *His hands are tied behind his back. He kneels with his back to us. The* **BAILIFF** *carries a brazier of hot coals with an iron poking from it.*

BISHOP *and* **MATHEW** *appear.*

LONLE
Hypocrites! You preach labourers should be freed from all estates except your own!

BISHOP
You will be branded here, before the church, a warning to others.

LONLE
The law says if I live in a town for a year and a day I've earned my freedom.

BISHOP
You were caught before then.

LONLE
Three days! Three more days!

BISHOP
And why should you have wanted to leave? The manor made you, rented you land, guarded you in sick times. Was I a bad lord? When labour is scarce, you run away! And why? To claim your freedom! No man's free! Responsibilities, duties, bind us all!

MATHEW (*Reads from manorial roll. His heart's not in it*)
Richard Lonle, bondsman to the manor of Henry, Lord Bishop of Norwich, you are charged with absconding from your place of work, withdrawing services, dispersing family, for which a right and proper jury found you guilty. In return for service, Henry has restored your lands. On your knees. Be grateful, be prepared. On your forehead with hot iron, must be branded a sign to neighbour and God that you had broken bond.

BISHOP (*Calling*)
Bailiff!

MATHEW holds the victim, and turns away in horror.

The BAILIFF plucks the hot iron and brands LONLE on the forehead.

He screams, faints. The BAILIFF drags him away.

BISHOP and MATHEW move up into the church.

BISHOP
You think I shouldn't brand a man.

MATHEW
The times are changing, Lord Bishop.

BISHOP
The church decides if times are changing.

MATHEW

The church did not decide a plague – robbing labour from the land.

BISHOP

God's plagues are God's affair. God's church is ours, to be obeyed no matter what John Wycliffe says. John Wycliffe! An intellectual! Destroy the power of priests, he says. Leave every man consult his conscience, he says. Well, let me say, give heed to him and you'll have chaos! Chaos!

(*Calmer*) Forgive me, rector. Talk too loud. Unsettled times. Learnt words. Pursued my duty – developed passions for the land. I love the earth and seasons. I must attend to what I love. And let me tell you something else. I don't approve of them! (*Pointing to the anchoress's cell*)

MATHEW

Says her prayers, eats little; from her window, gives advice, confesses through her quatrefoil. The 'old life' clings to her; hasn't found the new one yet.

BISHOP

Fervours! Tantrums and fervours! "She's called, Lord Bishop, her vocation, Lord Bishop". I always warned – some cannot bear the touch of God, they scream loud hymns and prayers to drown him out. Fervours! Tantrums and fervours!

SCENE 3

Light up on a cell and window. **ROBERT**, *alone, outside* **CHRISTINE**'s *cell.*

ROBERT (*Angry*)

It's not God you serve but a devil of your own. God didn't make you for that hole. He made you for the world, the world for you.

CHRISTINE

In here's the world, out there is clutter.

ROBERT

Cruelty, unreason, killing.
That's not God a-calling,
that's man, cruel man a-driving.

CHRISTINE
Don't taunt me Robert Lonle,
pray for me. You love me,
pray for me.

ROBERT
Black is white and white is black,
your words are wind and mist.

CHRISTINE
I have no other words.

ROBERT
Try village words, and fairground words!

CHRISTINE
Love, Robert, love!
I can't say more;
I'm filled with love for Him
who took upon himself great suffering and death,
so we might be redeemed.
That makes me weep.

Long pause

They tell a story. Mother and son. Lived at the foot of high mountains. The boy was drawn. Had to climb. The spirit of the mountains drew him. "No!" his mother begged. But come the day he knew his strength, he climbed! Climbed. His mother watched, watched and feared. The long days passed. She marvelled, proud, but Oh the ache, the ache, the helpless ache. For what was life without her lovely loving son? To be with him, to tread his road, share the pain, share the fate. Adored him, see? She would retrace his steps. There were no other way.

Sounds of taunting children.

CHILDREN'S VOICES
Christine, Christine, had a revelation yet? Had a vision, had a word, had a revelation yet? Had a vision, had a word?

ROBERT (*Shouting at the children*)
Get off! Get away with you! Get off! Off!

SCENE 4

Carpenter's workshop. WILLIAM *and* ROBERT *are answering the questions of the* TAX COLLECTOR, *who's writing on sheets propped on a sawn tree trunk. We don't need to hear all the questions and answers.*

TAX COLLECTOR *looks questioningly to* WILLIAM, *who nods, then* TAX COLLECTOR *writes. Repeat as often as music requires. Moves on to* AGNES, *same procedure, until:*

COLLECTOR
The anchoress! A chastening rebuke! But I confess, I am a mortal man, a tax collector full of sins and shames. Temptation shreds my soul. I struggle hard against excess and self, self-indulgent luxuries, but no control, no control! God's indignation flares, but what I am, I am. What's there to do?

WILLIAM
There speaks a city man.

COLLECTOR
Correct! The solitary life is not for me. I'm reverent and full of awe, but no control. You must be proud

His tone is casual. The men are silent. The TAX COLLECTOR *looks around and then at* WILLIAM *for confirmation.*

WILLIAM
Aye, carpenter.

COLLECTOR (*Writes*)
Carpentarius. Now, possessions! And I want to hear everything. You know the penalty for hoarding. Although – arrangements can be made; eyes closed, this and that ignored. (*Smiles*)

WILLIAM (*Coldly ignoring invitation of bribe*):
Three saws, two axes, a spokeshave, two adzes, two hammers, four oxen, seven steers, two cows, two and a half quarters of winter wheat, five quarters of oats …

SCENE 5

WILLIAM'*s voice dies away as* CHRISTINE'*s voice from the cell takes over.*

CHRISTINE
There was a oneness time,
I search that,
when my soul were with my body,
and my body were with me
and all was one with God
and nature.
And Oh!
There was peace.
A rightness
and a knowing of my place.
'Tis that I search, Lord Jesus.

Old MATILDE, *the busybody and gossip, enters and places her stool beneath the window, cards her wool and chatters.*

MATILDE
You crossed you mouth?
Your eyes?
You crossed your ears, you crossed your breasts?
This village here is filled with men
and idle hags
with soft tongues and long tongues,
and boys with taunts and lewd eyes.
Your mother brings you food? Good!
Now here's a story 'bout a Belgie saint,
I heard it from a Smithy who, in turn,
was told it by a pilgrim nun to Rome,
which as you know, is how my stories come.

Yvetta, named, poor girl,
at sixteen wedded, bedded, claimed,
and bearing many children long before
her husband die and leave her free to quit
the world and live a leper's life of pain.
Shouldn't catch me doing that!
Then she were enclosed
like you, enclosed.
Such tempting dreams of lust assailed her,
Oh she flog her poor 'ol limbs
and ate baked flour and prayed,
and genuflected, wept and struck her breasts,
and slept on pointed rocks. She were all bone!

And she did die the day she prophesy;
Her hand outstretched, with eyes upraised to heaven.
Three score and ten she were. And when she die,
it was the winter, but the birds, they say,
like summer sang, and on her face there gleamed
a brilliant, brilliant summer glow.
That was a day!

SCENE 6

Inside the church. MATHEW *by the quatrefoil taking confession from* CHRISTINE.

CHRISTINE
Oh all you blessed angels and saints of God! A most miserable sinner, pray for me
that I may turn from evil ways, and lock forever my poor heart with yours in eternal
love, nevermore to go astray. Amen.
I have sinned father, I have sinned.

MATHEW
What sins, daughter?

CHRISTINE
I find pleasure in my cell.

MATHEW
Who told you pleasure was a sin?

CHRISTINE
I look forward to each day.

MATHEW
That is a joy.

CHRISTINE
I feel my suffering is false. I feel a fraudulence, deceit; I feel an emptiness.

MATHEW
Be patient, child.

CHRISTINE
Not to suffer is a sin.

MATHEW
What foolishness is this, Christine?

CHRISTINE
Chains! Haircloth! I *want* my chains. I *want* my haircloth!

MATHEW
You want, you want! Those are the sins.

CHRISTINE
Chains! Haircloth!

MATHEW
Enfeebled bodies cannot sing the praise of God.

CHRISTINE
My body needs the pain to help me concentrate on Him.

MATHEW
What harmony can torn flesh know?

CHRISTINE
Our Lord's torn flesh brought harmony.
His suffering brought peace.

MATHEW
Suffering brings suffering.

CHRISTINE
I'm selfish. Wilful! I must destroy my selfish will.

MATHEW
For which you'll need your will again.

CHRISTINE
Do I have God or Satan here?

Pause

MATHEW
Beware, Christine. Into a life of solitude creep many evil bests; the serpent of venomous envy, the bear of sloth, the fox of covetousness …

CHRISTINE
… the swine of gluttony, the scorpion with the tail of stinking lechery!

MATHEW
The lion of pride, and the unicorn of wrath!

Pause

CHRISTINE
I know them!

MATHEW
I will come another time.

CHRISTINE calls after MATHEW as AGNES arrives with clothes and food for her daughter.

CHRISTINE
My chains! My haircloth! My chains! My haircloth!

AGNES (*To MATHEW*)
See! I warned! You thought an anchoress would grace your church. I thought her solitary life would free her for love of God. But love imprisons, intoxicates, clouds the truth of things.

Now moonlight falls on CHRISTINE's cell as she whispers desperately to herself.

CHRISTINE
A showing! A showing!
Give me, Lord, a showing!
Jesus Christ before me, weep!
Gentle crucifix before me, bleed!
Let Your passion touch me, Lord.
Let Your whispers reach me, Lord.
Christine craves, craves a showing, Lord.
Every day of darkness, Lord!
In her cell of darkness, Lord.
A showing, a showing!
Give me, Lord, a showing.

AGNES and MATHEW exchange looks of despair. She passes food and clothing into her daughter's cell.

AGNES turns to MATHEW.

AGNES
Why? Why? Why?

As they leave, MATILDE *arrives.*

SCENE 7

CHRISTINE*'s cell.* MATILDE *arrives, places her stool, cards her wool and listens.*

CHRISTINE
Rumours, rumours, I hear rumours whispered,
that another place exists;
that a state of grace could grow.

Nothing fit. Rumour come and say it could.
Never could I love myself.
Rumour whispered I was loved.
Sometimes, when I listened,
I imagined I could hear the truth.

That were echoes, echoes, echoes.
So I rage and weep and start again.
Beware echoes, but attend
The whispered rumours,
whispered rumours.

MATILDE
Rumours, rumours, whispered rumours,
Beware echoes but attend the rumours.

She leaves, shrugging, utterly bewildered.

CHILDREN'S VOICES (*Taunting*)
Christine, Christine, had a vision, had a word, had a revelation yet? Had a vision, had
a word, had a revelation yet? Christine, Christine, Christine …

SCENE 8

Carpenter's workshop. February 1379.

WILLIAM, AGNES *and* ROBERT *are arguing with the* TAX COLLECTOR.

AGNES
The King had tax from us, two years ago.

COLLECTOR
This money's needed for the safety of the realm, and to support the army in its wars abroad.

WILLIAM
The wars in France. Disastrous wars. Costly, disastrous, losing wars.

COLLECTOR
They pay me to collect the tax, not judge how it is spent.

ROBERT (*Threateningly*)
We hear from Kent a tax collector raped a farmer's girl.

COLLECTOR (*Frightened*)
Well that's in Kent, that was him. This is Norfolk, this is me.

ROBERT
The farmers hung him!

TAX COLLECTOR flees.

AGNES
I do believe this tax collector's shit himself!

Evening. AGNES lays out a meal.
The family sit over beer and cheese, animated by the events they discuss.

AGNES
I hear plans, I hear plotting.

WILLIAM
Grazing places gone, forbid to hunt and fish.

ROBERT
A third tax coming!

AGNES
There'll be killings.

WILLIAM
What's the sense?

AGNES
Sit on people, you get killings.

ROBERT
A third tax coming!

AGNES
I hear plans, I hear plotting.

MATHEW enters. AGNES pours him a drink. ROBERT eyes him anxiously.

MATHEW
No grammar for him, says the Bishop.

ROBERT
The yearly levy, that he'll take. And when we use his mill to grind his corn, he'll levy that. Of course the Bishop will refuse me grammar. If we study words, we leave!

AGNES
And have your forehead branded like your father?

ROBERT
That was then. But now he wants his son to read. The English word is born. The French has died, and Christine should have been my teacher, guide.

All sit in silence for a while.

MATHEW
She sits demanding visions. Now! At once! When some have waited sixty years and not been graced. She was not made for solitude.

AGNES
The dawn appears. She rises, genuflects.
And kneels upon that bed,
 and with bowed body prays,
and prays, and prays some more.
And praying still and mumbling still,
she dresses into God knows what.
I took her once a day a shift,
until she said: each week!

and now each month!
And soon she'll live a year in one foul dress
and Oh, the filth, the misery and pain.
For what? I ask myself, for what?
(*Weeps*) My girl, my girl, my own poor girl.

MATHEW
To give up now, she knows there's only excommunication, fire and hell.

WILLIAM
She was not made for solitude, nor you to be a priest, it seems.

MATHEW
For this church, no!

SCENE 9

Interior of church. MATHEW *at silent prayer.* CHRISTINE *is heard praying.*

CHRISTINE
We adore thee, O Christ, and bless Thee, because of Thy holy cross. Thou hast redeemed the world. We adore Thy cross, O Lord. Hail, O holy cross, worthy tree, whose precious wood bore the ransom of the world.

Hail O (*She breaks off in ecstasy*)
Oh! Oh! A showing!

(*She can hardly believe it*)

A showing! I have a showing! There, before me!

MATHEW *raises his head.*

[CHRISTINE:]   Shape! Lord Jesus shows me how the world has shape. I see its joins, I see its links, I see what clasps and holds it firm. The hole, the dowel, the dove-tail, mortise, tenon. I hear the flower blossom, oh I see the harvest grow, know the colour of the wind, the dark in the light. It joins and locks and fits and rhymes. That's not an echo, Lord, I see the truth, the shape. The mystery gone. I begged and prayed, the cross! The tree! The precious wood! And now the spark, divine and burning – you have give to me a showing! You have give to me a showing!

MATHEW
Beware, Christine, beware the vision.
Satan's stratagems delude, Christine.
Beware, beware the vision.

CHRISTINE
The dark in the light? Did I say "the dark in the light"?
(*Sadly realising the vision is false*) That were no showing, then?

Pause

CHRISTINE (*Brutally*)
Who'll rid my cell of its foul stench?

MATHEW
Christine? Christine? Are you alright? Shall I confess you?

CHRISTINE (*Hissing*):
Go away!

CHILDREN'S VOICES:
Christine, Christine, Christine, had a revelation yet?
Had a vision, had a word? Christine, Christine, Christine …

SCENE 10

Inside the church. June 17, 1381.

A TRAVELLING PRIEST is giving a 'sermon'. But not to the audience, rather from a pulpit to a congregation of those on stage.

PRIEST
"Blow ye the trumpet in Zion, and sound an alarm on my holy mountain". Thus saith the prophet Joel.

Beloved! In our land new sermons; to each man hath God given conscience! Therefore unto your priests say this: one vicar cannot be upon the earth, for each is vicar to himself.

"Beat your ploughshares into swords, your pruning hooks to spears: let the weak say, 'I am strong'". Thus saith the prophet Joel.

Wat Tyler leads one hundred, thousand men; Canterbury opens up her gates; the manor records burn, and mad John Ball is snatched from jail to sing his lovely sermons to us all.

"Good people, goods must be in common held. What right have Lords to Lordship, clothed in velvet, we in rags! When Adam delved and Eve span, who was then the gentleman?"

D'you like these songs? They sing them from the coast of Kent to the Wash.

"And it shall come to pass that I will pour my spirit on your flesh; and your sons and your daughters shall prophesy, your old shall dream dreams, your young men shall see visions." Thus saith the prophet Joel! And –

BISHOP HENRY storms in.

BISHOP (*Calling*):
In my church?
Blasphemy and treason in my church?

The TRAVELLING PRIEST tries to avoid him, dodging here and there.

BISHOP
Bailiff! Rector! Who opens God's house to the wandering blasphemer?

PRIEST
Now reigneth pride in place,
And covertise is counted wise,
And lechery withouten shame,
And gluttony withouten blame.

BISHOP
I'll have you hung, drawn and quartered!
You'll burn in hell!

The PRIEST flees.

CHRISTINE screams.

CHRISTINE (*Voice of dread*):
I do not have the vocation! Release me! I do not have it!

SCENE 11

MATILDE enters, places her stool, cards her wool.
CHRISTINE mocks and mimics MATILDE.

MATILDE
You crossed your mouth?

CHRISTINE (*Mocking*):
You crossed your mouth?

MATILDE (*Ignoring her tone*):
Good! An' your eyes?

CHRISTINE
An' you eyes?

MATILDE
An' your ears?

CHRISTINE
An' your ears?

MATILDE
An' your breasts?

CHRISTINE
An' your breasts?

MATILDE
Good!

CHRISTINE and MATILDE:
Your mother bring your food?

MATILDE
Good!

She senses something wrong. Waits.

MATILDE
Now here's a story.

She's uncertain what is wrong or what to do. Risks another story.

MATILDE
Now here's a story 'bout a holy soul.
No anchoress, no special saint or such,
but how shall I describe her? She was touched by God ...

CHRISTINE screams loudly three times

MATILDE goes off, unable to finish her tale ...

SCENE 12

Inside the church – lit away from the cell wall. The BISHOP is joined by MATHEW, who brings with him AGNES, WILLIAM and ROBERT.

BISHOP (*To ROBERT, pointing to the cell*)
See where books and reading lead? To notions which have lives that chain you, grab you, bind you, hold you.

Poverty, obedience and chastity she vowed. For unity with God! The perfect state! Upon her head the perfect state! A vow's a vow!

He pauses to collect his temper.

Tell me what you want.

*Now begins a **TRIO**.*

AGNES
She's our only child, Bishop, sir, our only child. Let her go. No sons to help our work, look after our old age and bring us heirs. This life on earth is hard. Let her go. A promised heaven then, a family now, what else is there? She give our Lord three precious years. She tried to please God and the church. Let them be pleased enough, Lord Bishop, sir. Let her go.

WILLIAM
What's to be gained from a reluctant solitary, Lord? Let her go. You want your folk to take example from your anchoress. She must give courage, light, a standard set. What standard can my poor girl set? Let her go. She've gone in there to fill her head and heart but, look, she've emptied them instead. No light, or standard, Lord, no use to God or church. Let her go.

ROBERT
She were betrothed to me for love of me. Let her go. She were betrothed to me for love of me, and I for love of her. There's not a week passed these three years I've not sat with her, and she talk, and talk. And I know that she loves me still. Let her go, and we'll be married. You'll hear nothing of us more if you relent. Let her go.

Pause.

BISHOP
We have no power to sanction breaking of a vow.
She cannot leave her cell.

The BISHOP leaves, followed by a distressed MATHEW.

WILLIAM, AGNES and ROBERT are shattered.

Now a red glow slowly grows like a house burning, as we hear the CHILDREN'S VOICES.

Time passes.

CHILDREN'S VOICES
Christine, Christine, had a revelation yet, had a vision, had a word, had a revelation yet?

CHRISTINE
Not fit, not fit! You have hell anchored to your church, Bishop Henry. Break down its walls, break them, break them. In the name of God, BREAK THEM DOWN!

ROBERT picks up her cry, but he is referring to unjust laws.

ROBERT
Break them down! Break them down!

WILLIAM tries to hold ROBERT back but he runs off to join the revolt.

WILLIAM consoles AGNES.

We hear drums and marching feet. The Peasants' Revolt is underway.

The red glow lingers. Time has passed. The TRAVELLING PRIEST enters, carrying the dead ROBERT in his arms. AGNES is in tears.
The PRIEST, himself in tatters and blood-stained, walks slowly, as though showing the carnage to onlookers.

PRIEST'S VOICE
London. The boy King met Wat Tyler at Mile End – agreed to his demands. Exhilerating. Shivers down my spine. Then the mood changed. Intoxicated with their gains and power, a people's court beheaded Sudbury and Hales, which intoxicated passions more, and then the crude and rough ones surfaced to pay off ancient scores.

I shouted, warned, but there were quick and easy tongues to call me traitor. We come to Smithfield where we give the King a second paper of demands. "Come talk to us", he says.

Wat Tyler, goaded by the quick and easy mob, stepped to the other side. The Mayor of London killed him. Quick and easy. That was that!

The 'Freedom Charters' were withdrawn. John Ball sang one last sermon, and was hung, drawn and quartered at St Albans – and the rest came home (*looking at* ROBERT's *dead body*) one way or another.

Slowly the funeral procession begins to move. The dead boy is carried off. WILLIAM *and* AGNES *follow. During this the wall revolves slowly. We see the inside of the cell. Backed against the wall is* CHRISTINE. *The sight of her is shocking. She is dirty, unkempt and terrified, as her eyes take in what she realises is to be her cell forever.*

The lights slowly fade on the funeral procession.

ACT TWO *(SCENE 13)*

CHRISTINE *in the corner of her cell, terrified.*

CHRISTINE (*intoning*)
I am nothing, I have nothing,
I desire nothing, save the love of Jesus only.

She moves to kneel before her crucifix.

Oh Jesus Christ, whose flesh were torn – comfort me. Deliver me and show me mercy, Lord. I tried, my Lord, I gave, my Lord, I thought I heard You speak, but that were Satan, Lord.

She returns to the corner of her cell.

(*intoning*) I am nothing, I have nothing, I desire nothing, save the love of Jesus only.

Sound of taunting children outside the grill window of her cell. She ignores them, sits in her corner.

CHILDREN'S VOICES
Christine, Christine, had a vision, had a word?
Had a revelation yet? Christine, Christine …

CHRISTINE
I must return to the living!

CHRISTINE *by the quatrefoil.*

Alone in the silence, in the dark!
I see the truth, that's noisy, truth.
Anchoresses hear the truth,
more than they can bear. Help me,
Father, or I'll go mad with all the noise.
Deliver me, deliver me ….
(*Intoning*) I am nothing, I have nothing,
save the love of Jesus only.

She lies on the bed, gazing upwards, motionless.

Suddenly she sits bolt upright and swivels round, her face alight with a new thought.

There's not one God, there's two!
Why put good *and* evil in the world?
There *must* be two! Both made the world!

She is incredulous at the thought – panic enters her voice.

Oh Lord! To which do I pray?
Kneeling before the crucifix.

(*Intoned with desperation*)
Hail Mary, full of grace!
The Lord is with Thee; blessed art Thou amongst women; blessed
is the fruit of Thy womb, Jesus.

She starts to pace up and down the cell.

That's a blasphemous thought, Christine Carpenter.
Two Gods! There are two Gods!

She continues to pace up and down her cell.
The BISHOP *and* MATHEW *talk to her through the quatrefoil. They can't be seen by the audience.*

BISHOP
That's heresy!

CHRISTINE
Let Christine go.

BISHOP
D'you still love Christ? Still long for union with God?

CHRISTINE
Not fit! Not fit!

BISHOP
It's not a temptation of the devil?

CHRISTINE
No! No! The Lord spoke,
A God of love, a God of hate.
"I am the good God's son, the evil One had Satan".

All you see, and all what's been,
and all that ever will be seen,
the two of them created.

BISHOP
Unprovable!

MATHEW
Like the teaching of our church.

BISHOP
You'll do well to find another parish …

MATHEW
Or another church!

CHRISTINE
There are no Gods, there are no sons.

Would a God of love put evil in your heart?
Answer me!

You have hell anchored in your church,
Father. Break down its walls.
In the name of God, break them down!

A LITTLE GIRL appears. CHRISTINE moves to the window grill and gives advice to the little girl.

When you are dead, your soul will go
to terrors which in life you sow.
If you can live without fear
your soul will soar to heavens dear.
You live like that, my little friend,
life without terror, till the end.

CHRISTINE runs to kneel before the crucifix. A routine must be established.

CHILDREN'S VOICES
Christine, Christine, had a revelation yet, had a vision, had a word? Christine, Christine …

CHRISTINE (*Fervent*):
Hail O Cross, dedicated to the body of Christ, and adorned with his limbs, as with pearls. Save the sound and heal the sick.

She strikes her breast hard.

CHRISTINE rises quickly from her kneeling position, and sits on the small wooden stool. She rises, and dusts the table, bed and stool with the end of her dress. She searches for her hairbrush. She combs her hair.

CHRISTINE (*To herself*):
They think you're mad, so comb your hair, and bring back the running girl, dancing girl, girl-at-the-fair, girl who made the village proud.

She laughs and moves to the window to speak to the little girl again.

There's no meaning, girl, purpose only, to do good.
A word, a deed, an act.
The poor fed.
A word forgiven in love …

The purpose is to love.
Lord Jesus Christ loved
you so, He died for you. Love, girl …

She is jubilant, and continues brushing her hair.

There, Christine! Mad?
She'll go away and say Christine gave her good advice.
Word will spread to the Bishop, then the Pope.
You'll see, you'll see …

CHRISTINE *runs to kneel before the crucifix.*

Hail Mary, full of grace! The Lord is with Thee;
blessed art Thou amongst women;
blessed is the fruit of Thy womb, Jesus.
The remedy for pride is humility, for envy, love.
For anger, patience,
For sloth, work,
For avarice, a generous heart.
The remedy for lust is mortification of the flesh.

Mortification of the (*screamed*) FLESH!
(*Shouted*) Help, mercy. O mother! Tell them I have no vocation.
I'm not fit. NOT FIT …

*She goes into the corner of her cell, picks up a heavy crucifix and offering it a bare
breast, she begins to rock it like a babe.*

The poor wail, the orphan sighs, the widow is desolate, the pilgrim needs water;
there's danger for the voyager, hardship for the soldier, cares for the Bishop.
Come to me, come to me.

LULLABY
I've loved him from cradle-time.
No smile like my baby's.
They humiliate him now. I can't comfort him.
No cry like my baby's.
There are thorns on his head.
I can't comfort him.
The smell of oil upon his skin; the trust in his eyes
as I wrapped him warm.
They give his poor body a cross to bear.

I can't comfort him.
They nail him now.
My own, my flesh, my blood.
Did I feed and watch and guard you for this?
Did we look at blue skies, the mare mating, the lamb sucking,
sun setting, the rivers run – for this?

ROBERT (*Voice offstage echoing in* CHRISTINE's *mind*):
Did we look at blue skies, the lamb sucking, sun setting, *for this*?

AGNES (voice offstage)
She gave our Lord three precious years. Let her go.

WILLIAM (*voice offstage*)
No use to God or Church. Let her go.

BISHOP (*voice offstage*)
May God put off from thee the old woman.

CHRISTINE
Put nails through me!
Pierce my hands, pierce my feet!
Me! Oh the helpless ache.

CHRISTINE by the quatrefoil, her back to the wall.

It's my thoughts, Father.
I can't put my thoughts on Him.
I see Him on the cross.
I see that sweet face suffering,
I see that poor body hanging limp on its nails.

She stretches out her arms as though welcoming an embrace.

I close my eyes and cry out:
"Lord Jesus, sweet Lord, I'm
with you, I feel the pain …"
And then, and then …

She stands, legs apart, arms outstretched.

Oh, forgive me, Father!
I think new thoughts. So sweet, so sweet. I'm naked.

My body open to the sky.
Ah! my skin in the grass, sun on my breasts; so sweet.
I feel cool winds bring scents; hawthorn, wild mint.
Birds sweep high.
Oh, those clouds, sweet scents; soft air.
Ah! They're not forms of the devil.
The spring, Father, the spring!
I am crucified upon the spring!

The CHILDREN's *hands wave through the grill.*

CHILDREN'S VOICES
Christine, Christine, had a vision, had a word, had a revelation yet?
(*Also heard is "Alleluia, Te martyrum", which gradually becomes louder and distorts – in many parts.*)

CHRISTINE *grabs a waving hand and plunges her teeth into it. There is a terrible scream which gradually fades.*

CHRISTINE *looks around her cell. She turns to a wall, places her hand on it and turns her head slowly, looking around the cell. The lights slowly fade, until only a faint glimmer comes through the grill. Then darkness.*

CHRISTINE (*Out of darkness*)
This is a wall … and this is a wall … and this is a wall … and this is a wall … and this is a wall … and this is a wall … and this is a wall … and this is a wall …

Select Bibliography

Books, Pamphlets and Reviews

Barraclough, Geoffrey (1968/1975) *The Medieval Papacy* (London: Thames and Hudson).

Brooke, Michael (1989) *Anchoress*. Booklet to VFD26538 (London: British Film Institute, see below).

Carmi, T, ed. (1981) *The Penguin Book of Hebrew Verse* (London and New York: Penguin Classics).

Clay, Rotha Mary (1914) *The Hermits and Anchorites of England* (London: Methuen).

Clements, Andrew (2005) 'Review of NMC D102', *BBC Music Magazine*, 1 February.

Davies, R.T., ed. (1963/1968/1971) *Medieval English Lyrics* (London: Faber and Faber).

Dean, James M. (1996) *Medieval English Political Writings* (Kalamazoo: Medieval Institute).

Doctor, Jennifer (2007) 'Saxton's Caritas' in *The Grove Dictionary of Opera* (Oxford: Grove Music Online).

Dronke, Peter (1984) *Women Writers of the Middle Ages: A Critical Study of Texts from Perpetua to Marguerite Porete* (Cambridge: Cambridge University Press).

— (1968/1977/1996) *The Medieval Lyric* (Woodbridge: Brewer).

Evans, Peter A. (1976/2002) *The Music of Benjamin Britten* (Oxford: Clarendon Press).

Griffiths, Paul (1985) *New Sounds; New Personalities* (London: Faber and Faber).

— (1986) 'A Little Light on Robert Saxton', *Musical Times* 127(1717), pp. 145–7.

Hayes, Malcolm (1991) 'Playing safe', *The Daily Telegraph*, 25 November.

Helm, Seigfied (1991) 'God's Hostage', *Die Welt*, 12 December.

Heym, Stefan (1984) *The Wandering Jew* (Illinois: Northwestern University Press).

Hopper, Vincent Foster (1938/2000) *Medieval Number Symbolism – Its Sources, Meaning, and Influence on Thought and Expression* (New York: Columbia University; reprint New York: Dover Publications).

Johnson, Stephen (1992) 'Charity without clarity', *The Independent*, 3 July.

Julian of Norwich (fourteenth-century) (1986) *A Revelation of Love*, ed. Marion Glasscoe (Exeter: University of Exeter).

Kennedy, Michael (1991) 'All walled up with somewhere to go', *Sunday Telegraph* (Review Supplement), 24. November.

Krochalis, J. and Peters, E, ed. (1975) *The World of Piers Plowman* (Pennsylvania: University of Pennsylvania Press).

Langland, William (fourteenth-century) (1978/1989) *The Vision of Piers Plowman*, ed. A.V.C. Schmidt (London: J.M. Dent).

Lebrecht, Norman (1991) 'A Fight at the Opera', *The Independent Magazine*, 16 November.

Leeming, Glenda (1983) *Wesker – The Playwright* (London: Methuen).

Lendvai, Ernö (1971) *Béla Bartók – an Analysis of his Music* (London: Kahn and Averill).

Leyser, Henrietta (1996) *Medieval Women – A Social History of Women in England, 450–1500* (London: Phoenix Press).

The Liber Usualis (1961), ed. The Benedictines of Solesmes (Tournai and New York: Desclee).

Moorcraft, Paul L. (2002) *Anchoress of Shere* (Scottsdale, USA: Poison Pen Press).

Morrison, Richard (1990) Record notes for EMI CDC7 499152.

Morton, James, ed. and trans. (1853) The Ancren(e) Riwle: *A Treatise on the Rules and Duties of Monastic Life* (London: Camden Society/books.google.com).

Ringer, Alexander L. (1990) *Arnold Schoenberg – The Composer as Jew* (Oxford: Clarendon Press).

Salu, M.B., trans. and ed. (1955/2001) *Ancrene Riwle* (Exeter: Exeter University Press).

Sandon, Nicholas, ed. (1984–99) *The Use of Salisbury* (Newton Abbot: Antico Edition).

Saxton, Robert (1994) 'Where do I Begin?', *Musical Times* cxxxv: 623–33 [an earlier version of Saxton (1998), below].

— (1998) 'The Process of Composition from Detection to Confection' in *Composition – Performance – Reception: Studies in the Creative Process in Music*, ed. W. Thomas (Aldershot: Ashgate).

— (1998) 'The Orchestral Composer' in *The Cambridge Companion to the Orchestra*, ed. C. Lawson (Cambridge: Cambridge University Press).

— (2002) *Programme Note – Brief Synopsis and Composer's Note for Caritas* (www.schirmer.com; accessed 27 October 2009).

— (2003) 'Darkness to Light, Cycles and Circles; The Sacred in My Music' in *Composing Music for Worship*, ed. S. Darlington and A. Kreider (Norwich: Canterbury Press).

— , ed. (with Archbold, P.) (2007) *Contemporary British Composers in their Own Words*. (Aldershot: Ashgate).

— (2010) 'My New Music', *Musical Opinion* July/August.

— (2011) *The Wandering Jew*. Introductory Essay to NMC D170.

Saxton Robert and Bruce, D. (2004) *Interview* (www.composition today.com/ interviews; accessed 17 September 2007).

Smith, John Arthur (2011) *Music in Ancient Judaism and Early Christianity* (Farnham: Ashgate).

Spearing, Elizabeth (2002) *Medieval Writings on Female Spirituality* (London: Penguin Classics).

Thomas, Wyndham, ed. (1998) *Composition – Performance – Reception: Studies in the Creative Process in Music* (Aldershot: Ashgate).

— (1998) 'Composing, Arranging and Editing: A Historical Survey' in *Composition – Performance – Reception: Studies in the Creative Process in Music*, ed. W. Thomas (Aldershot: Ashgate, 1998).

— , transcr./ed., (2001) *Plays for Christmas and Easter* in *The Fleury Playbook*, Vol. 2 (Newton Abbot: Antico Edition).

Wada, Yoko, ed. (2003–10) *A Companion to Ancrene Wisse* [aka *Riwle*] (Cambridge: D.S. Brewer; paperback: Woodbridge: Boydell & Brewer).

Warren, Raymond (1995) *Opera Workshop* (Aldershot/Ashgate).

Webster, Alan (1981) *Suffering – The Jews of Norwich and Julian of Norwich* (London: St Paul's Lecture).

Wesker, Arnold (1960/1973) *The Wesker Trilogy* (*Chicken Soup with Barley* (1959), *Roots* (1959), *I'm Talking about Jerusalem* (1960)) (London: Jonathan Cape).

— (1960) *Lady Othello and Other Plays* in *Arnold Wesker Plays*, Vol. 6 (London: Penguin Books).

— (1981) *Caritas* (London: Jonathan Cape).

— (1989) Libretto for the opera *Caritas* (CD Booklet: NMC D102, pp. 12–25).

— (1990) *Caritas* in *Arnold Wesker Plays*, Vol. 6 (London: Penguin Books).

— (1991) *Blood Libel* in *Arnold Wesker Plays*, Vol. 7 (London: Penguin Books).

— (1996) Programme notes for premiere of *Blood Libel* (Norwich Playhouse).

White, Michael (1992) 'A lifetime's search for the moment', *The Independent*, 5 July.

Winchester Register (1329/1332) *Christine Carpenter: The Anchoress of Shere*, ed. D.M.S. Dane (St. James' Church, Shere, 1986). [Also included in Brooke (1989).]

Woolf, Peter Grahame (n.d.) *Review of Robert Saxton's Caritas and other works* on NMC Anchora D102 (www.musicalpointers.co.uk; accessed 18 September 2007).

— (n.d.) *Review of A Yardstick to the Stars and other chamber works* on NMC D065 (Classical CD, April 2000) (www.musicweb.uk.net/2000/classrev/apr00/saxton.htm; accessed 17 September 2007).

Wright, David C.H. (1989) 'Invoking Apollo: Similarities and Contrast in 'Mainstream Music', *The Listener*, 13 April.

— (1990) 'At the Threshold of Eternity: Robert Saxton on Disc', *Musical Times* cxxxi: 363–4.

— (1993) 'Coming of Age', *Musical Times* cxxxiv: 596–8.

— (2000) *Robert Saxton – An Introduction* (CD booklet for NMC D065: *A Yardstick to the Stars*).

— (2001) 'Robert Saxton' (rev.), *The New Grove Dictionary of Music and Musicians*. (Basingstoke: MacMillan).

— (2001) *Robert Saxton in the 1990s*. Tempo: New series, 2–6 (Cambridge: Cambridge University Press).

Scores

Saxton, Robert (various dates), complete published works, courtesy of Chester/
    Novello and York University Press, especially:
— (1991) *Caritas*, orchestral score (London: Chester Music).
— (1997) *Caritas*, vocal score, prep. S. Gibson (London: Chester Music).
— (2010) *The Wandering Jew: Dramatic Radio Myth*, full score (Munich: Ricordi).

Recordings

Works by Robert Saxton

CDC 7 49915 2 (1990) Concerto for Orchestra (1984); *The Sentinel of the Rainbow*
    (1984); *The Ring of Eternity* (1983); Chamber Symphony: *The Circles of Light*
    (1986).
MSV CD 92009 (1995) Piano Sonata (1981).
MSV CD92008 (1995) *Chacony for Piano Left Hand* (1988).
QPRM 127D (1995) *Ring Time* for Symphonic Wind Ensemble.
CACD 77005 (1996) *Birthday Piece for Richard Rodney Bennett* (1986); *Elijah's
    Violin* (1988).
NMC D065 (2000) *Processions and Dances* (1980/81); *Chacony* (1988); *Fantazia*
    (1993); *Evocation, Dance and Meditation* (1991); *Eloge* (1980); *Arias* (1977); *A
    Yardstick to the Stars* (1994).
NMC D102 (2004) *Music to Celebrate the Resurrection* (1988*); I Will Awake the
    Dawn* (1986/87); Violin Concerto (1990); *In the Beginning* (1987); *Caritas*
    (1988–91).
MSV 28507 (2008) *Songs, Dances and Ellipses for String Quartet* (1997; rev.1998).
SIGCD 174 (2009) *Five Motets for Nine Voices*.
NMC D170 (2011) *The Wandering Jew*.

Video

Newby, Chris, dir. (1993) *Anchoress*, based on the story of Christine Carpenter of
    Shere (VFD26538) (London: British Film Institute).

Index